DISIDENTIFICATIONS

Cultural Studies of the Americas

Edited by George Yúdice, Jean Franco, and Juan Flores

Volume 3 *Latin Americanism*
Román de la Campa

Volume 2 *Disidentifications: Queers of Color and the Performance of Politics*
José Esteban Muñoz

Volume 1 *The Fence and the River: Culture and Politics at the U.S.–Mexico Border*
Claire F. Fox

DISIDENTIFICATIONS

Queers of Color and the Performance of Politics

josé esteban muñoz

Cultural Studies of the Americas, Volume 2

University of Minnesota Press — Minneapolis — London

"Famous and Dandy like B. 'n' Andy" was originally published in *Pop Out: Queer Warhol,* Jennifer Doyle, Jonathan Flatley, and José E. Muñoz, editors (Durham, N.C.: Duke University Press, 1996), 144–79. "Photographies of Mourning" was originally published in *Race and the Subject(s) of Masculinity,* Harry Stecopoulous and Michael Uebel, editors (Durham, N.C.: Duke University Press, 1997), 337–60. "The Autoethnographic Performance" was originally published in *Screen* 36, no. 2 (1995): 83–99; reprinted by permission of Oxford University Press. "The White to Be Angry" was originally published in *Social Text* 52–53 (fall–winter 1997): 801–3. Parts of "Sister Acts: Ela Troyano and Carmelita Tropicana" first appeared in *The Ethnic Eye: Latino Media Arts,* Chon A. Noriega and Ana M. López, editors (Minneapolis: University of Minnesota Press, 1996), and *Women and Performance: A Journal of Feminist Theory* 7:2, no. 14–15 (1995): 39–52. An earlier version of "Pedro Zamora's *Real World* of Counterpublicity: Performing an Ethics of the Self" was published in *Homosexuality and Hispanisms,* Sylvia Molloy, editor (Durham, N.C.: Duke University Press, 1998); the version that appears in this book was published in *Living Color: Race and Television,* Sasha Torres, editor (Durham, N.C.: Duke University Press, 1998).

Published by the University of Minnesota Press
111 Third Avenue South, Suite 290
Minneapolis, MN 55401-2520
http://www.upress.umn.edu

Printed in the United States of America on acid-free paper

Library of Congress Cataloging-in-Publication Data

Muñoz, José Esteban.
Disidentifications : queers of color and the performance of politics / José Esteban Muñoz.
p. cm. — (Cultural studies of the Americas ; v. 2)
Includes bibliographical references (p.) and index.
ISBN 978-0-8166-3014-1 (HC : acid-free paper). — ISBN 978-0-8166-3015-8 (PB : acid-free paper)
1. Minority gays—United States—Social conditions. 2. Minority lesbians—United States—Social conditions. 3. Hispanic American gays—Social conditions. 4. Hispanic American lesbians—Social conditions. 5. Gays—United States—Identity. 6. Lesbians—United States—Identity. 7. Performance art—Political aspects—United States. I. Title. II. Series.
HQ76.3.U5M87 1999
305.9'0664—dc21 98-54363

22 21 27 26 25 24 23 22 21 20 19 18 17 16 15 14 13

This book is for my families
and in loving memory of

Vivana Veloso (1919–97)

and

Brian Selsky (1967–97)

Carmelita Tropicana, Rebecca Sumner-Burgos, Ana Margaret Sanchez, and Uzi Parnes. Photo by Dona Ann McAdams.

Contents

Jack's Plunger

Normalcy is the evil side of homosexuality.
—Jack Smith

The phrase "queer theater" was spectacularly inaugurated in 1978 by Stefan Brecht in his weird and resplendent book *Queer Theatre.* Brecht's participant-observer chronicle of freaky performance in New York from the mid-sixties to the mid-seventies is the second volume of a nine-volume study of the New York avant-garde. It is through Brecht's accounts that I first learned of Jack Smith's legendary performance practice. Brecht's descriptions of Smith's durational performances were thick and functioned as performative writing inasmuch as the critic's prose rambled with a "moldy" excess that echoed the performer's own particular style. My own visualization of Smith's performances was enabled by the filmic documentations that existed of his work, including his own restored underground classics *Normal Love* and *Flaming Creatures* and Ela Troyano's *Bubble People.*[1] Years later, I would learn a lot more about Smith through the reminiscences of his friends Troyano and Carmelita Tropicana. The power of Smith's strange and opulent performances was conveyed to me over many meals and drinks with these friends. These conversations fostered a deep regret that I never witnessed Smith's work firsthand. The more I learned about Smith, the more I became convinced that his work was important to my understanding of the modality of performance I was theorizing as disidentification. It was my hunch that Smith's performances were especially useful for the project of unpacking and describing what I called the worldmaking power of disidentificatory performances. Smith once claimed that important acting did not change the actor but instead transformed the world.[2] Smith made worlds during his performances; he recycled schlock culture and remade it as a queer world.

As I learned more of Smith's performances, I became partly disturbed by what could be described as the orientalizing and tropicalizing aspects of the work, which is to say the way he played with over-the-top images of "exotic" Third World ethnoscapes. These reservations were significantly diminished when I looked closely at the available documentation of Smith's work. His work with images of Latin spitfires and cheesy Hollywood renditions of Scheherazade deserved more careful consideration. I began to think that Smith had little to do with actual Third World cultures and instead worked through Hollywood's fantasies of the other. The underground genius utilized these fantasies of the other in a reflective fashion. The excess affect of Maria Montez and the gaudy fantasies of harem culture were utilized to destabilize the world of "pasty normals" and help us imagine another time and place.[3] In Smith's cosmology, "exotic" was an antinormative option that resisted the overdetermination of pastiness. Hollywood's fetishized fantasies of the other were reenergized by Smith's performance. His performances of the "spitfire" and Scheherazade were inflected with disidentificatory difference that helped toxic images expand and become much more than quaint racisms. Disidentification is the process in which the artist reformulates the actual performativity of his glittering B movie archive, which is to say that the images that Smith cited were imbued with a performativity that surpassed simple fetishization. Glitter transformed hackneyed orientalisms and tropical fantasies, making them rich antinormative treasure troves of queer possibility.

My estimation of the political efficacy of Smith's performance is gleaned from my readings of Brecht's performance documentation. Yet, I take issue with his analysis of Smith's or queer theater as political project. Brecht wrote about what he perceived as the political limits of queer theater: "Since the queer artist, having no justification for it, cannot allow himself the disfigurement of care, his art is entirely dependent on energy. But since his energy is entirely dependent on an exuberance of rage, his art, an active rebellion, is prone to degenerate into good-humored comedy and unthinking repetition, and to fall apart."[4] Brecht's generalizations about queer theater are arrived at through readings of Smith, John Vaccaro, Charles Ludlam and the Ridiculous Theatrical Company, John Waters's cinema, and other white performers from the 1960s and the 1970s. I disagree with this particular assessment of queer theater's politics of performance on a few counts. The comedy of Smith and many of the other playwrights and performers considered in his text cannot be reduced to "good-humored" fun. To do so would be to ignore the scathing antinormative critiques that Smith performances enacted.

Jack Smith's performance of politics often had a materialist orientation. His discourse on "landlordism," for example, was a Marxian-tinged critique of capitalist constructions of private property. Property owners were depicted as moneygrubbing lobsters in the Smith bestiary. In his performance "Irrational Landlordism of Baghdad," Smith called for a modality of artistic production that insisted on art that educated as it entertained. The text of that performance begins by asking a flat-footed question that nonetheless haunts aesthetic philosophy: "Could art be useful?" He answered his own question with aplomb:

> Ever since the desert drifted over the burntout ruins of Plaster Lagoon thousands of artists have pondered and dreamed of such a thing, yet, art must not be used anymore as another elaborate means of fleeing from thinking because of the multiplying amount of information each person needs to process in order to come to any kind of decision on what kind of planet one wants to live on before business, religion, and government succeed in blowing it out of the solar system.[5]

The monologue is played as a taped voice-over accompanying a scene in which a scrubwoman, down on her knees, cleans the floor. At the end of the recording, she stands up triumphantly. Another woman, a "glamorous floorlady," enters the room and the worker once again drops to her knees. This performance, with all its camp and out-there glamour in place, nonetheless insisted on chronicling wage exploitation and class stratification. This performance is particularly illustrative of Smith's materialist aesthetic philosophy. Smith insisted on art that was "escapist, stunning, glamorous and NATURALISTIC."[6] "NATURALISTIC" for Smith meant that it served a politically pedagogical role, that it provided the spectator the material to resist "the Capitalism of Lobsterland," and instead disidentify with that world and perform a new one.

Smith's camp was not good-humored goofing. It insisted on social critique. Even his diva worship indexed something of a materialist ethos. Dominican-born Hollywood B movie actress Maria Montez was the principal goddess in the Church of Jack Smith. Smith had great contempt for Montez's replacement in the firmament of Hollywood stardom. Yvonne de Carlo was a competent actress where Montez was, from a conservative vantage point, a poor actress. Smith described de Carlo as a "walking career." The actress represented the loathsome corporate ethos of Hollywood. Smith's love of Montez had much to do with the way in which her performance eschewed the commercialized tenets of "good acting" and helped the performance artist imagine another mode of performing the world that was for him transformative.

I am also left to wonder what Brecht's more general conclusions about queer theater would look like if he considered the work of Carmelita Tropicana, Vaginal Davis, Marga Gomez, and many other queer performers of color who specialize in the interweaving of passion and comedy in intricate and self-sustaining fashions. Although they participate in the genre of comedy and satire, these performances do not lose sight of the fact that humor is a valuable pedagogical and political project. In this book, I will argue the opposite of Brecht's thesis in respect to queers of color: the work of these performers does not eventually become "good-humored," "unthinking," and it most certainly does not fall apart. Comedy does not exist independently of rage. It is my contention that rage is sustained and it is pitched as a call to activism, a bid to take space in the social that has been colonized by the logics of white normativity and heteronormativity. These logics are embodied for artists in the form of Smith's number one targets, the "pasty normals."

J. Hoberman has translated "pasty normals" as Smith's dismissal of heterosexuals.[7] But my reconstructions of Smith's lexicon lead me to read more into this idea of the "pasty normal." Smith, as the epigraph to this preface shows, saw normalcy as the dark side of homosexuality. Normalcy is therefore not constituted as strictly endemic to heterosexuality. The rise of assimilationist gay politics and its weak request for a place at the table prove Smith's point decades later. Normalcy might be better understood as normativity. The "normal" in the "pasty normal" might then be described as "normativity," as in Michael Warner's influential neologism "heteronormativity."[8] In Warner's formulations, lesbians and gay men might very well subscribe to heteronormative thinking and politics. Lisa Duggan's recent work on "homonormativity," a theory that deciphers the ways in which conservative and assimilationist gays and lesbians contribute to the privatization of mass culture, is especially relevant when considering Smith's work.[9]

But what of the "pasty" in the "pasty normal" equation? In the Smith cosmology, *pasty* would be the opposite of exotic. *Pasty* is the negative term. Smith himself had troubles with pastiness. One of his journal entries reads: "I overcame pastiness." I want to suggest that Smith's phrase is meant to index "whiteness" or, more nearly, *white normativity.* In Smith's ingenious phrase, white normativity and heteronormativity are shown to be adjacent and mutually informing ideological formations. Furthermore, they are not linked to predetermined biological coordinates.

The fact that I have never seen Smith's performances does not help authorize my disagreement with Brecht. After all, what do I know? I was not there. But I have been there for a lot of queer theater performance in the "wake" of Jack Smith. For instance, I have witnessed one particular homage to Smith many times. My most recent observation of this performance was at a benefit for P.S. 122, the hub of downtown performance in Manhattan. The bill included the upscale performance art of Meredith Monk and Spalding Gray. Downtown legends The Alien Comic and the marvelous Holly Hughes rounded off the evening along with the emcee, a noted performance artist in her own right. Carmelita Tropicana barrels onto the stage. She is wearing a blue wig, a tight red plastic bodice with fringes, black leggings, and leopard-print cowboy boots. She immediately sizes up the audience. She spots a woman with a hat and, in her thick pseudo-accent, she purrs that the hat is very sexy and very becoming. The flaming spitfire gets very close to the embarrassed woman, deliberately challenging her personal space. She asks the woman not to be upset because, after all, this is her job, she is a performance artist. She then launches into her own origin as a performance artist. She moves back from the audience and walks into a spotlight. Her voice booms as she takes the pressure off the blushing woman in the hat and inquires of the entire audience: "How many of you know performance art?" She explains that a telephone call from Ela Troyano alerted Carmelita (then mild-mannered Alina Troyano) of the existence of this practice. Alina asked her sister exactly what was performance art? Ela explained that there was a five-thousand-dollar grant available for performance art. Alina dashed off an application and was awarded the grant. Thus, Carmelita Tropicana was born, a fully born *chusma* performance deity.

Tropicana then proceeds to recite her personal performance manifesto. I have heard this many times, but I nonetheless laugh as she reads four quotations on what performance art is. She quotes Laurie Anderson's line that performance art is a performance by a live artist. Carmelita agrees, emphatically adding that it would most certainly not be performance art if the artist were dead. She then quotes Hughes, who has joked that 90 percent of performance art is the costume. She gestures to her own flashy attire. Her third citation is from herself: "Performance art is not music, is not dance, is not film but can contain all of these elements."

There is one more point to her manifesto, which she identifies as the most important part, and this is what I am most interested in considering here. Tropicana explains that performance art changes one's perception of the world. She turns from the audience and walks to a large shopping bag that is positioned a few feet behind her. She reaches into the bag and pulls out a plunger. With one hand she holds the plunger up high, as if she were displaying her patriotism to the People's Republic of Performance Art. She challenges the audience: "What is this?" Meek voices in the crowd respond by saying "a plunger." Carmelita lifts an eyebrow and glares at the spectators: "A plunger! I laugh at you wildly. Ha." Carmelita confesses that she too once mistook this object for a mere plunger. Because she is a superintendent as well as a performance artist, this is an understandable mistake. But she was disabused of this misconception after seeing a performance by Jack Smith. She then launches into a recounting of this performance:

> I was in the Village in a concrete basement. It was packed, eight of us wall to wall. There is a breeze blowing through the wall created by two fans. Beautiful Scheherazade music plays and out comes an Arabian Prince Jack Smith in a diaphanous material. He is dancing. He pours gasoline in the middle of the floor to make a black lagoon. He takes out a match and throws it in. The flames grow and we think we are going to die but he chases, revolves and demi-pliés to the corner and grabs this [she brandishes the plunger] and continues his dance, putting the flames out with this. No, ladies and gentlemen, this to me, a superintendent and performance artist, has changed from a plunger to an objet d'art. I remember Jack Smith, who died of AIDS in 1989.

With this recitation over, she holds the object firmly in her fist and then bows, introducing the first performer and leaving the stage.

Charles Ludlam was quoted as saying that Jack was the father of us all. In this homage by Carmelita Tropicana we see Jack Smith as a precursor to her own performance practice. In much of Tropicana's work, traces of Jack are evidenced in her over-the-top "exoticism," her deep investment in gaudy and toxic stereotypes of the Latina, her red feather boas, and the occasional splash of glitter that might punctuate her performances. In this performance of a performance, or a performance of memory, the student of queer theater can glimpse an alternative rendering of the queer performance of politics than the one theorized by Brecht. Queer performance from Smith to Tropicana and beyond is about transformation, about the powerful and charged transformation of the world, about the world that is born through performance. Smith's flaming black lagoon scared his spectators, it made them think that they would perish in that small downtown basement, but they soon learned that the performance was a ritual of transformation. Smith's exotic dance, his graceful dousing of the flames, signaled a world to come and called attention to a world that was already there. It made a queer world for those eight snug spectators. Years later, Tropicana rehearses that performance and adds to the continuously disidentifying process of performing a queer world.

A plunger is remade into an art object. The subtitle of this book speaks to the performance of politics. The study itself is a contribution to the formation of a queer performance-studies lens. That lens is interested in theorizing the political force of performance and performativity by queers of all races. In this book, I will look at disidentificatory performances of politics, acts that I will describe as reformulating the world *through* the performance of politics. The Introduction looks at various performances that remake the world, prominent among them Marga Gomez's remaking of stigmatized televisual lesbian stereotypes into lush sites of erotic investment. In chapter 1, I consider Jean-Michel Basquiat's disidentification with both pop guru Andy Warhol and the practice of pop art. Chapter 2 examines Isaac Julien's cinematic performance of diasporic black queer identity through redeployment of black mourning and melancholia. Chapter 3 surveys Richard Fung's recycling of porn and ethnography as powerful autoethnographic performance. Chapter 4 chronicles Vaginal Davis's terrorist drag and its fierce disidentification with white supremacist militiamen from Idaho. The final four chapters focus on Cuban America. Chapter 5 takes a closer look at the remaking of camp performance in the work of Troyano and Tropicana. The activist performance of Pedro Zamora is the topic of chapter 6. Chapter 7 further inquires into disidentificatory performances in the public sphere by looking at the disidentity fashioned in the conceptual art of Felix Gonzalez-Torres. In chapter 8, Carmelita Tropicana's *Chicas 2000,* a theater production, enables me to further elaborate a discussion of queer worldmaking through the example of disidentificatory performances of Latina *chusmería.* All of these case studies are stories of transformation and political reformulation. In divergent and complicated ways, all of these cultural workers, like Smith before them, choreograph and execute their own metaphoric dances in front of the flaming black lagoon, stamping out fires with grace and political efficacy, and, in the process, building worlds.

Acknowledgments

This project was made possible by the seemingly limitless support and encouragement from the communities I have lived in over the last few years. I am deeply indebted to the vigorous and enabling intellectual climate at Duke University and New York University.

The committee that directed this project in its most protean incarnation as a dissertation was extremely generous with its time and feedback. Karla F. C. Halloway and Walter Mignolo valiantly signed on without having previously known me as a student. I benefited from their knowledge, insight, and experience. Jane M. Gaines offered me a wealth of both critical and bibliographical knowledge in her field of expertise. Michael Moon's insistence on a high level of scholarship helped push this project forward when it was in desperate need of propulsion. Eve Kosofsky Sedgwick has not only been an extraordinary dissertation director, but also an invaluable friend. I continue to be inspired by her work, her example, and her presence.

Other friends in the Duke matrix that I need to thank include Sandy Mills, whose friendship, institutional mastery, and wit made graduate school a much more pleasant place. I also wish to express my appreciation to Sandy Swanson, Priscila Lane, and Joan McNay for all their help. I also want to thank Thomas Sherrat for his support through those years.

I feel fortunate to have worked beside and lived among Brian Selsky, Jonathan Flatley, Gustavus Stadler, Katie Kent, Mandy Berry, Celeste Fraser Delgado, Hank Okazaki, Jennifer Doyle, Johannes von Molthke, Eleanor Kaufman, John Vincent, Renu Bora, and Ben Weaver. Many of these friends were the first people to engage these ideas. Their confidence in me and assurances that this was not just crazy talk made this book possible.

The presence of Brian Selsky, who read this book before it was anywhere near readable, haunts every page.

I am very grateful to this book's series editors for their interest in the project and their helpful suggestions. George Yúdice has been an especially good editor. I want to thank Jennifer Moore for her amazing competence.

Thanks to the Andrea Rosen Gallery (especially Andrea Rosen and John Connelly) for permissions. Donna McAdams's images and documentation add considerably to the texture of this book.

New York University has been a fantastic place to do my work. I thank performance-studies colleagues Barbara Browning, May Joseph, Barbara Kirshenblatt-Gimblett, Fred Moten, Peggy Phelan, Richard Schechner, and Diana Taylor for their support. Sylvia Molloy and Andrew Ross have also been supportive colleagues. The members of the Faculty Working Group in Queer Studies at New York University, including Carolyn Dever, Lisa Duggan, Philip Brian Harper, and Chris Straayer, have been ideal colleagues.

Other "show-business" friends (or friends I met through the business) whom I need to thank include Sasha Torres, who has supported my work with intelligence and love; Judith Halberstam, who has been a superlative intellectual and political ally; Ann Pellegrini, who is my brilliant coconspirator; and my dear friend Josh Kun, who has taught me how to listen to sounds of disidentification. David Román has taught me a great deal about intellectual generosity. Alberto Sandoval has been an important model for me and my generation of queer Latina/o scholars. Ana López and Chon Noriega did some important Latino mentoring out of the kindness of their hearts. Licia Fiol-Mata was one of this book's "anonymous readers" and her tough yet generous appraisal of this project made a world of difference. I am grateful to Marcos Becquer for reading and responding to my work with such intellectual force and brilliance. Other amazing divas whom I need to send humble shout-outs to include Stephen Best, Jennifer Brody, Ondine Chavoya, Ann Cvetkovich, David Eng, Beth Freeman, Coco Fusco, Joseba Gabilondo, Gayartri Gopinath, Miranda Joseph, Alex Juhasz, Tiffany Ana Lopez, Martin Manalansan, Mandy Merck, Ricardo Ortiz, Geeta Patel, José Quiroga, Robert Reid-Pharr, B. Ruby Rich, Amy Robinson, Alisa Solomon, and Patty White. My comrades at *Social Text* and the Boards of Directors for the Center for Gay and Lesbian Studies at the City University of New York and the New Festival have been a delight to work with.

This book is deeply indebted to the cultural workers whose performances and productions ground my theoretical ruminations. I have had the good fortune of getting to know many of these artists after I began working on them. I have discovered that Marga Gomez, Isaac Julien, Richard Fung, Vaginal Davis, Ela Troyano, Carmelita Tropicana, Rebecca Sumner-Burgos, Uzi Parnes, and Ana Margaret Sanchez are as rewarding to know as they are to write about. Other superlative artists who inspire me include Luis Alfaro, Nayland Blake, Justin Bond and Kenny Mellman,

La Ricardo Bracho, Jorge Ignacio Cortiñas, Cheryl Dunye, Brian Freeman, Holly Hughes, and Tony Just.

My students have enabled my scholarship in productive and beautiful ways. They have heard much of this in its earliest incarnations and have responded with intelligence, wit, and political clarity. I offer them a heartfelt thank you. The research support of Berta Jottar has been invaluable. I have been very fortunate to work with the talented young scholar Paul Scolieri, to whom I owe a substantial debt. Another debt is owed to John Wiggins for his work on the index.

A list of dear friends in New York whom I take pleasure in acknowledging includes V. S. Brody, Luke Dowd, Andrew Gebhardt, Jennifer Sharpe, Nicolas Terry, Frida and Rose Troche (a k a the singing Troche sisters), and Abe Weintraub. Antonio Viego Jr. and Guin Turner have kept me sharp and mean. These best friends and sometimes tormentors/arch-foes have made me laugh and cry and kept the living deep and real. Tony got me into this line of work and it is almost certain that I would not have achieved much if he had not shown me how to disidentify with just about everything.

It is especially hard to find the words to thank Ari Gold, who has meant so much to this book and my life. His patience, love, and concern have been instrumental to this project and so much more. He has read these pages and offered me a steady flow of valuable feedback and precious support.

The "Lady" Bully is joy.

My family in Hialeah has aided and abetted me in crucial ways, despite the fact that we are separated by an expansive ideological gulf that makes the ninety miles between Cuba and Miami look like a puddle. Their support of me has never waned. *Gracias.*

Introduction

Performing Disidentifications

Marga's Bed

There is a certain lure to the spectacle of one queer standing onstage alone, with or without props, bent on the project of opening up a world of queer language, lyricism, perceptions, dreams, visions, aesthetics, and politics. Solo performance speaks to the reality of being queer at this particular moment. More than two decades into a devastating pandemic, with hate crimes and legislation aimed at queers *and* people of color institutionalized as state protocols, *the act* of performing and theatricalizing queerness *in public* takes on ever multiplying significance.

I feel this lure, this draw, when I encounter Marga Gomez's performances. *Marga Gomez Is Pretty, Witty, and Gay,* a 1992 performance by the Cuban and Puerto Rican-American artist, is a meditation on the contemporary reality of being queer in North America. Gomez's show is staged on a set that is meant to look like her bedroom. Much of her monologue is delivered from her bed. The space of a queer bedroom is thus brought into the public purview of dominant culture. Despite the *Bowers v. Hardwick* U.S. Supreme Court decision, which has efficiently dissolved the right to privacy of all gays and lesbians, in essence opening all our bedrooms to the state, Gomez willfully and defiantly performs her pretty, witty, and gay self in public. Her performance permits the spectator, often a queer who has been locked out of the halls of representation or rendered a static caricature there, to imagine a world where queer lives, politics, and possibilities are representable in their complexity. The importance of such public and semipublic enactments of the hybrid self cannot be undervalued in relation to the formation of counterpublics that contest the hegemonic supremacy of the majoritarian public sphere. Spectacles such as those that Gomez presents offer the minoritarian subject a space to situate itself in history and thus seize social agency.

Marga Gomez. Courtesy of Marga Gomez.

I want to briefly consider a powerful moment in her performances that demonstrates disidentification with mainstream representations of lesbians in the media. From the perch of her bed, Gomez reminisces about her first interaction with lesbians in the public sphere at the age of eleven. Marga hears a voice that summons her down to the living room. Marga, who at this age has already developed what she calls "homosexual hearing," catches the voice of David Susskind explaining that he will be interviewing "lady homosexuals" on this episode of his show *Open End*. Gomez recounts her televisual seduction:

> [I] sat next to my mother on the sofa. I made sure to put that homophobic expression on my face. So my mother wouldn't think I was mesmerized by the lady homosexuals and riveted to every word that fell from their lips. They were very depressed, very gloomy. You don't get that blue unless you've broken up with Martina. There were three of them. All disguised in raincoats, dark glasses, wigs. It was the wigs that made me want to be one.

She then channels the lesbian panelists:

> Mr. Susskind, I want to thank you for having the courage to present Cherene and Millie and me on your program. Cherene and Millie and me, those aren't our real names. She's not Cherene, she's not Millie, and I'm not me. Those are just our, you know, synonyms. We must cloak ourselves in a veil of secrecy or risk losing our employment as truck drivers.

Gomez luxuriates in the seemingly homophobic image of the truck-driving closeted diesel dykes. In this parodic rendering of pre-Stonewall stereotypes of lesbians, she performs her disidentificatory desire for this once toxic representation. The phobic object, through a campy over-the-top performance, is reconfigured as sexy and glamorous, and not as the pathetic and abject spectacle that it appears to be in the dominant eyes of heteronormative culture. Gomez's public performance of memory is a powerful disidentification with the history of lesbian stereotyping in the public sphere. The images of these lesbian stereotypes are rendered in all their abjection, yet Gomez rehabilitates these images, calling attention to the mysterious erotic that interpellated her as a lesbian. Gomez's mother was apparently oblivious to this interpellation, as a later moment in the performance text makes patent. Gomez's voice deepens as she goes into bulldagger mode again, mimicking the lesbian who is known as "me and not me":

> Mr. Susskind. When you are in the life, such as we, it's better to live in Greenwich Village or not live at all! At this time we want to say "hello" to a new friend who is watching this at home with her mom on WNEW-TV in Massapequa, Long Island. Marga Gomez? Marga Gomez, welcome to the club, *cara mía.*

Despite the fact that the lesbian flicks her tongue at Marga on the screen, her mother, trapped in the realm of deep denial, does not get it. Of course, it is probably a good thing that she did not get it. The fact that Marga was able to hear the lesbian's call while her mother tuned out, that she was capable of recognizing the *cara* being discussed as her own face, contributed, in no small part, to her survival as a lesbian. Disidentification is meant to be descriptive of the survival strategies the minority subject practices in order to negotiate a phobic majoritarian public sphere that continuously elides or punishes the existence of subjects who do not conform to the phantasm of normative citizenship. In this instance, Marga's disidentification with these damaged stereotypes recycled them as powerful and seductive sites of self-creation. It was, after all, the wigs that made her want to be one.

I possess my own hazy memories of Susskind's show and others like it. I remember being equally mesmerized by other talk-show deviants who would appear long after I was supposed to be asleep in my South Florida home. Those shows were, as Gomez described them, smoky and seedy spectacles. After all, this was during my own childhood in the 1970s, before the flood of freaks that now appear on *Oprah* and her countless clones. I remember, for instance, seeing an amazingly queeny Truman Capote describe the work of fellow writer Jack Kerouac as not writing but, instead, typing. I am certain that my pre-out consciousness was completely terrified by the swishy spectacle of Capote's performance. But I also remember feeling a deep pleasure in hearing Capote make language, in "getting" the fantastic bitchiness of his quip. Like Gomez, I can locate that experience of suburban spectatorship as having a disidentificatory impact on me. Capote's performance was as exhilarating as it was terrifying. This memory was powerfully reactivated for me when I first saw *Marga Gomez Is Pretty, Witty, and Gay.* Her performance, one that elicited disidentificatory spectatorship, transported me to a different place and time. Her performance did the work of prying open memory for me and elucidating one important episode of self-formation.

In writing this Introduction, I went back to check my sources to determine exactly when and on which show Capote first made this statement. I was surprised to discover, while flipping through a Capote biography, that while the writer did indeed make this cutting remark on the *David Susskind Show,* that remark aired during a 1959 episode dedicated to the Beats in which established writers Capote, Norman Mailer, and Dorothy Parker were evaluating the worth of the then younger generation of writers. Capote's quip was in response to Mailer's assertion that Kerouac was the best writer of his generation. The original broadcast, which was the same year as the Cuban Revolution, aired eight years before my own birth and six years before my parents emigrated to Miami. I mention all of this not to set the record straight but to gesture to the revisionary aspects of my own disidentificatory memory of Capote's performance. Perhaps I read about Capote's comment, or I may have seen a rerun of that broadcast twelve or thirteen years later. But I do know this: my memory and subjectivity reformatted that memory, letting it work within my own internal narratives of subject formation. Gomez's performance helped and even instructed this re-

remembering, enabling me to somehow understand the power and shame of queerness. Now, looking through the dark glass of adulthood, I am beginning to understand why I needed that broadcast and memory of that performance, which I may or may not have actually seen, to be part of my self.

The theoretical conceptualizations and figurations that flesh out this book are indebted to the theoretical/practical work of Gomez's performance. For me there would be no theory, no *Disidentifications,* without the cultural work of people such as Gomez. Such performances constitute the political and conceptual center of this study. I want to note that, for me, the making of theory only transpires *after* the artists' performance of counterpublicity is realized for my own disidentificatory eyes.

It is also important to note at the beginning of this book that disidentification is *not always* an adequate strategy of resistance or survival for all minority subjects. At times, resistance needs to be pronounced and direct; on other occasions, queers of color and other minority subjects need to follow a conformist path if they hope to survive a hostile public sphere. But for some, disidentification is a survival strategy that works within and outside the dominant public sphere simultaneously. The remainder of this Introduction will elaborate disidentification through a survey of different theoretical paradigms.

Dissing Identity

The fiction of identity is one that is accessed with relative ease by most majoritarian subjects. Minoritarian subjects need to interface with different subcultural fields to activate their own senses of self. This is not to say that majoritarian subjects have no recourse to disidentification or that their own formation as subjects is not structured through multiple and sometimes conflicting sites of identification. Within late capitalism, all subject citizens are formed by what Néstor García Canclini has called "hybrid transformations generated by the horizontal coexistence of a number of symbolic systems."[1] Yet, the story of identity formation predicated on "hybrid transformations" that this text is interested in telling concerns subjects whose identities are formed in response to the cultural logics of heteronormativity, white supremacy, and misogyny—cultural logics that I will suggest work to undergird state power. The disidentificatory performances that are documented and discussed here circulate in subcultural circuits and strive to envision and activate new social relations. These new social relations would be the blueprint for minoritarian counterpublic spheres.

This study is informed by the belief that the use-value of any narrative of identity that reduces subjectivity to either a social constructivist model or what has been called an essentialist understanding of the self is especially exhausted. Clearly, neither story is complete, but the way in which these understandings of the self have come to be aligned with each other as counternarratives is now a standard protocol of theory-making processes that are no longer of much use. Political theorist William E. Connolly argues that

> [t]o treat identity as a site at which entrenched dispositions encounter socially constituted definitions is not to insist that any such definition will fit every human being equally well or badly. Some possibilities of social definition are more suitable for certain bodies and certain individuals, particularly after each had branded into it as "second nature" a stratum of dispositions, proclivities, and preliminary self-understandings.[2]

Connolly understands identity as a site of struggle where fixed dispositions clash against socially constituted definitions. This account of identity offers us a reprieve from the now stale essentialism versus antiessentialism debates that surround stories of self-formation.[3] The political theorist's formulations understand identity as produced at the point of contact between essential understandings of self (fixed dispositions) and socially constructed narratives of self. The chapters that make up this study attempt to chart the ways in which identity is enacted by minority subjects who must work with/resist the conditions of (im)possibility that dominant culture generates. The cultural performers I am considering in this book must negotiate between a fixed identity disposition and the socially encoded roles that are available for such subjects. The essentialized understanding of identity (i.e., men are like this, Latinas are like that, queers are that way) by its very nature must reduce identities to lowest-common-denominator terms. There is an essential blackness, for example, in various strains of black nationalist thinking and it is decidedly heterosexual.[4] Socially encoded scripts of identity are often formatted by phobic energies around race, sexuality, gender, and various other identificatory distinctions. Following Connolly's lead, I understand the labor (and it is often, if not always, *work*) of making identity as a process that takes place at the point of collision of perspectives that some critics and theorists have understood as essentialist and constructivist. This collision is precisely the moment of negotiation when hybrid, racially predicated, and deviantly gendered identities arrive at representation. In doing so, a representational contract is broken; the queer and the colored come into perception and the social order receives a jolt that may reverberate loudly and widely, or in less dramatic, yet locally indispensable, ways.

The version of identity politics that this book participates in imagines a reconstructed narrative of identity formation that locates the enacting of self at precisely the point where the discourses of essentialism and constructivism short-circuit. Such identities use *and* are the fruits of a practice of disidentificatory reception and performance. The term *identities-in-difference* is a highly effective term for categorizing the identities that populate these pages. This term is one of the many figurations that I borrow from Third World feminists and radical women of color, especially Chicana theorists, who have greatly contributed to discourses that expand and radicalize identity. Gloria Anzaldúa and Cherríe Moraga, in their individual writings and in their groundbreaking anthology *This Bridge Called My Back: Writings by Radical Women of*

Color, have pushed forward the idea of a radical feminist of color identity that shrewdly reconfigures identity for a progressive political agenda. The thread that first emanated from those writers is intensified and made cogent for an academic discourse by Chela Sandoval in her theory of *differential consciousness.* All of these writers' ideas about identity are taken up by Norma Alarcón in her influential articles. In one particular essay, Alarcón synthesizes the work of Anzaldúa, Moraga, and Sandoval, along with the other theories of difference put forward by Audre Lorde and Jacques Derrida (who employs the term *différance*), in an attempt to describe and decipher identity-in-difference:

> By working through the "identity-in-difference" paradox, many radical women theorists have implicitly worked in the interstice/interface of (existentialist) "identity politics" and "postmodernism" without a clear cut modernist agenda. Neither Audre Lorde nor Chela Sandoval's notion of difference/differential consciousness subsumes a Derridean theorization—though resonances cannot be denied and must be explored—so much as represents a process of "determined negation," a nay-saying of the variety of the "not yet, that's not it." The drive behind that "not yet/that's not it" position in Sandoval's work is termed "differential consciousness," in Lorde's work, "difference," and in Derrida's work, *différance.* Yet each invokes dissimilarly located circuits of signification codified by the site of emergence, which nevertheless does not obviate their agreement on the "not yet," which points towards a future.[5]

Alarcón's linking of these convergent yet dissimilar models is made possible by the fact that these different paradigms attempt to catalog "sites of emergence." The disidentificatory identity performances I catalog in these pages are all emergent identities-in-difference. These identities-in-difference emerge from a failed interpellation within the dominant public sphere. Their emergence is predicated on their ability to disidentify with the mass public and instead, through this disidentification, contribute to the function of a counterpublic sphere. Although I use terms such as "minoritarian subjects" or the less jargony "people of color/queers of color" to describe the different culture workers who appear in these pages, I do want to state that all of these formations of identity are "identities-in-difference."

The strict psychoanalytic account of identification is important to rehearse at this point. Jean Laplanche and Jean-Bertrand Pontalis define "identification" in the following way: "[A] psychological process whereby the subject assimilates an aspect, property or attribute of the other and is transformed, wholly or partially, after the model the other provides. It is by means of a series of identifications that the personality is constituted and specified."[6] Can a self or a personality be crafted without proper identifications? A disidentifying subject is unable to fully identify or to form what Sigmund Freud called that "just-as-if" relationship. In the examples I am engaging, what stops identification from happening is always the ideological restrictions implicit in an identificatory site.

The processes of crafting and performing the self that I examine here are not best explained by recourse to linear accounts of identification. As critics who work on and with identity politics well know, identification is not about simple mimesis, but, as Eve Kosofsky Sedgwick reminds us in the introduction to *The Epistemology of the Closet,* "always includes multiple processes of identifying with. It also involves identification as against; but even did it not, the relations implicit in identifying with are, as psychoanalysis suggests, in themselves quite sufficiently fraught with intensities of incorporation, diminishment, inflation, threat, loss, reparation, and disavowal."[7] Identification, then, as Sedgwick explains, is never a simple project. Identifying with an object, person, lifestyle, history, political ideology, religious orientation, and so on, means also simultaneously and partially counteridentifying, as well as only partially identifying, with different aspects of the social and psychic world.

Although the various processes of identification are fraught, those subjects who are hailed by more than one minority identity component have an especially arduous time of it. Subjects who are outside the purview of dominant public spheres encounter obstacles in enacting identifications. Minority identifications are often neglectful or antagonistic to other minoritarian positionalities. This is as true of different theoretical paradigms as it is of everyday ideologies. The next section delineates the biases and turf-war thinking that make an identity construct such as "queer of color" difficult to inhabit.

Race Myopias/Queer Blind Spots: Disidentifying with "Theory"

Disidentifications is meant to offer a lens to elucidate minoritarian politics that is not monocausal or monothematic, one that is calibrated to discern a multiplicity of interlocking identity components and the ways in which they affect the social. Cultural studies of race, class, gender, and sexuality are highly segregated. The optic that I wish to fashion is meant to be, to borrow a phrase from critical legal theorist Kimberle William Crenshaw, *intersectional.*[8] Crenshaw's theory of intersectionality is meant to account for convergences of black and feminist critical issues within a paradigm that factors in both of these components and replaces what she has referred to as monocausal paradigms that can only consider blackness at the expense of feminism or vice versa. These monocausal protocols are established through the reproduction of normative accounts of woman that always imply a white feminist subject and equally normativizing accounts of blackness that assume maleness.

These normativizing protocols keep subjects from accessing identities. We see these ideological barriers to multiple identifications in a foundational cultural studies text such as Frantz Fanon's *Black Skins, White Masks,* the great twentieth-century treatise on the colonized mind. In a footnote, Fanon wrote what is for any contemporary antihomophobic reader an inflammatory utterance: "Let me observe at once that I had no opportunity to establish the overt presence of homosexuality in Martinique. This must be viewed as the absence of the Oedipus complex in the Antilles. The schema of homosexuality is well enough known."[9] In his chapter on colonial identity, Fanon dismisses the possibility of a homosexual component in such an identic formation. This move is not uncommon; it is basically understood as an "it's a white thing" dismissal of queerness. Think, for a moment, of the queer revolutionary from the Antilles, perhaps a young woman who has already been burned in Fanon's text by his writing on the colonized woman. What process can keep an identification with Fanon, his politics, his work possible for this woman? In such a case, a disidentification with Fanon might be one of the only ways in which she is capable of reformatting the powerful theorist for her own project, one that might be as queer and feminist as it is anticolonial. Disidentification offers a Fanon, for that queer and lesbian reader, who would not be sanitized; instead, his homophobia and misogyny would be interrogated while his anticolonial discourse was engaged as a *still* valuable yet mediated identification. This maneuver resists an unproductive turn toward good dog/ bad dog criticism and instead leads to an identification that is both mediated and immediate, a disidentification that enables politics.

The phenomenon of "the queer is a white thing" fantasy is strangely reflected in reverse by the normativity of whiteness in mainstream North American gay culture. Marlon Riggs made this argument with critical fierceness in his groundbreaking video *Tongues Untied* (1989), where he discussed being lost in a sea of vanilla once he came out and moved to San Francisco. A segment in the video begins a slow close-up on a high-school yearbook image of a blond white boy. The image is accompanied by a voice-over narration that discusses this boy, this first love, as both a blessing and, finally, a curse. The narrative then shifts to scenes of what seems to be a euphoric Castro district in San Francisco where semiclad white bodies flood the streets of the famous gay neighborhood. Riggs's voice-over performance offers a testimony that functions as shrewd analysis of the force of whiteness in queer culture:

> In California I learned the touch and taste of snow. Cruising white boys, I played out adolescent dreams deferred. Patterns of black upon white upon black upon white mesmerized me. I focused hard, concentrated deep. Maybe from time to time a brother glanced my way. I never noticed. I was immersed in vanilla. I savored the single flavor, one deliberately not my own. I avoided the question "Why?" Pretended not to notice the absence of black images in this new gay life, in bookstores, poster shops, film festivals, my own fantasies. I tried not to notice the few images of blacks that were most popular: joke, fetish, cartoon caricature, or disco diva adored from a distance. Something in Oz, in me, was amiss, but I tried not to notice. I was intent on the search for love, affirmation, my reflection in eyes of blue, gray, green. Searching, I found something I didn't expect, something decades of determined assimilation could not blind me to: in this great gay mecca I was an invisible man; still, I had no shadow, no substance. No history, no place. No reflection. I was alien, unseen, and seen, unwanted. Here, as in Hepzibah, I was a nigga, still. I quit—the Castro was no longer my home, my mecca (never was, in fact), and I went in search of something better.

Marlon Riggs in *Tongues Untied*. Courtesy of Frameline.

This anecdotal reading of queer culture's whiteness is a critique that touches various strata of queer culture. *Tongues Untied* has been grossly misread as being a "vilification" of white people and the S/M community in general. Consider John Champagne's apologist defense of the mainstream gay community's racism as a standard maneuver by embattled white gay men when their account of victimization is undercut by reference to racial privilege.[10]

A survey of the vast majority of gay and lesbian studies and queer theory in print shows the same absence of colored images as does the powerful performance in *Tongues Untied.* Most of the cornerstones of queer theory that are taught, cited, and canonized in gay and lesbian studies classrooms, publications, and conferences are decidedly directed toward analyzing white lesbians and gay men. The lack of inclusion is most certainly not the main problem with the treatment of race. A soft multicultural *inclusion* of race and ethnicity does not, on its own, lead to a progressive identity discourse. Yvonne Yarbro-Bejarano has made the valuable point that "[t]he lack of attention to race in the work of leading lesbian theorists reaffirms the belief that it is possible to talk about sexuality without talking about race, which in turn reaffirms the belief that it is necessary to talk about race and sexuality only when discussing people of color and their text."[11] When race is discussed by most white queer theorists, it is usually a contained reading of an artist of color that does not factor questions of race into the entirety of their project. Once again taking up my analogy with Riggs's monologue, I want to argue that if the Castro was Oz for some gay men who joined a great queer western migration, the field of scholarship that is emerging today as gay and lesbian studies is also another realm that is over the rainbow. The field of queer theory, like the Castro that Riggs portrays, is—and I write from experience—a place where a scholar of color can easily be lost in an immersion of vanilla while her or his critical faculties can be frozen by an avalanche of snow. The powerful queer feminist theorist/activists that are most often cited—Lorde, Barbara Smith, Anzaldúa, and Moraga, among others—are barely ever critically engaged and instead are, like the disco divas that Riggs mentions, merely adored from a distance. The fact that the vast majority of publications and conferences that fill out the discipline of queer theory continue to treat race as an addendum, if at all, indicates that there is something amiss in this Oz, too.

The Pêcheuxian Paradigm

The theory of disidentification that I am offering is meant to contribute to an understanding of the ways in which queers of color identify with ethnos or queerness despite the phobic charges in both fields. The French linguist Michel Pêcheux extrapolated a theory of disidentification from Marxist theorist Louis Althusser's influential theory of subject formation and interpellation. Althusser's "Ideology and Ideological State Apparatuses" was among the first articulations of the role of ideology in theorizing subject formation. For Althusser, ideology is an inescapable realm in which subjects are called into being or "hailed," a process he calls interpellation. Ideology is the imaginary relationship of individuals to their real conditions of existence. The location of ideology is always within an *apparatus* and its practice or practices, such as the state apparatus.[12]

Pêcheux built on this theory by describing the three modes in which a subject is constructed by ideological practices. In this schema, the first mode is understood as "identification," where a "Good Subject" chooses the path of identification with discursive and ideological forms. "Bad Subjects" resist and attempt to reject the images and identificatory sites offered by dominant ideology and proceed to rebel, to "counteridentify" and turn against this symbolic system. The danger that Pêcheux sees in such an operation would be the counterdetermination that such a system installs, a structure that validates the dominant ideology by reinforcing its dominance through the controlled symmetry of "counterdetermination." Disidentification is the third mode of dealing with dominant ideology, one that neither opts to assimilate within such a structure nor strictly opposes it; rather, disidentification is a strategy that works on and against dominant ideology.[13] Instead of buckling under the pressures of dominant ideology (identification, assimilation) or attempting to break free of its inescapable sphere (counteridentification, utopianism), this "working on and against" is a strategy that tries to transform a cultural logic from within, always laboring to enact permanent structural change while at the same time valuing the importance of local or everyday struggles of resistance.

Judith Butler gestures toward the uses of disidentification when discussing the failure of identification. She parries with Slavoj Žižek, who understands disidentification as a breaking down of political possibility, "a fictionalization to the point of political immobilization."[14] She counters Žižek by asking the following question of his formulations: "What are the possibilities of politicizing disidentification, this experience of misrecognition, this uneasy sense of standing under a sign to which one does and does not belong?" Butler answers: "it may be that the affirmation of that slippage, that the failure of identification, is itself the point of departure for a more democratizing affirmation of internal difference."[15] Both Butler's and Pêcheux's accounts of disidentification put forward an understanding of identification as never being as seamless or unilateral as the Freudian account would suggest.[16] Both theorists construct the subject as *inside* ideology. Their models permit one to examine theories of a subject who is neither the "Good Subject," who has an easy or magical identification with dominant culture, or the "Bad Subject," who imagines herself outside of ideology. Instead, they pave the way to an understanding of a "disidentificatory subject" who tactically and simultaneously works on, with, and against a cultural form.

As a practice, disidentification does not dispel those ideological contradictory elements; rather, like a melancholic subject holding on to a lost object, a disidentifying subject works to hold on to this object and invest it with new life. Sedgwick, in her work on the affect, shame, and its role in queer performativity, has explained:

> The forms taken by shame are not distinct "toxic" parts of a group or individual identity that can be excised; they are instead integral to and residual in the process in which identity is formed. They are available for the work of metamorphosis, reframing, refiguration, *trans*figuration, affective and symbolic loading and deformation; but unavailable for effecting the work of purgation and deontological closure.[17]

To disidentify is to read oneself and one's own life narrative in a moment, object, or subject that is not culturally coded to "connect" with the disidentifying subject. It is not to pick and choose what one takes out of an identification. It is not to willfully evacuate the politically dubious or shameful components within an identificatory locus. Rather, it is the reworking of those energies that do not elide the "harmful" or contradictory components of any identity. It is an acceptance of the necessary interjection that has occurred in such situations.

Disidentifications is, to some degree, an argument with psychoanalytic orthodoxies within cultural studies. It does not represent a wholesale rejection of psychoanalysis. Indeed, one's own relationship with psychoanalysis can be disidentificatory. Rather than reject psychoanalytic accounts of identification, the next section engages work on identification and desire being done in the psychoanalytic wing of queer theory.

Identification beyond and with Psychoanalysis

The homophobic and racist vicissitudes of psychoanalysis's version of identification have been explored by various critics. Diana Fuss, for instance, has shown the ways in which Freud constructed a false dichotomy between desire and identification. Desire is the way in which "proper" object choices are made and identification is a term used to explicate the pathological investment that people make with bad object choices.[18] Fuss proposes a new theory of identification based on a vampiric understanding of subjectivity formation:

> Vampirism works more like an inverted form of identification—identification pulled inside out—where the subject, in the act of interiorizing the other, simultaneously reproduces externally in the other. Vampirism is both other-incorporating and self-reproducing; it delimits a more ambiguous space where desire and identification appear less opposed than coterminous, where the desire to be the other (identification) draws its very sustenance from the desire to have the other.[19]

The incorporation of the other in this account is in stark opposition to Freud's version, in which identification is distributed along stages, all teleologically calibrated toward (compulsory) heterosexuality. Fuss's revisionary approach to psychoanalysis insists on desire's coterminous relationship with identification.

Fuss's groundbreaking work on identification has been met with great skepticism by Teresa de Lauretis, who discounts this theory on the grounds that it will further blur the lines between specifically lesbian sexuality and subjectivity and feminist takes on female sexuality and subjectivity.[20] De Lauretis's approach, also revisionary, takes the tack of substituting desire for identification in the narrative of psychoanalysis. For de Lauretis, lesbian desire is not predicated by or implicated within any structure of identification (much less cross-identifications). Her approach to desire is to expand it and let it cover and replace what she sees as a far too ambiguous notion of identification. On this point, I side with Fuss and other queer theorists who share the same revisionary impulse as de Lauretis but who are not as concerned with ordering the lines of proper, reciprocal desire against what she views as oblique cross-identifications. A substantial section of chapter 1, "Famous and Dandy like B. 'n' Andy," is concerned with the power of cross-identifications between two artists, Jean-Michel Basquiat and Andy Warhol, who do not match along the lines of race, sexuality, class, or generation. This strategy of reading the two artists together and in reaction to each other is informed by a politics of coalition antithetical to the politics of separatism that I see as a foundational premise of de Lauretis's project. The political agenda suggested here does not uniformly reject separatism either; more nearly, it is wary of separatism because it is not always a feasible option for subjects who are not empowered by white privilege or class status. People of color, queers of color, white queers, and other minorities occasionally and understandably long for separatist enclaves outside of the dominant culture. Such enclaves, however, are often politically disadvantageous when one stops to consider the ways in which the social script depends on minority factionalism and isolationism to maintain the status of the dominant order.

Disidentification works like the remaking of identification that Fuss advocates. Counteridentification, the attempt at dissolving or abolishing entrenched cultural formations, corresponds to de Lauretis's substitution of desire for identification. In *Identification Papers,* her book on Freud, psychoanalysis, and identification, Fuss succinctly historicizes the long-standing confusion between the terms *desire* and *identification.* She puts pressure on the distinction between wanting the other and wanting to be the other. Fuss marks the distinction between these terms as "precarious" at best.[21]

Valentín, a documentary subject in Augie Robles's groundbreaking short documentary *Cholo Joto* (1993), comes to recognize an early communal identification with Che Guevara as being, on both a subjective and a communal level, about desiring El Che. Robles's video interviews three young Chicano men in their early twenties. The documentary subjects expound on the quotidian dimensions of queer Chicano life in *el barrio* and the white gay ghetto. *Cholo Joto*'s final sequence features a performance by Valentín. Valentín, hair slicked back and lips reddened with a dark lipstick, turns in a captivating performance for the video camera. He sits in a chair throughout his monologue, yet the wit and charm of his performed persona defy the conventions of "talking head"; which is to say that he is not so much the talking head as he is a performer in collaboration with the video artist. After reflecting on the "tiredness" of Chicano nationalism's sexism and homophobia, he tells an early childhood story that disidentifies with the script of Chicano nationalism.

> And I grew up in Logan Heights. We had murals, Chicano park was tremendous. Now that I'm not there I know what it is. But at the time you would walk through and see these huge murals. There was a mural of Che Guevara, that is still there, with the quote "A true rebel is guided by deep feelings of love." I remember reading that as a little kid and thinking, what the fuck does that mean? Then I realized, yeah, that's right. That I'm not going to fight out of anger but because I love myself and I love my community.

For Valentín, this remembering serves as a striking reinvention of Che Guevara. By working through his queer child's curiosity from the positionality of a gay Chicano man, Valentín unearths a powerful yet elusive queer kernel in revolutionary/liberationist identity. Guevara, as both cultural icon and revolutionary thinker, had a significant influence on the early Chicano movement, as he did on all Third World movements. In this video performance, Guevara stands in for all that was promising and utopian about the Chicano movement. He also represents the entrenched misogyny and homophobia of masculinist liberation ideologies. Valentín's locution, his performance of memory, reads that queer valence that has always subliminally charged such early nationalist thought. His performance does not simply undermine nationalism but instead hopes to rearticulate such discourses within terms that are politically progressive.

Indeed, Valentín knows something that Fuss and other queer and feminist commentators on Freud know: that the story we are often fed, our prescribed "public" scripts of identification and our private and motivating desires, are not exactly indistinguishable but blurred. The point, then, is not to drop either desire or identification from the equation. Rather, it is to understand the sometimes interlocking and coterminous, separate and mutually exclusive nature of both psychic structures.

Ideology for de Lauretis seems to be an afterword to desire. In this book, I will be teasing out the ways in which desire and identification can be tempered and rewritten (not dismissed or banished) through ideology. Queers are not always "properly" interpellated by the dominant public sphere's heterosexist mandates because desire for a bad object offsets that process of reactionary ideological indoctrination. In a somewhat analogous fashion, queer desires, perhaps desires that negate self, desire for a white beauty ideal, are reconstituted by an ideological component that tells us that such modalities of desire and desiring are too self-compromising. We thus disidentify with the white ideal. We desire it but desire it with a difference. The negotiations between desire, identification, and ideology are a part of the important work of disidentification.

Disidentification's Work

My thinking about the power and poignancy of crisscrossed identificatory and desiring circuits is as indebted to the work of writers such as James Baldwin as it is to psychoanalytic theorists such as Fuss or de Lauretis. For instance, Baldwin's *The Devil Finds Work,* a book-length essay, discusses young Baldwin's suffering under a father's physical and verbal abuse and how he found a refuge in a powerful identification with a white starlet at a Saturday afternoon matinee screening. Baldwin writes:

> So here, now, was Bette Davis, on the Saturday afternoon, in close-up, over a champagne glass, pop-eyes popping. I was astounded. I had caught my father not in a lie, but in an infirmity. For here, before me, after all, was a movie star: white: and if she was white and a movie star, she was rich: and she was ugly. . . . Out of bewilderment, out of loyalty to my mother, probably, and also because I sensed something menacing and unhealthy (for me, certainly) in the face on the screen, I gave Davis's skin the dead white greenish cast of something crawling from under a rock, but I was held, just the same, by the tense intelligence of the forehead, the disaster of the lips: and when she moved, she moved just like a nigger.[22]

The cross-identification that Baldwin vividly describes here is echoed in other wistful narratives of childhood described later in this Introduction. What is suggestive about

Valentín in Augie Robles's *Cholo Joto.* Courtesy of Augie Robles.

Baldwin's account is the way in which Davis signifies something both liberatory and horrible. A black and queer belle-lettres queen such as Baldwin finds something useful in the image; a certain survival strategy is made possible via this visual disidentification with Bette Davis and her freakish beauty. Although *The Devil Finds Work* goes on to discuss Baldwin's powerful identifications with Hollywood's small group of black actors, this mediated and vexed identification with Davis is one of the most compelling examples of the process and effects that I discuss here as disidentification.

The example of Baldwin's relationship with Davis is a disidentification insofar as the African-American writer transforms the raw material of identification (the linear match that leads toward interpellation) while simultaneously positioning himself within and outside the image of the movie star. For Baldwin, disidentification is more than simply an interpretative turn or a psychic maneuver; it is, most crucially, a survival strategy.

If the terms *identification* and *counteridentification* are replaced with their rough corollaries *assimilation* and *anti-assimilation,* a position such as disidentification is open to the charge that it is merely an apolitical sidestepping, trying to avoid the trap of assimilating or adhering to different separatist or nationalist ideologies. The debate can be historicized as the early twentieth-century debate in African-American letters: the famous clashes between Booker T. Washington and W. E. B. Du Bois. Washington, a writer, national race leader, and the founder of the Tuskegee Institute, proposed a program for black selfhood that by today's post–civil-rights standards and polemics would be seen as assimilationist. Washington proposed that blacks must prove their equality by pulling themselves up by their bootstraps and achieving success in the arenas of economic development and education before they were allotted civil rights. Du Bois was the founder of the Niagara Movement, a civil-rights protest organization that arose in response to Washington's conciliatory posture accommodating and justifying white racism. Du Bois's separatist politics advocated voluntary black segregation during the Depression to consolidate black-community power bases, and eventually led to his loss of influence in the National Association for the Advancement of Colored People (NAACP), an organization he helped found in 1910. Washington's and Du Bois's careers came to embody assimilation and anti-assimilation positions. In Chicano letters, Richard Rodriguez's autobiography, *Hunger of Memory* (1982), came to represent an assimilationist position similar to the one proposed in Washington's *Up from Slavery* (1901). Some of the first interventions in contemporary Chicano cultural studies and literary theory were critiques of Rodriguez's antibilingualism tract.[23]

Disidentification is not an apolitical middle ground between the positions espoused by intellectuals such as Washington and Du Bois. Its political agenda is clearly indebted to antiassimilationist thought. It departs from the antiassimilationist rhetoric for reasons that are both strategic and methodological. Michel Foucault explains the paradox of power's working in relation to discourse in *The History of Sexuality,* volume 1:

> [I]t is in discourse that power and knowledge are joined together. And for this very reason, we must conceive discourse as a series of discontinuous segments whose tactical function is neither uniform nor stable. To be more precise, we must not imagine a world of discourse divided between accepted discourse and excluded discourse, or between the dominant discourse and the dominated one; but as a multiplicity of discursive elements that can come into play in various strategies. . . . Discourses are not once and for all subservient to power or raised up against it, any more than silences are. We must make allowance for the complex and unstable process whereby discourse can be both an instrument and an effect of power, but also a hindrance, a stumbling-block, a point of resistance and a starting point for an opposing strategy. Discourse transmits and produces power; it reinforces it, but also undermines and exposes it, renders it fragile and makes it possible to thwart it.[24]

The Foucauldian theory of the polyvalence of discourse informs the theory of disidentification being put forth here inasmuch as disidentification is a strategy that resists a conception of power as being a fixed discourse. Disidentification negotiates strategies of resistance within the flux of discourse and power. It understands that counterdiscourses, like discourse, can always fluctuate for different ideological ends and a politicized agent must have the ability to adapt and shift as quickly as power does within discourse.

Listening to Disidentification

The Devil Finds Work received considerable praise and helped revitalize what was, at the time, Baldwin's somewhat faltering career. It was released right before the author commenced what he called his "second life" as an educator. David Leeming's biography cites an interview with Baldwin in which he discusses what he imagines to be the link between *The Devil Finds Work* and the text that followed it, Baldwin's final and longest novel, *Just Above My Head*:

> He told Mary Blume that the book "demanded a certain confession of myself," a confession of his loneliness as a celebrity left behind by assassinated comrades, a confession of compassion and hope even as he was being criticized for being passé, a confession of his fascination with the American fantasy, epitomized by Hollywood, even as he condemned it. It was "a rehearsal for something I'll deal with later." That something, *Just Above My Head,* would be the major work of his later years.[25]

For Baldwin, nonfiction, or, more nearly, autobiography, is a rehearsal for fiction. Stepping back from the autobiographer's statement, we might also come to understand the writer's disidentificatory practice to extend to the ideological and structural grids that we come to understand as genre. Baldwin's fiction did not indulge the project of camouflaging an authorial surrogate. Instead, he produced a fiction that abounded with stand-ins. *Just Above My Head* includes the central character of Arthur, who is representative of a familiar thematic in the author's work, the trope of the bluesboy who is a bluesman in process. Arthur is a black gay man whose intense relationship with his brother David clearly mirrors the author's close tie with his own brother, David Baldwin. But there is also a Jimmy in the novel, who is also a black gay man, and represents a younger version of the author. Jimmy has a sister, Julia, who, like Baldwin, was a renowned child preacher, famous throughout the black church community of Harlem.

With this posited, we begin to glimpse an understanding of fiction as "a technology of the self." This self is a disidentificatory self whose relation to the social is not overdetermined by universalizing rhetorics of selfhood. The "real self" who comes into being through fiction is not the self who produces fiction, but is instead produced by fiction. Binaries finally begin to falter and fiction becomes the real; which is to say that the truth effect of ideological grids is broken down through Baldwin's disidentification with the notion of fiction—and it does not stop here: fiction then becomes a contested field of self-production.

Let me attempt to illustrate this point by substituting the word *fiction* used thus far with the word *song*. Furthermore, I want to draw a connecting line between fiction/song and ideology in a similar fashion. With this notion of the song in place, I want to consider an elegant passage near the end of *Just Above My Head*. Up to this point, the novel has been narrated by Hall, Arthur's brother. The narrative breaks down after Arthur passes away on the floor of a London pub. At this pressured moment, the narrative voice and authority are passed on to Jimmy, Arthur's last lover. The baton is passed from Hall to Jimmy through a moment of performative writing that simultaneously marks Arthur's passing and Hall's reluctance to give up command over the fiction of Arthur, his brother:

> Ah. What is he doing on the floor in a basement of the historical city? That city built on the principle that he would have the grace to live, and, certainly, to die somewhere outside the gates?
>
> Perhaps I must do now what I most feared to do: surrender my brother to Jimmy, give Jimmy's piano the ultimate solo: which must also now, be taken as the bridge.[26]

Jimmy, who is certainly another manifestation of the ghost of Jimmy Baldwin, is given his solo. It is a queer lover's solitary and mournful song. The queer solo is a lament that does not collapse into nostalgia but instead takes flight:

> The song does not belong to the singer. The singer is found by the song. Ain't no singer, anywhere, ever *made up* a song—that is not possible. He *hears* something. I really believe, at the bottom of my balls, baby, that something hears him, something says, come here! and jumps on him just how you jump on a piano or a sax or a violin or a drum and you make it sing the song you hear: and you love it, and you take care of it, better than you take care of yourself, can you

> dig it? but you don't have no mercy on it. You can't. You can't have mercy! That sound you hear, that pound you try to pitch with the utmost precision—and did you hear me? Wow!—is the sound of millions and millions and, who knows, now, listening, where life is, where is death?[27]

The singer is the subject who stands inside and, in the most important ways, outside—of fiction, ideology, "the real." He is not its author and never has been. He hears a call and we remember not only the "hey, you" of Althusser's ideology cop but also the little white girl in Fanon who cries out "Look, a Negro." But something also *hears* this singer who is not the author of the song. He is heard by something that is a shared impulse, a drive toward justice, retribution, emancipation—which permits him to disidentify with the song. He works on the song with fierce intensity and *the utmost precision.* This utmost precision is needed to rework that song, that story, that fiction, that mastering plot. It is needed to make a self—to disidentify despite the ear-splitting hostility that the song first proposed for the singer. Another vibe is cultivated. Thus, we hear and sing disidentification. The relations between the two are so interlaced and crisscrossed—reception and performance, interpretation and praxis—that it seems foolish to straighten out this knot.

Baldwin believed that *Just Above My Head* was his greatest novel, but he also experienced it as a failure. In a letter to his brother David, he wrote: "I wanted it to be a great song, instead it's just a lyric."[28] It was ultimately a lyric that mattered. It was a necessary fiction, one like the poetry that was not a luxury for Audre Lorde. It was a lyric that dreamed, strove, and agitated to disorder the real and wedge open a space in the social where the necessary fictions of blackness and queerness could ascend to something that was and was not fiction, but was, nonetheless, utterly heard.

Marginal Eyes: The Radical Feminist of Color Underpinnings of Disidentification

When histories of the hermeneutic called queer theory are recounted, one text is left out of most origin narratives. Many would agree that Foucault's discourse analysis or Roland Barthes's stylized semiology are important foundational texts for the queer theory project. Monique Wittig's materialist readings of the straight mind are invoked in some genealogies. Many writers have traced a line to queer theory from both Anglo-American feminism and the French feminism that dominated feminist discourse in the 1980s. But other theory projects have enabled many scholars to imagine queer critique today. This book is influenced, to various degrees, by all of those theoretical forerunners, yet it is important to mark a text and a tradition of feminist scholarship that most influence and organize my thinking. I am thinking of work that, like Foucault's and Barthes's projects, help us unpack the ruses and signs of normativity; I am calling on a body of theory that, like Wittig's critiques, indexes class as well as the materialist dimensions of the straight mind; I am invoking a mode of scholarship that also emerged from the larger body of feminist discourse. Cherríe Moraga and Gloria Anzaldúa's 1981 anthology *This Bridge Called My Back: Writings by Radical Women of Color* is too often ignored or underplayed in genealogies of queer theory.[29] *Bridge* represented a crucial break in gender studies discourse in which any naive positioning of gender as the primary and singular node of difference within feminist theory and politics was irrevocably challenged. Today, feminists who insist on a unified feminist subject not organized around race, class, and sexuality do so at their own risk, or, more succinctly, do so in opposition to work such as *Bridge.* The contributors to that volume set out to disrupt the standardized protocols of gender studies and activism; and, although the advancements of white feminists in integrating multiple sites of difference in their analytic approaches have not, in many cases, been significant, the anthology has proved invaluable to many feminists, lesbians, and gay male writers of color.

This Bridge Called My Back serves as a valuable example of disidentification as a political strategy. Alarcón, a contributor to that volume, suggested in a later article that *This Bridge Called My Back* served as a document that broke with previous feminist strategies of identification and counteridentification.[30] She carefully describes the ways in which the first wave of feminist discourse called for a collective *identification* with the female subject. That female subject was never identified with any racial or class identity and was essentially a desexualized being; thus, by default, she was the middle-class straight white woman. Alarcón described the next stage of evolution for pre-*Bridge* feminist discourse as a moment of *counteridentification.* She turns to Simone de Beauvoir and *The Second Sex* and proposes that de Beauvoir "may even be responsible for the creation of Anglo-American feminist theory's 'episteme': a highly self-conscious ruling-class white Western female subject locked in a struggle to the death with 'Man.'"[31] This endless struggle with "man" is indicative of a stage in feminist discourse in which counteridentification with men is the only way in which one became a woman. Alarcón identifies the weakness of this strategy as its inability to speak to lesbians and women of color who must negotiate multiple antagonisms within the social, including antagonisms posed by white women. Queers of color experience the same problems in that as white normativity is as much a site of antagonism as is heteronormativity. If queer discourse is to supersede the limits of feminism, it must be able to calculate multiple antagonisms that index issues of class, gender, and race, as well as sexuality.

Alarcón argues that *Bridge* has enabled the discourse of gender studies to move beyond politics of identification and counteridentification, helping us arrive at a politics of disidentification. I agree with her on this point, and in this book, begun almost seventeen years after the publication of *This Bridge Called My Back,* I will consider the critical, cultural, and political legacy of *This Bridge Called My Back.*

Although this book tours a cultural legacy that I understand as post-*Bridge,* I want briefly to consider a text that I think of as a beautiful addendum to that project. The video work of Osa Hidalgo has always dared to visualize the politics of disidentification that *This Bridge Called My Back* so bravely outlined. Hidalgo's most recent tape infuses humor into the fierce political legacy of that classic anthology. Her sensual lens injects the work with a defiant political imagination that moves us from activist manifesto to the expansive space of political humor and satire.

Osa Hidalgo's 1996 video *Marginal Eyes* or *Mujería Fantasy 1* presents a farcical and utopian fantasy of a remade California in which Chicanas, Native women, and other women of color, like the women who populated the *Bridge,* have ascended to positions of power. The video tells the story of Dr. Hidalgo dela Riva Morena Gonzalez, a fictional Chicana archaeologist who discovers the matrilinial origins to Western culture in the form of small red clay figurines that she unearths during a dig. The discovery serves to boost what is an already remade state of California. In Hidalgo's fantasy play, the Chicana scientist is celebrated by the entire state. The celebration includes a press conference attended by the mayor of Los Angeles, another Latina, and the governor of California, a dark-skinned mestiza named Royal Eagle Bear. (The governor is played by the director.) This emphasis on work has alienated the protagonist's lover—a woman who has felt neglected during her partner's rise to fame and prominence.

The video's first scene is found footage of an early educational film that chronicles the discovery of the Olmec civilization. The film stock is scratchy 8 mm and its appearance reminds the U.S.-based ethnic subject of the national primary education project that force-fed them Eurocentric history and culture. The video shifts from grainy images of the dig to a new archaeological quest led by Dr. Hidalgo dela Riva Morena Gonzalez. Her entire team is composed of Latinas and Latinos. The video cuts back to the educational footage, and one witnesses the discovery of tiny figurines that connote the patriarchal origins of Western culture. This is followed by a sequence in which the Chicana team discovers its own statuettes. These artifacts have breasts and, within the video's camp logic, cast a picture of a utopian matriarchal past.

The video offers a public and a private description of the archaeologist's life. The private world represented is an intimate sphere of Latina love and passion that calls attention to the quotidian pressures that besiege Chicana dykes who must negotiate the task of being public intellectuals and private subjects. The video's final scene concludes with the two lovers finally finding time to make love and reconnect, as they have sex in a candlelit room full of red roses while the educational film plays on the television set. The film represents the "real world" of masculinist archaeology that is being disidentified with. In this instance, disidentification is a remaking and rewriting of a dominant script. The characters can ignore this realm and symbolically recreate it through their sex act. This final scene offers a powerful utopian proposition: it is through the transformative powers of queer sex and sexuality that a queerworld is made.

The public component helps one imagine a remade public sphere in which the minoritarian subject's eyes are no longer marginal. In the fantasy ethnoscape, the world has been rewritten through disidentificatory desire. The new world of Hidalgo's

Marginal Eyes. Courtesy of Osa Hidalgo.

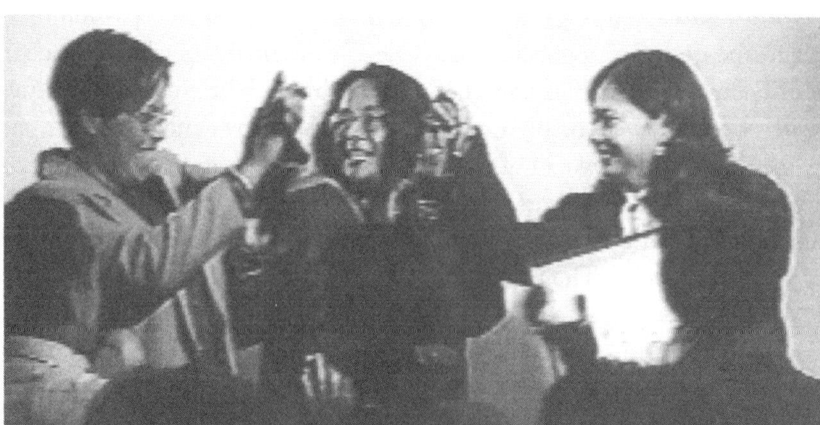

video is a utopian possibility; it is here where we begin to glimpse the importance of utopianism for the project of disidentification. Disidentificatory performances and readings require an active kernel of utopian possibility. Although utopianism has become the bad object of much contemporary political thinking, we nonetheless need to hold on to and even *risk* utopianism if we are to engage in the labor of making a queerworld.

Hidalgo's project also remakes utopianism into something different. Her utopianism is infused with humor and progressive camp sensibilities. In chapter 5, I discuss the way in which Ela Troyano and Carmelita Tropicana disidentify with camp, a predominantly gay white male project, and recast it as a view to a fabulous and funky Latina life-world. Hidalgo offers a camp utopianism that rejects the utopianism of somber prophecies of liberation and instead reimagines a radical future replete with humor and desire.

Her utopianism looks into the past to critique the present and helps imagine the future. The past that is represented in the video is the imagined past of Mesoamerican antiquity; the present that the film critiques is the current climate of immigrant scapegoating that targets Latinas and other women and men of color; and the future that the film imagines is a queer world that is as brown as it is bent. Theodor Adorno once commented that "utopia is essentially in the determined negation of that which merely is, and by concretizing itself as something false, it always points, at the same time, to what should be."[32] Hidalgo's project points to the "should be" with elegance, humor, and political ferocity.

Hidalgo's project and my own owe a tremendous debt to the writing of radical women of color that emerged in the 1970s. It is in those essays, rants, poems, and manifestos that we first glimpsed what a queer world might look like. The bridge to a queer world is, among other things, paved by *This Bridge Called My Back.*

Performing Disidentifications

Throughout this book, I refer to disidentification as a hermeneutic, a process of production, and a mode of performance. Disidentification can be understood as a way of shuffling back and forth between reception and production. For the critic, disidentification is the hermeneutical performance of decoding mass, high, or any other cultural field from the perspective of a minority subject who is disempowered in such a representational hierarchy. Stuart Hall has proposed a theory of encoding/decoding that has been highly influential in media and cultural studies. He postulates an understanding of broadcast television as yielding an encoded meaning that is both denotative and connotative of different ideological messages that reinforce the status quo of the majority culture. These codes are likely to seem natural to a member of a language community who has grown up in such a system. For Hall, there are three different options on the level of decoding. The first position for decoding is the dominant-hegemonic position where a "viewer takes the connoted from, say, a television newscast, full and straight and decodes its message in terms of the reference code in which it has been encoded, we might say the viewer is operating within the dominant code."[33] The second vantage point from which to decode is the negotiated position that, to some degree, acknowledges the constructed nature of discourse but does not, within its interpretative project, challenge its authorization. As Hall puts it: "Negotiated codes operate through what we might call particular or situated logics: and these logics are sustained by their differential and unequal logics of power."[34] The third and final position that Hall touches on is the oppositional one. This mode of reading resists, demystifies, and deconstructs the universalizing ruse of the dominant culture. Meanings are unpacked in an effort to dismantle dominant codes. As an approach to the dominant culture, disidentification is analogous to the paradigm of oppositional reception that Hall constructs within his essay.

The mode of cultural production that I am calling disidentification is indebted to earlier theories of revisionary identification. These foundational theories emerged from fields of film theory, gay and lesbian studies, and critical race theory. Although these different fields do not often branch into one another's boundaries, they have often attempted to negotiate similar methodological and theoretical concerns. The term "revisionary identification" is a loose construct that is intended to hold various accounts of tactical identification together. "Revisionary" is meant to signal different strategies of viewing, reading, and locating "self" within representational systems and disparate life-worlds that aim to displace or occlude a minority subject. The string that binds such different categories is a precariously thin one and it is important to specify the influence of different critical traditions on my own formulations by surveying some of the contributions they make to this project.

Film theory has used a psychological apparatus to figure identification in the cinematic text. Although the story of disidentification is decidedly *not* aligned with the orthodoxies of psychoanalysis in the same way that different branches of literary and film theory are, it does share with the psychoanalytic project an impulse to discern the ways in which subjectivity is formed in modern culture. Christian Metz, a French pioneer in psychoanalytic approaches to cinema, elaborated an influential theory of cinematic identification in the early seventies.[35] Drawing heavily from the Lacanian theory of the mirror stage, Metz outlines two different registers of filmic identification. Primary cinematic identification is identification with the "look" of the technical apparatus (camera, projector). The spectator, like the child positioned in front of the mirror constructing an imaginary ideal of a unified body, imagines an illusionary wholeness and mastery. Secondary identification, for Metz, is with a person who might be a star, actor, or character. Feminist film theorist Laura Mulvey posed a substantial challenge to Metz's formulation by inquiring as to the gender coordinates of the "bearer-of-the-look" and the object of the look.[36] Mulvey described standardized patterns of fascination in classical narrative cinema structure that placed the female spectator in the masochistic position of identifying with the female subject, who is either a scopophilic fetish in the narrative or a brutalized character on the screen. The other remaining option for Mulvey's female spectator is a cross-identification with the male protagonist who is, by the gender coding of the cinematic apparatus, placed in the dominant position of control. Implicit in Mulvey's argument is an understanding of any identification across gender as pathologically masochistic. Mulvey's and Metz's theories, when considered together, offer a convincing model of spectatorship and its working. Their models fall short insofar as they unduly valorize some very limited circuits of identification.[37]

Mulvey later refined her argument by once again returning to Freud and further specifying the nature of female desire along the lines pioneered by the founder of psychoanalysis. "Afterthoughts on 'Visual Pleasure and Narrative Cinema,' Inspired by *Duel in the Sun*" argues that the female spectator undergoes a certain regression that returns her to the transsexed site of her childhood identification that every young girl passes through.[38] The identification here is clearly encoded in the terminology of transvestism, a brand of degayed[39] transvestism that is positioned to disallow the possibility of reading a homosexual spectator. Psychoanalytic theorizations of cross-gender identification such as Mulvey's never challenge the normativity of dominant gender constructions.

Miriam Hansen, in her impressive study of early cinema and emergent practices of spectatorship, calls for a reworking of the Mulveyan paradigm to figure various oscillations in spectatorship between masculine and feminine.[40] In her chapter on Rudolph Valentino and "scenarios" of identification, Hansen writes:

> If we can isolate an instance of "primary" identification at all—which is dubious on theoretical grounds—Valentino's films challenge the assumption of perceptual mastery implied in such a concept both on account of the star system and because of the particular organization of the gaze. The star not only promotes a dissociation of scopic and narrative registers, but also complicates the imaginary self-identity of the viewing subject with an exhibitionist and collective dimension. . . . The Valentino films undermine the notion of unified position of scopic mastery by foregrounding the reciprocity and ambivalence of the gaze as an erotic medium, a gaze that fascinates precisely because it transcends the socially imposed subject-object hierarchy of sexual difference.[41]

Hansen moves away from the monolithic and stable spectator that was first posited by Metz and then gendered as masculine by Mulvey. The gaze itself is the site of identification in Hansen's study, and that gaze is never fixed but instead always vacillating and potentially transformative in its possibilities. Hansen also moves beyond Mulvey's theorizations of the female spectator as having the dismal options of either finding her lost early masculine identification or taking on a masochistic identification. Hansen's work, along with that of other film theorists in the 1980s, took the notion of spectatorial identification in more complicated and nuanced directions where the problem of identification was now figured in terms of instability, mobility, oscillation, and multiplicity.[42] Disidentification is, at its core, an ambivalent modality that cannot be conceptualized as a restrictive or "masterfully" fixed mode of identification. Disidentification, like Hansen's description of identification, is a survival strategy that is employed by a minority spectator (the female spectator of the early twentieth century in Hansen's study) to resist and confound socially prescriptive patterns of identification.

Scholars of color and gay and lesbian scholars also brought important and transformative urgencies to questions of spectatorship and identification. Manthia Diawara, for example, offered the historically relevant corrective to Mulvey's foundational theory:

> Laura Mulvey argues that the classical Hollywood film is made for the pleasure of the male spectator. However, as a black male spectator I wish to argue, in addition, that the dominant cinema situates Black characters primarily for the pleasure of White spectators (male or female). To illustrate this point, one may note how Black male characters in contemporary Hollywood films are made less threatening to Whites either by White domestication of Black customs and culture—a process of deracination and isolation—or by the stories in which Blacks are depicted playing by the rules of White society and losing.[43]

Contributions such as Diawara's made it clear that difference has many shades and any narrative of identification that does not account for the variables of race, class, and sexuality, as well as gender, is incomplete.[44] Queer film theory has also made crucial challenges to the understanding of identification. Chris Straayer outlines the reciprocity of identification in queer spectatorship, the active play of elaborating new identifications that were not visible on the surface. Straayer's "hypothetical lesbian heroine" is just such a disidentificatory construct: "The lesbian heroine in film must be conceived of as a viewer construction, short-circuiting the very networks that forbid her energy. She is constructed from the contradictions within the text and between text and viewer, who insists on assertive, even transgressive, identification and seeing."[45] The process Straayer narrates, of reading between the dominant text's lines, identifying as the classical text while actively resisting its encoded directives to watch and identify as a heterosexual, can be understood as the survival tactic that queers use when navigating dominant media. Such a process can be understood as disidentificatory in that it is not about assimilation into a heterosexual matrix but instead a partial disavowal of that cultural form that works to restructure it from within. The disidentification, in this instance, is the construction of a lesbian heroine that changes the way in which the object is inhabited by the subject.

My thinking on disidentification has also been strongly informed by the work of critical race theorists, who have asked important questions about the workings of identification for minority subjects within dominant media. Michele Wallace has described the process of identification as one that is "constantly in motion."[46] The flux that characterizes identification for Hansen when considering female spectatorship and identification is equally true of the African-American spectator in Wallace's article. Wallace offers testimony to her own position as a spectator:

> It was always said among Black women that Joan Crawford was part Black, and as I watch these films again today, looking at Rita Hayworth in *Gilda* or Lana Turner in *The Postman Always Rings Twice,* I keep thinking "she is so beautiful, she looks Black." Such a statement makes no sense in current feminist film criticism. What I am trying to suggest is that there was a way in which these films were *possessed* by Black female viewers. The process may have been about problematizing and expanding one's racial identity *instead* of abandoning it. It seems important here to view spectatorship as not only potentially bisexual but also multiracial and multiethnic. Even as "The Law of the Father" may impose its premature closure on the filmic "gaze" in the coordination of suture and classical narrative, disparate factions in the audience, not equally well indoctrinated in the dominant discourse, may have their way, now and then, with interpretation.[47]

The wistful statement that is central to Wallace's experience of identification, "she is so beautiful, she looks Black," is a poignant example of the transformative power of disidentification. White supremacist aesthetics is rearranged and put in the service of historically maligned black beauty standards. In this rumination, the Eurocentric conceit of whiteness and beauty as being naturally aligned (hence, straight hair is "good hair" in some African-American vernaculars) is turned on its head. Disidentification, like the subjective experience Wallace describes, is about expanding and problematizing identity and identification, not abandoning any socially prescribed identity component. Black female viewers are not merely passive subjects who are possessed by the well-worn paradigms of identification that the classical narrative produces; rather, they are active participant spectators who can mutate and restructure stale patterns within dominant media.

In the same way that Wallace's writing irrevocably changes the ways in which we consume forties films, the work of novelist and literary theorist Toni Morrison offers a much-needed reassessment of the canon of American literature. Morrison has described "a great, ornamental, prescribed absence in American literature,"[48] which is the expurgated African-American presence from the North American imaginary. Morrison proposes and executes strategies to reread the American canon with an aim to resuscitate the African presence that was eclipsed by the machinations of an escapist variant of white supremacist thought that is intent on displacing nonwhite presence. The act of locating African presence in canonical white literature is an example of disidentification employed for a focused political process. The mobile tactic (disidentification) refuses to follow the texts' grain insofar as these contours suggest that a reader play along with the game of African (or, for that matter, Asian, Latino, Arab, Native American) elision. Instead, the disidentificatory optic is turned to shadows and fissures within the text, where racialized presences can be liberated from the protective custody of the white literary imagination.

One of queer theory's major contributions to the critical discourse on identification is the important work that has been done on cross-identification. Sedgwick, for example, has contributed to this understanding of decidedly queer chains of connection by discussing the way in which lesbian writer Willa Cather was able to, on the one hand, disavow Oscar Wilde for his "grotesque" homosexuality while at the same moment uniquely invest in and identify with her gay male fictional creations: "If Cather, in this story, does something to cleanse her own sexual body of the carrion stench of Wilde's victimization, it is thus (unexpectedly) by identifying with what seems to be Paul's sexuality not in spite of but through its saving reabsorption in a gender liminal (and a very specifically classed) artifice that represents at once a particular subcultural and cultural self."[49] This is only one example of many within Sedgwick's oeuvre that narrates the nonlinear and nonnormative modes of identification with which queers predicate their self-fashioning. Judith Butler has amended Sedgwick's reading of Cather's cross-identification by insisting that such a passage across identity markers, a passage that she understands as being a "dangerous crossing," is not about being *beyond* gender and sexuality.[50] Butler sounds a warning that the crossing of identity may signal erasure of the "dangerous" or, to use Sedgwick's word when discussing the retention of the shameful, "toxic." For Butler, the danger exists in abandoning the lesbian or female in Cather when reading the homosexual and the male. The cautionary point that Butler would like to make is meant to ward off reductive fantasies of cross-identification that figure it as fully achieved or finally reached at the expense of the points from which it emanates. Although Sedgwick's theorizations about cross-identification and narrative crossing are never as final as Butler suggests, the issues that Butler outlines should be heeded when the precarious activity of cross-identification is discussed. The tensions that exist between cross-identification as it is theorized in Sedgwick's essay and Butler's response is one of the important spaces in queer theory that has been, in my estimation, insufficiently addressed. The theory of disidentification that I am putting forward responds to the call of that schism. Disidentification, as a mode of understanding the movements and circulations of identificatory force, would always foreground that lost object of identification; it would establish new possibilities while at the same time echoing the materially prescriptive cultural locus of any identification.

Operating within a very subjective register, Wayne Koestenbaum, in his moving study of opera divas and gay male opera culture, discusses the ways in which gay males can cross-identify with the cultural icon of the opera diva. Koestenbaum writes about the identificatory pleasure he enjoys when reading the prose of an opera diva's autobiographies:

> I am affirmed and "divined"—made porous, open, awake, glistening—by a diva's sentences of self-defense and self-creation.
>
> I don't intend to prove any historical facts; instead I want to trace connections between the iconography of "diva" as it emerges in certain publicized lives,

> and a collective gay subcultural imagination—a source of hope, joke, and dish. Gossip, hardly trivial, is as central to gay culture as it is to female cultures. From skeins of hearsay, I weave an inner life, I build queerness from banal and uplifting stories of the conduct of famous and fiery women.[51]

A diva's strategies of self-creation and self-defense, through the crisscrossed circuitry of cross-identification, do the work of enacting self for the gay male opera queen. The gay male subculture that Koestenbaum represents in his prose is by no means the totality of queer culture, but for this particular variant of a gay male lifeworld, such identifications are the very stuff on which queer identity is founded. Koestenbaum's memoir explains the ways in which opera divas were crucial identificatory loci in the public sphere before the Stonewall rebellion, which marked the advent of the contemporary lesbian and gay rights movement. Koestenbaum suggests that before a homosexual civil-rights movement, opera queens were the sole pedagogical example of truly grand-scale queer behavior. The opera queen's code of conduct was crucial to the closeted gay male before gay liberation. Again, such a practice of *transfiguring* an identificatory site that was not meant to accommodate male identities is to a queer subject an important identity-consolidating hub, an affirmative yet temporary utopia. Koestenbaum's disidentification with the opera diva does not erase the fiery females that fuel his identity-making machinery; rather, it lovingly retains their lost presence through imitation, repetition, and admiration.

Disidentification is about recycling and rethinking encoded meaning. The process of disidentification scrambles and reconstructs the encoded message of a cultural text in a fashion that both exposes the encoded message's universalizing and exclusionary machinations and recircuits its workings to account for, include, and empower minority identities and identifications. Thus, disidentification is a step further than cracking open the code of the majority; it proceeds to use this code as raw material for representing a disempowered politics or positionality that has been rendered unthinkable by the dominant culture.

Hybrid Lives/Migrant Souls

The cultural work I engage here is hybridized insofar as it is cultivated from the dominant culture but meant to expose and critique its conventions. It is no coincidence that the cultural workers who produce these texts all identify as subjects whose experience of identity is fractured and split. The type of fragmentation they share is something more than the general sense of postmodern fragmentation and decenteredness.[52] *Hybridity* in this study, like the term *disidentification,* is meant to have an indexical use in that it captures, collects, and brings into play various theories of fragmentation in relation to minority identity practices. Identity markers such as *queer* (from the German *quer* meaning "transverse") or *mestizo* (Spanish for "mixed") are terms that defy notions of uniform identity or origins. *Hybrid* catches the fragmentary subject formation of people whose identities traverse different race, sexuality, and gender identifications.

Queers of color is a term that begins to describe most of the cultural performers/makers in every chapter of *Disidentifications.* These subjects' different identity components occupy adjacent spaces and are not comfortably situated in any one discourse of minority subjectivity. These hybridized identificatory positions are always in transit, shuttling between different identity vectors. Gayatri Chakravorty Spivak has suggested that migrant urban public culture, by its very premise, hybridizes identity.[53] A theory of migrancy can potentially help one better understand the negotiation of these fragmentary existences. The negotiations that lead to hybrid identity formation are a traveling back and forth from different identity vectors.

Arturo Islas's second novel, *Migrant Souls,* provides an opportunity to consider the idea of migrancy. The novel tells of two "black sheep" cousins in a large Chicano family. The female cousin's divorce, disrespect for the church, and sexually emancipated attitude alienate her from the family. But it is the male cousin, Miguel Chico, who is of especial interest in this project. Miguel, like the Richard Rodriguez of *Hunger of Memory,* is the scholarship boy who gets out of the barrio because of his academic excellence. Unlike Rodriguez, Miguel is at least partially out about his homosexuality.[54] Miguel's trip home, from his out existence as an academic Chicano to the semicloseted familial space of identity formation, exemplifies the kind of shuttling I describe. Of course, this movement is not only a by-product of Miguel's status as queer son; all of the family, in some way, experience migrancy. The text explains as much when it articulates the family ethos: "They were migrant, not immigrant, souls. They simply and naturally went from one bloody side of the river to the other and into a land that just a few decades earlier had been Mexico. They became border Mexicans with American citizenship."[55] I want to identify a deconstructive kernel in these three sentences by Islas. The idea of a border is scrutinized in this locution. The migrant status can be characterized by its need to move back and forth, to occupy at least two spaces at once. (This is doubly true for the queer Latino son.) The very nature of this migrant drive eventually wears down the coherency of borders. Can we perhaps think of Miguel, a thinly camouflaged authorial surrogate, as a border Mexican with citizenship in a queer nation or a border queer national claiming citizenship in Aztlán?

Marga's Life

After this tour of different high-theory paradigms, I find myself in a position where I need to reassert that part of my aim in this book is to push against reified understanding of theory. The cultural workers whom I focus on can be seen as making theoretical points and contributions to the issues explored in ways that are just as relevant and useful as the phalanx of institutionally sanctioned theorists that I promiscuously invoke throughout these pages. To think of cultural workers such as Carmelita Tropicana, Vaginal Creme Davis, Richard Fung, and the other artists who are considered here as not only culture makers but also theory producers is not to take an antitheory position. My chapter on Davis's terrorist drag employs Antonio Gramsci's theory of organic intellectuals in an effort to emphasize the theory-making power of performance. It should be understood as an attempt at opening up a term whose meaning has become narrow and rigid. Counterpublic performances let us imagine models of social relations. Such performance practices do not shy away from the theoretical practice of cultural critique.

Consider, once again, the example of Marga Gomez's performance piece *Marga Gomez Is Pretty, Witty, and Gay.* When the lesbian calls out to the young Marga, lasciviously flicking her tongue at the girl, the story of interpellation is reimagined with a comical and critical difference. One possible working definition of queer that we might consider is this: queers are people who have failed to turn around to the "Hey, you there!" interpellating call of heteronormativity. A too literal reading of Althusser's ideology cop fable suggests one primary moment of hailing. Such a reading would also locate one primary source or mechanism that hails the subject. But the simple fact is that we are continuously hailed by various ideological apparatuses that compose the state power apparatus. No one knows this better than queers who are constantly being hailed as "straight" by various institutions—including the mainstream media. The humor and cultural critique that reverberate through this moment in the performance are rooted in Gomez's willful disidentification with this call; she critiques and undermines the call of heteronormativity by fabricating a remade and queered televisual hailing. Through her disidentificatory comedic "shtick," she retells the story of interpellation with a difference.

After Gomez explains how she was "hailed" into lesbianism by the talk-show sapphists, she paces the stage and ruminates on her desire for the life-world these women represented:

> Mr. Susskind and the lady homosexuals chain-smoked through the entire program. I think it was relaxing for them. I don't think they could have done it without the smokes. It was like they were in a gay bar just before last call. And all the smoke curling up made *the life* seem more mysterious.
>
> *The life*—that's what they called it back then when you were one of us. You were in *the life*! It was short for *the hard and painful life.* It sounded so dramatic. I loved drama. I was in the drama club in high school. I wanted to be in *the life,* too. But I was too young. So I did the next best thing. I asked my mother to buy me Life cereal and *Life* magazine. For Christmas I got the game of Life.

Gomez paints a romantic and tragic picture of pre-Stonewall gay reality. She invests this historical moment with allure and sexiness. The performer longs for this queer and poignant model of a lesbian identity. This longing for *the life* should not be read as a nostalgic wish for a lost world, but instead, as the performance goes on to indicate, as a redeployment of the past that is meant to offer a critique of the present. After all the talk of smoking, she pulls out a cigarette and begins to puff on it.

> And as I moved the lonely game pieces around the board, I pretended I was smoking Life cigarettes and living *the life.* By the time I was old enough, no one called it the life anymore. It sounded too isolating and politically incorrect. Now they say *the community. The community* is made up of all of us who twenty-five years ago would have been in *the life.* And in the community there is no smoking.

She concludes the narrative by stamping out an imaginary cigarette. The performance, staged in many gay venues and for a crowd who might be called "the converted," does more than celebrate contemporary queer culture. Gomez's longing for a pre-Stonewall version of queer reality is a look toward the past that critiques the present and helps us envision the future. Although it might seem counterintuitive, or perhaps self-hating, to desire this moment before the quest for lesbian and gay civil rights, such an apprehension should be challenged. Marga's look toward the mystery and outlaw sensibility of *the life* is a critique of a sanitized and heteronormativized *community.* In Gomez's comedy, we locate a disidentificatory desire, a desire for a queer life-world that is smoky, mysterious, and ultimately contestatory. More than that, we see a desire to escape the claustrophobic confines of "community," a construct that often deploys rhetorics of normativity and normalization, for a life. *The life,* or at least Gomez's disidentification with this concept, helps us imagine an expansive queer *life*-world, one in which the "pain and hardship" of queer existence within a homophobic public sphere are not elided, one in which the "mysteries" of our sexuality are not reigned in by sanitized understandings of lesbian and gay identity, and finally, one in which we are all allowed to be drama queens and smoke as much as our hearts desire.

Part I
The Melancholia of Race

Chapter 1

Famous and Dandy like B. 'n' Andy: Race, Pop, and Basquiat

Disidentifying in the Dark

I always marvel at the ways in which nonwhite children survive a white supremacist U.S. culture that preys on them. I am equally in awe of the ways in which queer children navigate a homophobic public sphere that would rather they did not exist. The survival of children who are both queerly and racially identified is nothing short of staggering. The obstacles and assaults that pressure and fracture such young lives are as brutally physical as a police billy club or the fists of a homophobic thug and as insidiously disembodied as homophobic rhetoric in a rap song or the racist underpinnings of Hollywood cinema. I understand the strategies and rituals that allow survival in such hostile cultural waters, and I in turn feel a certain compulsion to try to articulate and explicate these practices of survival. These practices are the armaments such children and the adults they become use to withstand the disabling forces of a culture and state apparatus bent on denying, eliding, and, in too many cases, snuffing out such emergent identity practices. Sometimes these weapons are so sharply and powerfully developed that these same queer children and children of color grow up to do more than just survive. And sometimes such shields collapse without a moment' s notice. When I think about Andy Warhol, I think about a sickly queer boy who managed to do much more than simply survive. Jean-Michel Basquiat, painter and graffitist, a superstar who rose quickly within the ranks of the New York art scene and fell tragically to a drug overdose in 1988, is for me another minority subject who managed to master various forms of cultural resistance that young African-Americans needed to negotiate racist U.S. society and its equally racist counterpart in miniature, the 1980s art world.[1]

These practices of survival are, of course, not anything like intrinsic attributes that a subject is born with. More nearly, these practices are learned. They are not figured out alone, they are informed by the examples of others. These identifications with others are often mediated by a complicated network of incomplete, mediated, or crossed identifications. They are also forged by the pressures of everyday life, forces that shape a subject and call for different tactical responses. It is crucial that such children are able to look past "self" and encounter others who have managed to prosper in such spaces. Sometimes a subject needs something to identify with; sometimes a subject needs heroes to mimic and to invest all sorts of energies in. Basquiat's heroes included certain famous black athletes and performers, four-color heroes of comic books, and a certain very white New York artist. These identifications are discussed in a recollection of the artist by *Yo MTV Raps!* host Fab Five Freddy:

> We [also] talked about painting a lot. And that was when Jean-Michel and I realized we had something in common. There were no other people from the graffiti world who knew anything about the painters who interested us. Everybody was interested by comic book art-stuff sold in supermarkets with bright colors and bold letters. Jean-Michel discovered that my favorite artists were Warhol and Rauschenberg, and I found out that Jean-Michel's favorite artists were Warhol and Jasper Johns. Which was great because we could talk about other painters as well as the guys painting on trains.[2]

In this nostalgic narrative identification with highbrow cultural production, coupled with a parallel identification with the lowbrow graphic genre of the comic book, is what sets Basquiat apart from the rest of the subculture of early eighties New York graffiti artists. This double identification propelled Basquiat into the realm of "serious" visual artist. This powerful and complex identification is what made the movement from talking *about* Warhol to talking *to* Warhol so swift for Basquiat.

For Basquiat, Warhol embodied the pinnacle of artistic and professional success. One does not need to know this biographical information to understand the ways in which Basquiat's body of work grew out of pop art. But biographical fragments are helpful when we try to understand the ways in which this genius child from Brooklyn was able to meet his hero, and gain access to and success in the exclusive halls of that New York art world where Warhol reigned. At the same time, a turn to biography is helpful when we try to call attention to the white supremacist bias of the eighties art world and the larger popular culture that the pop art movement attempted to capture in its representations. Although it should be obvious to most, there is still a pressing need to articulate a truism about pop art's race ideology: there are next to no people of color populating the world of pop art—either as producers or as subjects. Representations of people of color are scarce, and more often than not worn-out stereotypes. Warhol's work is no exception: one need only think of the portrait of a Native American titled *American Indian,* the drag queens of *Ladies and Gentlemen,* and the mammy from the *Myths Series.* The paintings reproduce images that are ingrained in the North American racist imagination. There is no challenge or complication of these constructs on the level of title or image. Pop art's racial iconography is racist. A thesis/defense of these images is an argument that understands these representations as calling attention to and, through this calling out, signaling out the racist dimensions of typical North American iconography. I find this apologetic reading politically dubious in that it fails to contextualize these images within the larger racial problematics of pop art.

With this posited, I will swerve back to the story this chapter wants to tell, the story of how a middle-class black child of Haitian and Puerto Rican parents from Brooklyn becomes famous like Andy Warhol. The line I want to trace is one that begins with identifying with one's heroes, actually becoming like one's role model and then moving on. This line is not easy to follow inasmuch as it is neither linear nor in any way straight. It is, in fact, a very *queer* trajectory. There are some identifications that the culture not only reinforces but depends on. An example of this would be the way in which some young black males identify with famous black athletes and entertainment media stars. Such a normativized chain of associations transmits valuable cultural messages while, at the same time, depending on the identifying subject, it reinforces traditional ideas of "masculinity." Other identifications are harder to trace: how does this young African-American identify with a muscular red, blue, and gold—and yes, white—"superman," not to mention the pastiest of art-world megastars?

In what follows, I will consider these different identity-informing fixations and the ways in which they resurfaced in Basquiat's body of work. Central to this project is an understanding of the process of "disidentification" and its significance to Basquiat's artistic practices. I understand the survival strategies that subjects such as Basquiat and Warhol utilize as practices of disidentification.

Disidentification for the minority subject is a mode of *recycling* or re-forming an object that has already been invested with powerful energy. It is important to emphasize the transformative restructuration of that disidentification. With this notion of disidentification posited, I will be suggesting that it is simply not enough to say that Basquiat identified with his subject matter or "heroes," be they Batman or Warhol. Beyond that, it is not enough to say that Basquiat identified with the movement known as pop art or any of its derivatives. This is not to say that he rejected these previous cultural players, forms, and practices. Instead, he acknowledged and incorporated their force and influence; *transfigured,* they inform his own strategies and tactics in powerful ways.

Superheroes and Supremacists

Only now is cultural studies beginning to address the tremendous impact of superheroes, cartoons, and comic books in contemporary culture. Basquiat, like Warhol, was fascinated by the persistence and centrality of these characters in the cultural imaginary. Warhol, Roy Lichtenstein, and others blew up such images, calling attention to the art that goes into creating these seemingly artless productions. They zoomed in on every zip dot and gaudy color that made these characters larger than life. Michael Moon and Sasha Torres have forcefully explained the powerful homosocial and homosexual charges that animate these characters in our contemporary cultural mythologies.[3] Although I do not want to foreclose similar inquiries into Basquiat's identification with such images, I want to investigate another salient characteristic of these graphic figures: race. By examining the origins and aesthetics of the superhero, I will suggest that the twentieth-century myth of the superhero was, in its earliest manifestation, a disidentifying cultural formation that informed pop art and its legacy.

The American icon Superman first appeared in *Action Comics* in June 1938. It is important to contextualize this first appearance alongside early twentieth-century racist imaginings of a race of supermen. In their history of the comic book superhero, Greg S. McCue and Clive Bloom outline some of the cultural forces that helped form the Man of Steel:

> The multitude of supermen in the air was not limited to adventurers. In the early twentieth century, America was becoming aware of Nietzsche's *Übermensch* from *Thus Spoke Zarathustra.* Shaw's allusion to the idea in *Man and Superman* had made "superman" the translation of choice, replacing "overman" or "beyond-man." Two young Jewish men [Superman's creators Jerry Siegal and Joe Shuster] in the United States at the time could not have been unaware of an idea that would dominate Hitler's National Socialism. The concept was certainly well discussed.[4]

McCue and Bloom allude to a connection between the comic creators' status as Jews and the transfiguration of the anti-Semitic possibility encoded within the popular notion of a "superman." I would push their point further and suggest that the young writer and artist team not only was "aware" of all the notions of supermen saturating both North American and European culture but actively strove to respond to it by reformulating the myth of Superman outside of anti-Semitic and xenophobic cultural logics. The writers go on to suggest the character's resemblance to other important figures within the Judeo-Christian tradition: "Superman, as a religious allusion, has been indicated as a contributing factor in his creation and continued popularity. The infant Kal-El's [who would eventually grow up to be Superman] spaceship can be seen as a modern-day cradle of Moses on the cosmic Nile."[5] I want to suggest that within the myth of Superman, a myth that Basquiat and Warhol both utilized in powerful ways, a disidentificatory kernel was already present. The last son of Krypton is not only a popularized *Übermensch.* He is, at the same time, the rewriting of Moses, who led the Jews out of Egypt and through such obstacles as the Red Sea and the wilderness. For the young Jewish comic creators and the countless fans who consumed their work, the dark-haired alien superman was a powerful reworking and reimagining of a malevolent cultural fantasy that was gaining symbolic force.

If one decodes the signifiers of Jewish ethnicity that are central to Superman's mythic fabric it becomes clear that, working through the Superman character, its creators were able to intervene in another phobic anti-Semitic fantasy that figured the Jew's body as weak and sickly. Sander Gilman has addressed this issue in his study *The Jew's Body.* Gilman describes the racist science of eugenics's need to figure morphological difference when discussing the Jew's difference. Such discourses fed scientific discourse during the Nazi era. Gilman explains the ways in which the Jew's body as weak and sickly was first registered and the Zionist call for a new Jewish body that was proposed as an antidote to this stereotype:

> Elias Auerbach's evocation of sport as the social force to reshape the Jewish body had its origins in the turn-of-the-century call of the physician and Zionist leader Max Nordau for a new "Muscle Jew." This view became the commonplace of the early Zionist literature which called upon sport, as an activity, as one of the central means of shaping the new Jewish body.[6]

With Gilman's valuable historical analysis we can begin to understand the unique process of ethnic disidentification, a process, once again, of transfiguration and reorganization on the level of identification. Siegal and Shuster displaced dominant racist images of the Jew as pathological and weak by fusing together the dangerous mythologies of the *Übermensch* with something like Nordau's fantasy of the "Muscle Jew." The Superman character held on to both of these images, like lost objects that could not be dispelled no matter how hateful or self-hating their particular origin points might be. What is left at the end of this disidentificatory process is a new model of identity and a newly available site of identification.

The 1980s saw a painful resurgence of white supremacist activity in the subcultural models of the skinhead and neo-Nazi. With this in mind, I want to consider Basquiat's rewriting/reimagining of Superman.[7] His painting titled *Action Comics* is a reproduction of the original cover art for *Action Comics.* Stylistically, the painting strays from the earlier pop practice of reproducing and magnifying the hyperreal perfection of these images.[8] Basquiat's Superman is stripped of its fantasy aura of white male perfection. Instead of faultless lines we encounter rough and scrawl-like lines that translate this image to the graphic grammar of a child's perception. The disidentificatory strokes here retain the vibrancy of this fantasy of wanting to be Superman, of wanting to be able to accomplish awe-inspiring feats that only the Man of Steel can accomplish, without retaining the aestheticism of the image. In this painting, Superman is, in a manner of speaking, brought back to his roots. Basquiat's rendition of the character and the classic cover art works to resuscitate the disidentificatory force of the character's first incarnation and appearance.

The same childlike technique is deployed in Basquiat's rendition of Batman and Robin in *Piano Lesson.* The title implies the disidentificatory locus of such production, a space that might be imagined as the mandatory childhood piano lesson, a moment where fantasizing about superheroes is a tactic to transcend the boredom of childhood. Batman and Robin appear as though they are being rebuilt in the painting.

Jean-Michel Basquiat, *Television and Cruelty to Animals* (1983). Copyright 1998 Artists Rights Society (ARS), New York/ADAGP, Paris. Photo courtesy of Christie's Images.

The familiar superheroes' bodies are fragmented and incomplete. Such a representation connotes the revisionary and transformative effect of disidentification. The half-finished figures connote *process,* which is exactly how the *process* of disidentification should be understood.

This disidentificatory impulse is even more prominent in a later painting. The 1983 *Television and Cruelty to Animals* presents a mangled menagerie of cartoon characters. The canvas is populated by a large moose head that we might imagine as Bullwinkle, a stray black eight ball, the familiar Superman insignia, a curious conflation of that insignia and the bat signal and two crossed-out swastikas. We can say the barrage of images represents a pop media overload that characterizes postmodern North American childhood and adulthood. But I am more interested in the word images found near the top right-hand section of the painting. Here we see the phrase "Popeye versus the Nazis" written with a shaky black oil stick. This double-voiced articulation explicates the schoolyard fantasies of which mythological figure is mightier, "who can beat who up." More important, it reveals the ideologies of white supremacy that are never too distant from the "good guys" of this collective imaginary. Ideologies that Basquiat's disidentificatory process brings into a new visibility. Ideologies that can be, like the Batman insignia in *Television and Cruelty to Animals*, temporarily crossed out. The superhero insignia is just one of many of the symbols in contemporary culture that Basquiat worked with, other types of signifiers that the artist focused on were those that indicated ownership, such as the trademark sign and the copyright symbol. The next section will focus on Basquiat's disidentification with the commodity form and its signifiers.

Brand Basquiat

Basquiat's disidentification with the cartoon genre was certainly more radical than, but not altogether dissimilar from, the disidentification that characterized pop art's first wave. The variance is the intensity of the disidentificatory impulse and its relation to the image's aesthetic "realism." A 1984 collaboration between Warhol and Basquiat sharply contrasts these strategies. The right side of the canvas displays the classic pop disidentificatory stance. This strategy was described by Lucy Lippard as the tension that is produced because of the narrow distance between the original and the pop art piece.[9] Warhol's Arm & Hammer symbol on the right has the appearance of a seamless reproduction. But the relationship to the original design or "model" is strictly disidentificatory. In Warhol's distinctly postmodern practice, the image's disjunctive relocation calls attention to the trace of human labor, personified in the rolled-up worker's arm that has always been central to the design. This strategy disrupts the normative protocols of the commodity form. Susan Stewart explains the workings of the commodity system in her important study of outlaw representational strategies: "For it is the nature of the commodity system, of its compelling systematicity per se, to replace labor with magic, intrinsicality with marketing, authoring with ushering."[10] The refiguration of the trademark on Warhol's side of the canvas interrupts the erasure of labor by calling attention to the trademark's very inscription, one that, when properly scrutinized, reveals the thematics of labor that the commodity system works to elide.

Basquiat deals with the same subject matter but approaches a critique of the commodity form from a vastly different perspective that is still, within the terms of this analysis, disidentificatory. The circular center in Basquiat's half of the painting is occupied by a dime that features a black man playing the saxophone. This image calls attention to the often effaced presence of black production. An intervention such as this interrogates the ways in which the United States is, at bottom, a former slave economy that still counts on and factors in the exploitation and colonization of nonwhite labor. This is especially true in the arenas of cultural labor. Basquiat's intervention does more than call attention to the artifice and "constructedness" of these images. His half of the painting explodes a racial signifier that is often erased in the empire of signs that is the world of U.S. advertising.

Although the compulsive need to periodize different stages and levels of modernity is often the quickest route to stale and static conceptual grids, I do find some of Paul Gilroy's theorizations about the "premodern" in modernity a useful apparatus for contemplating the black horn-blowing body in the center of Basquiat's half of the painting. In an essay whose title asks the provocative question "Whose Millennium Is This?" Gilroy writes:

> Benjamin says that remembering creates the chain of tradition. His concern is with "perpetuating remembrance," and here, this modern black consciousness shares something with his blend of Jewish eschatology and Marxism. They converge, for example, in a concern with dissonance, negativity, redemption, and aesthetic stress on pain and suffering. Looking at modern black art and the social relations that support it can reveal how this remembering is socially and politically organized in part through assertive tactics which accentuate the symbolism of the pre-modern as part of their anti-modern modernism.[11]

The black face, starkly juxtaposed to the white arm, displays the vastly different cultural habitus of the two artists. The face, cartoonish and primitive, but primitive not in a contrived jungle fashion, but rather, with the primitivity of childhood, harks back to a "pre" moment that might be understood as premodern, but is also "pre" the congealing of subject formation. Its reference point is black music, which, as Gilroy has argued, is a key signifying practice within black Atlantic culture: "Music and its attendant rituals provide the most important locations where the unspeakable and unwriteable memory of terror is preserved as a social and cultural resource."[12] In the same way that shame cannot be expurgated in Sedgwick's understanding of the affect shame's relation to identity formation, this terror, this "unspeakable" terror that Gilroy identifies as being central to diaspora aesthetics and cultural practices, must, like the melancholic subject's lost object, be retained in the matrix of identity and its representations. Basquiat's figure, a shirtless, crudely sketched black male who plays a saxophone, is a melancholic reverberation that vibrates through the contemporary pop art project. Its "sound" evokes and eulogizes a lost past, a childhood, and a memory of racial exploitation and terror.

In Basquiat's disidentificatory project one encounters a proliferation of trademarks and copyright symbols. Such symbols remind the viewer that the history of consumer culture that Basquiat is signifying upon is an economy that was, in no small part, formulated on the premise that the ownership of other human beings was entirely possible. The quotidian dimensions of the commodity form are continually called attention to in paintings such as *Quality Meats for the Public,* where words such as *swine, poultry,* or *animated pig* are trademarked. Lauren Berlant, in an essay on national brands and the racialized body, reminds us that "A trademark is supposed to be a consensual mechanism. It triangulates with the consumer and the commodity,

Jean-Michel Basquiat, *Quality Meats for the Public* (1982). Copyright 1998 Artists Rights Society (ARS), New York/ADAGP, Paris. Photo courtesy of the Gagosian Gallery.

providing what W. F. Haug calls a 'second skin' that enables the commodity to appear to address, to recognize, and thereby to love the consumer."[13] I want to argue that the Basquiat brand trademark disrupts the triangulating mediation of consumer and commodity. It does so by producing an effect that Greg Tate has described, when writing about Basquiat's painting, as "an overloaded sensorium counterattacking the world via feedback loop."[14] If all the world's swine and poultry are exposed as always already trademarked, the special imaginary relationship that the trademark mediates is then short-circuited. The second skin is skinned.

Near the end of his too brief career, Basquiat began employing the trademark IDEAL. IDEAL, as used in his 1987 painting *Victor 25448,* clearly represents the na-

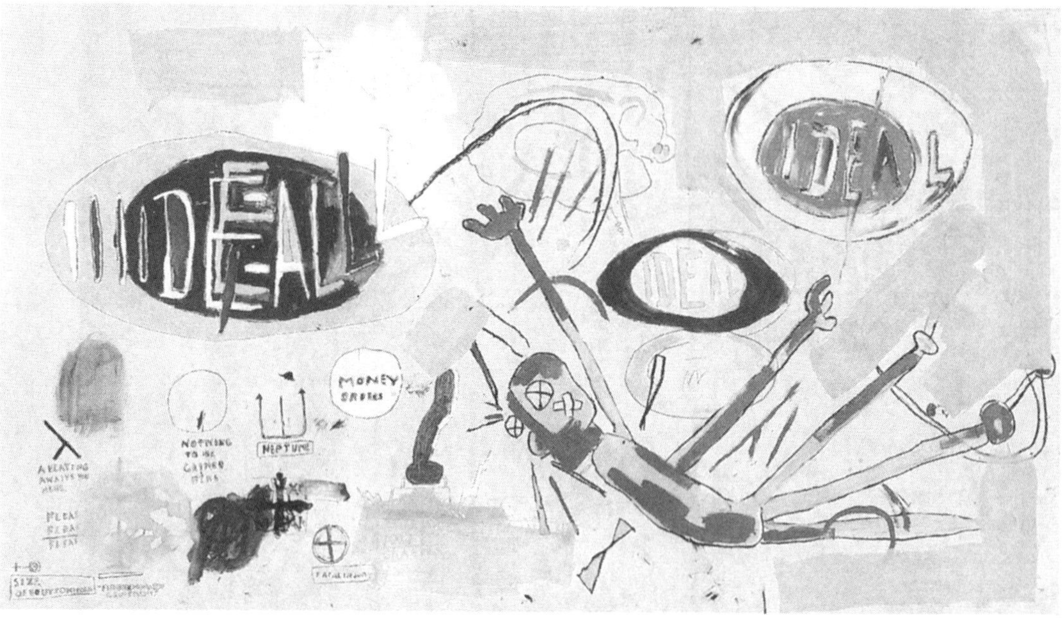

Jean-Michel Basquiat, *Victor 25448* (1987). Copyright 1998 Artists Rights Society (ARS), New York/ADAGP, Paris. Photo courtesy of the Brant Foundation.

tional toy brand, but one is also left to think that the statement is reflective of the trademark's status as "consensual mechanism" that makes the commodity object the *ideal* that the consumer is always shooting for. The particular plight of the black male consumer is embodied in the black figure stumbling and falling in the direction of the floating ideal symbols. The black male's flailing limbs and "x-ed-out" eyes are descriptive of the figure's betrayal by the "consensual mechanism" contract. IDEAL is, of course, also reflective of Basquiat's own participation in such a process. Indeed, none of his paintings can be understood as counteridentifications, including straightforward attacks, on commodity culture's iconography insofar as he too deals in such practices. The "I" in *ideal* is a Basquiat who also "deals" like an art dealer or drug pusher in the same consumer public sphere. He is, I have argued, working on and against a cultural pattern, a pattern that he, through his disidentificatory process, can transfigure.

Stewart has forcefully argued that the connections to be made between "real" graffiti writers and graffiti artists such as Basquiat who showed their work in galleries instead of subway trains are nearly nonexistent. I argue that his mass proliferation of the copyright and trademark sign works in similar ways as the "tags" of the urban graffiti writers she discusses. I make this claim, in part, because Basquiat began, as the testimony of Fab Five Freddy attests, as a graffiti artist on the trains and derelict walls of abandoned buildings in New York City. Stewart explains that the graffiti writer's use of the brand name has a disruptive effect on the symbolic economy of the commodity system:

> They have borrowed from the repetitions of advertising and commercial culture as antiepitaph: the names' frequent appearance marks the stubborn ghost of individuality and intention in mass culture, the ironic restatement of the artist as "brand name." Graffiti celebrates the final victory of the signature over the referent, by making claims on the very subjectivity invented by consumerism. In this sense they have gone beyond pop art, which always took on the abstractions of the exchange economy solely as a matter of thematic.[15]

Basquiat's repetitions of trademarks, brand names, figures, and words set up a parallel commodity system that, using the logic of Stewart's argument, produces an individual subject who disidentifies (restructures) the social holding pattern that is the mass-produced subject. Specificities, such as race, that are meant to be downplayed or whitewashed in consumer culture rise to the forefront of his production. I do not detect a victory of consumerism in Basquiat's project in the ways in which Stewart sees the graffiti writer's project as being a triumph over consumer capitalism. Instead, I see Basquiat's practice as a strategy of disidentification that retools and is ultimately able to open up a space where a subject can imagine a mode of surviving the nullifying force of consumer capitalism's models of self.

Stewart's charge that pop art, because of its location and complicity within consumerism, has made its critique operational only on the level of iconography and thematics is ultimately too sweeping an indictment. The notion that one is either coopted by consumerism or fighting the "real" fight against it poses a reductive binarism between representation and "reality." If Stewart's locution is uncontested, the work of making queer culture in a homophobic world, as in the case of Warhol, or representing black male youth culture in places where it has been systematically erased (such as the Soho gallery), would only register as the rumblings of bourgeois society's assimilation machine.

Famous

This section deals with questions of Warhol's and Basquiat's interpersonal identifications and their collaborations as both celebrities and artists, and with the thematic of fame that links their two personas. Before considering Basquiat's unstable identifications, disidentifications, and counteridentifications with Warhol, I want to briefly gloss some of the ways in which Jean-Michel meant a lot to Andy. First the art. In 1984, Warhol explained that "Jean-Michel got me into painting differently, so that's a good thing." Indeed, if we look at Warhol's work after his collaboration with Basquiat, we see a renewed interest in painting by hand, a process he had not done very much of, beyond some abstract backgrounds, since 1962. Warhol's star status was equally revitalized by Basquiat. Few would deny that making appearances with hot young art-world superstars Basquiat and Keith Haring upped Andy's glamour ratings. Basquiat also provided Andy's infamous diary with many a juicy gossip tidbit. The following passage from Warhol's diary recounts a story that is uncharacteristically sentimental:

> Saturday, May 5, 1984
>
> It was beautiful and sunny, did a lot of work. Called Jean-Michel and he said he'd come up. He came and rolled some joints. He was really nervous, I could tell, about how his show was opening later on at Mary Boone's. Then he wanted a new outfit and we went to this store where he always buys his clothes. He had b.o. We were walking and got to Washington Square Park where I first met him when he was signing his name "SAMO" and writing graffiti and painting T-shirts. That area brought back bad memories for him. Later on his show was great, though, it really was.[16]

This passage reveals a bit of the complexity of Warhol's identification with Basquiat. Warhol's sensitivity to Basquiat's "bad memories" of his seedy days as a graffiti artist selling hand-painted T-shirts in Washington Square Park might very well echo his own discomfort with his past, his own inability to completely reconcile that past with his present. The mention of joints also further signifies with Andy's later disavowal of the crazy people and drug addicts who populated the Factory days. We also hear Warhol's bitchy b.o. comment, which served to temper his identification with Basquiat. But finally, Basquiat's victory at Mary Boone's is, for the older artist, both an identification with Warhol's former early successes and a victory for him because of his current investment in the twenty-four-year-old artist. Warhol also records a much more poignant identification in the diaries. He recounts an August 5, 1984, party at the Limelight for Jermaine Jackson. The bouncers are described as "dumb Mafia-type of guys who didn't know anyone." After being rejected at the door, Basquiat turned to Warhol and exclaimed, "Now you see how it is to be Black."[17]

Basquiat's formal disidentification, his simultaneous working with, against, and on Warhol's production, is uniquely thematized in a collaboration with Warhol that depicts one of Warhol's motorcycle images and one of Basquiat's distinctive distorted figures. The enlarged image of the motorcycle from a newspaper ad is one that Warhol repeated throughout his mid-1980s black-and-white and Last Supper series. The black figures that Basquiat contributes to the frame work once again to show the black presence that has been systematically denied from this representational practice. These primitive jet black images look only vaguely human and bare sharp fangs. Through such representations, Basquiat ironizes the grotesque and distortive African-American presentations in consumer culture. In this canvas, like many of the other Warhol collaborations, the smooth lines of Warhol's practice work as *a vehicle* for Basquiat's own political and cultural practice.

The title for this chapter is a riff stolen from the Disposable Heroes of Hiphoprisy. In their 1992 song "Famous and Dandy like Amos 'n' Andy," the fictional characters are an entry point into a hip-hop meditation on the history of black media representation and the price of fame for African-Americans. These are, of course, important thematics for Basquiat. (Basquiat used and trademarked names of characters from the early radio and TV show in some of his paintings.) Fame is of tremendous import for both of this chapter's subjects, but a comparison of one of Basquiat's Famous Negro Athletes images to Warhol's portraits illustrates the world of difference between these two disidentificatory impulses and the aesthetic effects they produce. Warhol's portraits of Liza, Marilyn, Liz Taylor, Elvis, and so on, are not so much portraits of celebrities as of fame itself. Although it can be argued that Basquiat's paintings also treat fame as a subject, his formulations enact the disturbing encounter between fame and racist ideology that saturates North American media culture. The Famous Negro Athletes series reflects the problematic of being a famous black image that is immediately codified as a trademark by a white entertainment industry. The deployment of the word *Negro* is a disidentification with the racist cultural history that surrounds the history both of sports in the United States and of the contested lives of African-Americans in general. The simplicity of the following image exposes these dynamics of being famous and ethnically identified in U.S. culture; we see a trinity of three images: a hastily scrawled black head, a crown symbol that accompanied most of the painting in this series, and a baseball. The controversy that ensued in 1992 when one major baseball team executive, Marge Schott of the Cincinnati Reds, referred to one of her players as "a million-dollar nigger" makes a point that Basquiat was making in this series: the rich and famous black athlete is not immune to the assaults of various racisms. Within such racist imaginings, the famous black athlete is simply equated with the ball and other tools of the trade. Basquiat interrupts this trajectory by inserting the crown symbol between the man and object. The crown was an image that Basquiat frequently used to symbolize the rich history of Africans and African-Americans. The crown, or the title of "King," is, as Stewart explains, used to designate the supremacy of graffiti artists who were able to best proliferate and disseminate their tags.

Fab Five Freddy explained Basquiat's Famous Negro Artists series as follows: "And like a famous Negro athlete, Jean-Michel slid into home. He stole all three bases, actually, and then slid in to home. Home being Mary Boone's gallery."[18] I want to further engage this metaphor and speculate that home base was also embodied in

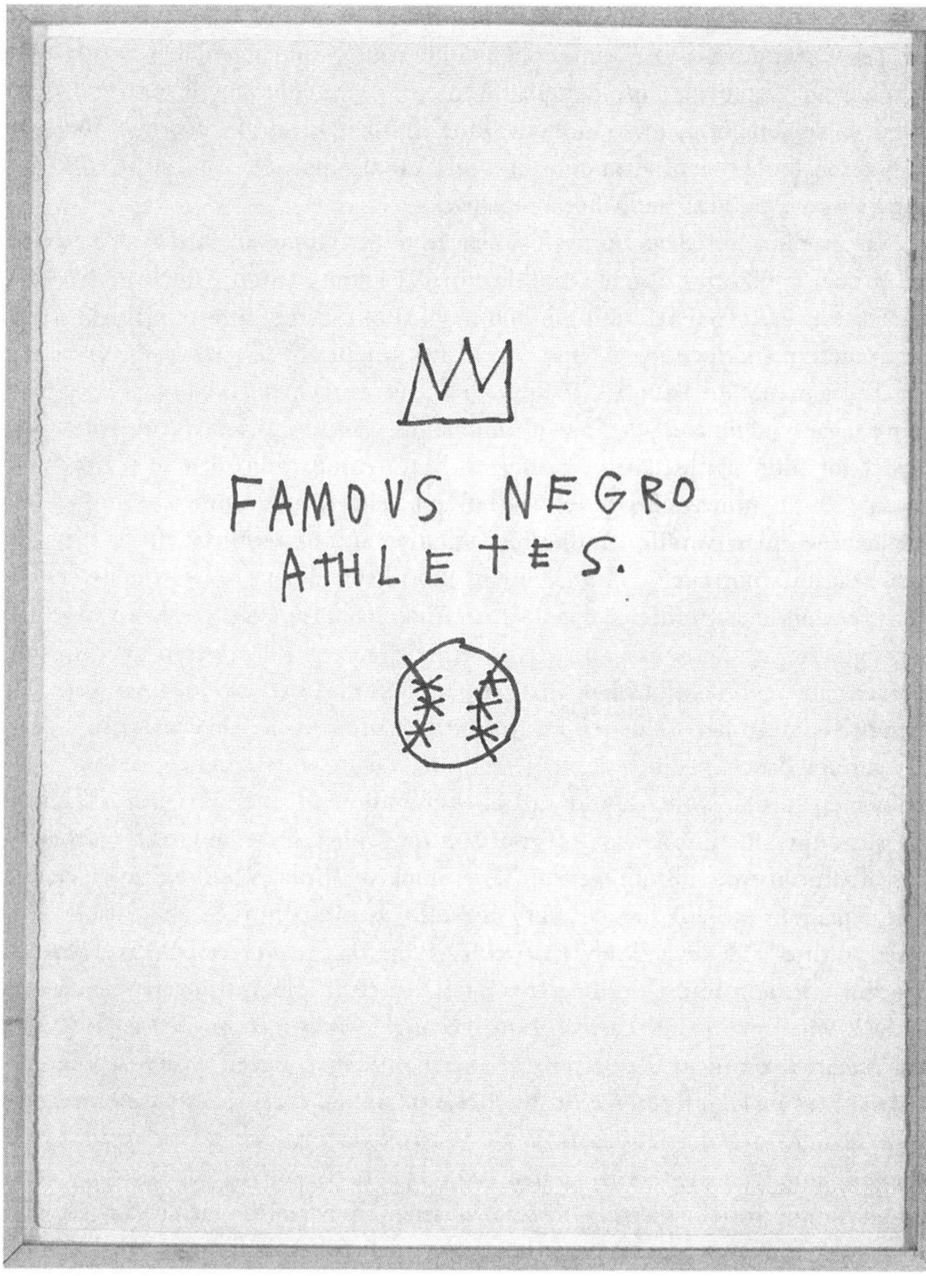

Jean-Michel Basquiat, *Untitled (Famous Negro Athletes)* (1981). Copyright 1998 Artists Rights Society (ARS), New York/ADAGP, Paris. Photo courtesy of the Brant Foundation.

Basquiat's relationship with Warhol. The painting *Dos Cabezas* depicts two rough sketches of both artists' faces lined up side by side, on an equal level. It also translates Andy's head into Spanish, setting up a moment of interculturation that is typical of both Basquiat's work and other examples of disidentification that can be found in U.S. culture.

The ways in which these two artists cross-identified, disidentified, and learned with and from each other also suggest the political possibilities of collaboration. The relationship of queerness and race is often a vexed and complicated one within progressive political arenas. When these identity shards are positioned as oppositional, they often split and damage subjects whose identifications vector into both identificatory nodes. The models and examples set by pop art in general, and Andy Warhol in particular, influenced Basquiat in innumerable ways. In turn, Basquiat rejuvenated both pop art and Warhol by exploding racial signifiers that had been erased, obstructed, or rendered dormant by the discourse. These disidentificatory cultural practices and the coterminous interpersonal identificatory crossings and crisscrossing that Basquiat made with Warhol and Warhol with Basquiat were, for both marginalized men, indispensable survival practices.

Melancholia's Work

My theoretical understanding of disidentification has been, as I have stated, informed by the structure of feeling that is melancholia. I now investigate the relationship of melancholia to disidentification within Basquiat's work, in an effort to make these connections more salient. Consider a portrait of Jean-Michel Basquiat that was one of the last photographs taken by the famous Harlem-based studio photographer James Van DerZee, whose career spanned more than five decades. The younger artist seems strangely comfortable in the gilded Edwardian trappings of Van DerZee's studio. His look away from the camera and the heaviness of his head, being held up by his hand, connote this quality of melancholia—a structure of feeling. I look at this image and feel the call of mourning. I reflect on the subject's short life in the New York avant-garde scene, his early death from a drug overdose, the loss of the artist, and all the paintings that were left undone. In this final stage of his career, Van DerZee produced many portraits of important African-Americans, including Muhammad Ali, Romare Bearden, Lou Rawls, Eubie Blake, Ruby Dee and Ossie Davis, and Max Robinson, the first African-American to land a position as a national newscaster. Robinson died in 1988 from AIDS complications. To look at his portrait now is indeed to summon up the dead, to put a face and voice on the countless black bodies that have been lost in the epidemic.[19] Basquiat, who was killed by a drug overdose the same year Robinson died, also embodies this moment of crisis in communities of color in which its young men are mercilessly cut down by the onslaught of the virus, the snares of a too often deadly drug addiction and a criminal justice system that has declared open season on young male bodies of color.

Basquiat understood the force of death and dying in the culture and tradition around him; his work was concerned with working through the charged relation between black male identity and death. Like Van DerZee, he understood that the situation of the black diaspora called on living subjects to take their dying with them. They were baggage that was not to be lost or forgotten because ancestors, be they symbolic or genetically linked, were a deep source of enabling energy that death need not obstruct.

Disidentification shares structures of feeling with Freudian melancholia, but the cultural formations I am discussing are not, in the Freudian sense, the "work of mourning." Jean Laplanche and Jean-Bertrand Pontalis describe the work of mourning as an "intrapsychic process, occurring after the loss of a loved object, whereby the subject gradually manages to detach itself from this object."[20] The works of mourning that I am discussing offer no such escape from the lost object. Rather, the lost object returns with a vengeance. It is floated as an ideal, a call to collectivize, an identity-affirming example. Basquiat saw the need to call up the dead, to mingle the power of the past with the decay of the present. Bell hooks has commented on the paintings of famous Negro athletes in Basquiat: "It is much too simplistic a reading to see works like Jack Johnson or Untitled (Sugar Ray Robinson), 1982, and the like, as solely celebrating black culture. Appearing always in these paintings as half-formed or somehow mutilated, the black male body becomes, iconographically, a sign of lack and absence."[21] Hooks is correct to shut down any reading that suggests that these twisted shapes are anything like purely celebratory. I disagree, however, with her reading of lack in the work. The lines that Basquiat employs are always crude and half-formed, and although they do signify a radical lack of completeness, they also hark back to a moment when a child takes a pencil to paper and, in a visual grammar that is as crude as it is beautiful, records the image of a beloved object, of a person or thing that serves as a node of identification, an object that possesses transcendent possibilities. The power of this painting has to do with the masterful way lack and desire are negotiated. The painting itself stands in for another lost object, childhood. The Famous Negro Athletes series works as a disidentification with the stars of an era when black representations were only the distorted images of athletes and the occasional performer that the white media deemed permissible.

Jazz great Charlie Parker was another of Basquiat's heroes, and Basquiat produced a creation that works as gravestone/mourning shrine for a lost hero. Again, the lines are, as bell hooks would put it, half-formed. In these half-formed lines we find a eulogy of great power and elegance. The structure (a tied-together wooden pole structure) records Parker's name and gives his place of death (Stan Hope Hotel) and the month and day he was memorialized at Carnegie Hall. The artist bestows royal status on the musician by renaming him Charles the First. Such a shrine is not as elegant and gilded as James Van DerZee's tributes to the dead, but this option is not available to Basquiat because the hurried pace of postmodernity no longer allows for the wistful and ethereal spaces of Van DerZee's portraits. Basquiat's objects also display the impulse to mourn, remember, and flesh out, but this is achieved through different strategies than the portrait photographer's. Basquiat's paintings achieve this mourning affect through urgency, speed, and frantic energized lines.

One of the artist's last finished paintings, *Riding with Death* (1988), poses the

Jean-Michel Basquiat, *Untitled (Sugar Ray Robinson)* (1982). Copyright 1998 Artists Rights Society (ARS), New York/ADAGP, Paris. Photo courtesy of the Brant Foundation.

black male body as death's horseman, riding and manipulating the pale specter. Many critics have read this painting in the light of Basquiat's death and found it ironic and delusional. I read *Riding with Death* under the pressure of the epidemics that now massacre millions of people of color. I read the painting as a call to do what Basquiat was able to do in his practice: to acknowledge and respond to the power of death and the dead in our lives. The black body mounting the white skeleton is brown and fleshed out in ways that many of his black male figures are not.[22] But the body is also highly abstracted, the face is crossed out by a black scrawl, the hands and arms are only traces in black oil stick. This incompleteness is also true of the skeleton, which

Jean-Michel Basquiat, *CPRKR* (1982). Copyright 1999 Artists Rights Society (ARS), New York/ADAGP, Paris. Courtesy of Artists Rights Society.

is missing a torso. The skeleton is a bright white that is almost illuminated by the gray-green background. Its whiteness is reminiscent of Warhol's own overwhelming whiteness. This whiteness can, then, stand in for a fantasy of black bodies not being burdened and mastered by whiteness, a fantasy space where the artist asserts his own agency in the relations of power he is imbricated in through his associations with the mainstream art world. I am not suggesting that whiteness is simply white people or the "white establishment." Instead, I read this painting as being about the complicated function of disidentification in which oppressive, shameful, and sometimes dangerous cultural influences and forces are incorporated, mediated, and transfigured.

Hooks has written that "Basquiat paintings bear witness, mirror this almost spiritual understanding. They expose and speak the anguish of sacrifice. It is amazing that so few critics discuss configurations of pain in his work, emphasizing instead its playfulness, its celebratory qualities."[23] Hooks is, again, right to point out the problems in the artist's critical reception. To look at Basquiat as a ludic painter is to put the mask of the minstrel show on him. Like hooks, I see the pain and anguish in his productions. To this I would add that there is also a powerful impulse in the artist's work to record a black life-world that is complex and multilayered.[24] *Riding with Death* is an excellent example; in it we see black bodies tarrying with death and destruction. But Basquiat's images do more than connote the destruction of the black body. They also strategize survival and imagine assertions of self in a cultural sphere that is structured to deny visibility to such bodies.

Hooks's greatest reservation about Basquiat's body of work is what she understands as his gender trouble:

> What limits body in Basquiat's work is the construction of maleness as lack. To be male, caught up in the endless cycle of conquest, is to lose out in the endless cycle of fulfillment.
>
> Significantly, there are few references in Basquiat's work that connect him to a world of blackness that is female or a world of influences and inspirations that are female.[25]

Because Basquiat chose to represent black males almost exclusively, and almost always in crisis, hooks figures the masculinity depicted in his oeuvre as lack primarily because of the absence of the female.[26] This line of argument echoes a previous theoretical maneuver by Hortense Spillers, who, in her influential essay "Momma's Baby, Papa's Maybe: An American Grammar Book," argues that African-American culture in the United States has been misnamed as matriarchal by such manifestations of white male patriarchy as the Moynihan Report.[27] The Moynihan Report figured the black family as dysfunctional because of what was perceived as the weakness of black male role models and the dominance of the black woman.[28] Spillers challenges this cultural myth, arguing that

> when we speak of the enslaved person, we perceive that the dominant culture, in a fatal misunderstanding, assigns a matriarchist value where it doesn't belong:

> actually misnames the power of the female regarding the enslaved community. Such naming is false because the female could not, in fact, claim her child, and false once again, because "motherhood" is not perceived in the prevailing social climate as a legitimate procedure of cultural inheritance.[29]

Spillers's valuable appraisal of the way in which the dominant culture figures an overabundance of black womanhood as *the* problem when discussing the status of African-Americans within U.S. culture leads me to suggest that hooks's thesis is a reversal of the very same logic that Moynihan Report disseminated in the mid-1960s. This inversion (African-American men as lack instead of African-American women as excess) still subscribes to the ideology of black men and black masculinity as "an absence and a negation." It also positions black women as something of a magical excess that can correct the failings of black men. Hooks's point thus seems like a reversal of psychoanalysis's understanding of woman as lack—an inversion that seems just as unproductive. Representing the complicated and dire situation of black masculinity in U.S. culture is important cultural work that should not be disavowed as a limitation. It is also important to note that the logic of hooks's argument relies on a presumption that, if the artist incorporated more female influences and inspirations (assuming that a spectator or critic can ever *know* what such forces might be), his lack would be filled. This formulation comes dangerously close to reinscribing a heterosexist fantasy that the fulfilling of a normative male and female dyad would flesh out the incompleteness of the artist's production. I do not mean to imply that there is no need for potentially productive alliances across gender (and sexuality) to be formed in the African diaspora, but I nonetheless see problems with hooks's formulation. The danger lies precisely at the point when any enslaved person, to use Spillers's description of people of color in the United States, is understood as incomplete because he or she chose to deal with the specificities of gender and race coordinates without involving the opposite sex. Such gender-normative thinking, when not checked for its heterosexist presumptions, leads to unproductive ends.

A certain quality of melancholia was intrinsic to the African-American male cultural worker, a quality that was absolutely necessary to navigate his way through a racist and genocidal landscape—which is not to say that mourning and genocide are salient thematics in the cultural production of African-American women.[30] It is to say, however, that a recent history of African-American masculinity would read like Van DerZee's funeral book.[31] This is especially true of Basquiat's painting. The shrines, altars, and portraits that Basquiat produced are not limited to the status of works of mourning, but within them is the potential to become meditative texts that decipher the workings of mourning in our culture. They are melancholic echoes, queer reverberations, that make possible an identity or cluster of communal identifications that are presently under siege.

Chapter 2

Photographies of Mourning: Melancholia and Ambivalence in Van DerZee, Mapplethorpe, and *Looking for Langston*

Deciphering a Dream Deferred

Black gay male cultural productions experienced a boom of sorts in the late 1980s and early 1990s. No one single type of cultural production trailblazed the way. Joseph Beam's now classic anthology *In the Life,* the videos of the late Marlon Riggs, the cultural criticism of Kobena Mercer, the music of Blackberri, the poetry of the late Essex Hemphill, the fiction of Melvin Dixon, the photos of Rotimi Fani-Kayode, the dance and choreography of Bill T. Jones, the performance art of Po-Mo Afro Homos, to name a handful of representatives from across a black queer diaspora, all informed and helped form one another. If one were to describe the unifying concepts, potencies, and tensions that bind these artists as something we might call a movement, beyond and beside the simple fact of their "identities," it would be the complicated work that they attempt to accomplish. This task can be summed up as the (re)telling of elided histories that need to be both excavated and (re)imagined, over and above the task of bearing the burden of representing an identity that is challenged and contested by various forces, including, but not limited to, states that blindly neglect the suffering bodies of men caught within a plague, the explosion of "hate crime" violence that targets black and gay bodies, and a reactionary media power structure that would just as soon dismiss queer existence as offer it the most fleeting reflection. In this shifting field of artistic performance and production, I would point out what might be thought of as a slippery center: Isaac Julien's *Looking for Langston* (1989). I use the term *center* in this instance to describe the way that film, as a primarily collaborative art form, incorporates and displays other modes of black queer cultural production such as music, performance, poetry, prose, cultural criticism, and photography.

In this chapter, I resist the term *masculinity.* Masculinity has been and continues to be a normative rubric that has policed the sex/gender system. I see very little advantage in recuperating the term *masculinity* because, as a category, masculinity has normalized heterosexual and masculinist privilege. Masculinity is, among other things, a cultural imperative to enact a mode of "manliness" that is calibrated to shut down queer possibilities and energies. The social construct of masculinity is experienced by far too many men as a regime of power that labors to invalidate, exclude, and extinguish faggotry, effeminacy, and queerly coated butchness. This is not to discount the possibility that a discourse on masculinity might produce some theoretical traction for scholars working in the field of gender theory. But I do aim to suggest that any such project that fails to factor in and interrogate heteronormativity and masculinist contours of such a discourse reproduces the phobic ideology of masculinity. An exemplary critical project that has reanimated the term *masculinity* is Judith Halberstam's writing on "female masculinity."[1] Halberstam dislodges masculinity from biological maleness, and in doing so opens up and reterritorializes the concept. Such a reterritorialization of masculinity can be understood as a disidentification with the sign of masculinity, which is to say a critical recycling of the term.

This chapter offers a reading that I hope will contribute to an understanding of both where this crucial wave of black queer work is coming from and where it currently stands, as well as a decipherment of this exemplary and central text's densely layered, aestheticized, and politicized workings. In this analysis, I intend to carry out Sylvia Wynter's call for a turn toward *decipherment* as opposed to the dominant scholarly mode of "interpretation" of the "play" of "meanings" and significations that a text produces. This decipherment of *Looking for Langston* (and what I see as its influential "co-texts") will attempt to carry out the program for film studies outlined by Wynters in her article "Rethinking 'Aesthetics': Notes Towards a Deciphering Practice":

> Rather than seeking to "rhetorically demystify" a deciphering turn seeks to decipher what a process of rhetorical mystification *does.* It seeks to identify not what texts and their signifying practices can be interpreted to *mean* but what they can be deciphered to *do,* it also seeks to evaluate the "illocutionary force" and procedures with which they do what they do.[2]

This chapter maps out two different tropes or structures of feeling—melancholia and ambivalence—that are central to a comprehension of the inner (textual) and external (social and political) work that the texts under consideration do.[3]

A grand and glowing mythotext, *Looking for Langston* makes no stale claims to documentary objectivity. It is, in Julien's own words at the beginning of the film, a "meditation" on "Langston Hughes and the Harlem Renaissance." The word *meditation* implies a text that is not dealing with clouded imperatives to tell what "really" happened or to give the reader a plastic "you were there" sensation. The text is instead profoundly evocative, suggestive, and, as I will argue in depth later, ambivalent. A meditation like this invites a reader to join the author in a contemplative position. The invitation reads: imagine, remember, flesh out.

Julien's film is a challenge to more terminal histories that work to dispel and undermine anything but flat empirical, historiographical facts. An example of this mode of history writing, one that more often than not excludes nonconventional, and especially queer, historiography, is Arnold Rampersad's biography of Langston Hughes.[4] Rampersad dismisses considerations of the poet as gay writer for a lack of empirical evidence: the biographer was unable to find any living person (male or female) who would admit to having had sex with Hughes. Such naive reasoning from such an otherwise sophisticated critic is unsettling. This blindness to both the different economies of desires and the historical and concurrent bonds of gay intertextuality that Hughes shares with other gay cultural workers can only be construed as heterosexist. (Rampersad's text is deserving of a long and rigorous inquiry that would take on the task of looking into the heterosexist logic of a study that dismisses a subject's sexual identity altogether before considering a homosexual possibility that, for any attentive reader, is far from opaque.)[5] I would argue that Julien's dynamic film offers all the "evidence" needed to make a case that Langston Hughes was queer.

The evidence of Julien's film is not that of rigorous historical fact; it is, rather, the evidence of revisionary history that meditates on queer cadences that can be heard in Hughes when studying Hughes's life and work. It is a mode of history reading that listens with equal attention to silences and echoes that reverberate through the artist's production. I understand the historiographical project of *Looking for Langston* to be in line with the program called for by the historian of "difference" Joan W. Scott. Scott explains that it is insufficient and risky to propose historiographical salvage operations that troll for some "lost" and essential "experience." Scott has explicated the implicit danger of such projects:

> History is a chronology that makes experience visible, but in which categories appear as nonetheless ahistorical: desire, homosexuality, heterosexuality, femininity, masculinity, sex and even sexual practices become so many fixed entities being played out over time, but not themselves historicized. Presenting the story this way excludes, or at least understates, the historically variable interrelationship between the meanings "homosexual" and "heterosexual," the constitutive force each has for the other, and the contested nature of the terrain that they simultaneously occupy.[6]

Julien's cinematic practice defies the lure of simply propping up a newly found history of what the queer Harlem Renaissance might have been. Instead, this cinematic meditation does not confine itself to single meanings, but instead works to explain the lack of fixity of such terms as *queer, black,* and *male,* within the temporal space that is being represented. Indeed, the film itself works to undermine any static or rigid definitions of these concepts.

One of the first of many "key" Hughes phrases that one catches in the film is "montage of a dream deferred," and the film, in its fluid dimensions, takes up the challenge of this image and attempts to imagine what it might look like. The classical cinematic theory of montage, first theorized and deployed by the Soviet filmmaker

Sergei Eisenstein as "a montage of attractions," speaks quite fluidly to Julien's project. The variation in the latter's interpretation of cinematic montage is his reliance on the juxtaposing of "attractions" that are not just "shots" but fabrics not traditionally enfolded within the tapestry of montage cinema—materials such as poems, experimental fiction, still photographs, vintage newsreels, and blues songs. Montage cinema creates a certain rhythm in its stark juxtapositions of images that, on a level of traditional novelistic narrative logic, clash and set each other off. *Looking for Langston,* though stylistically elegant and apparently seamless, calls on this tried-and-true calculus of juxtapositions. Although the textures of the "attractions" that are used are not traditional film fodder, they do roughly line up around different poles. The poles are connected to the project of black gay male self-representation sketched earlier, a project that is carried out against a heterosexist culture's hegemonic mandate that these lives not be seen, heard, or known. One of the two poles is the "historical self" that is represented by chiefly archival images from the Harlem Renaissance; the other is the contemporaneous self that produces images that represent an "under siege" reality. Both poles are embattled ones. The historical one is a counterhistory that must constantly define itself against "larger" more official and oppressive histories; the contemporary identity pole is populated by images that depict the dangers (and, of course, pleasures) of occupying a black and gay subject position during this particular moment of crisis. I do not wish to reify this dichotomy between "then" and "now": the film certainly does not commit such an error. A successful montage—and *Looking for Langston* is definitely that—eventually uses the current produced by the binary juxtapositions to meld the very same binary into what might seem like an autonomous whole. This "wholeness effect" is enacted through the dialectical interplay of these conflicting elements.

In his essay "A Dialectic Approach to Film Form," Eisenstein explains that it is not only the visible elements of shots that can be juxtaposed in a montage system. There is also the strategy of emotional combination that produces what the early film theorist has called "emotional dynamization." According to Eisenstein, this brand of montage, if successful, ultimately leads to the "liberation of the whole action from the definition of time and space."[7] The transhistorical crosscutting in Julien's film achieves, through its use of evocative and sometimes elusive contrasts and similarities, just such a liberation. The concept of time and space that is generated occupies overlapping temporal and geographic coordinates that we can understand as a queer black cultural imaginary. It is important to keep in mind that this queer black cultural imaginary is in no way ahistorical. Its filaments are historically specific and the overall project is more nearly *trans*historical.

Fredric Jameson, in writing about the triumph of Eisenstein's cinema, sums up the "payoff" that montage can yield when trying to depict history: "Montage thus assumes the existence of the time between shots, the process of waiting itself, as it reaches back and encompasses the two poles of its former dynamic, thereby embodying itself as emptiness made visible—the line of Russian warriors in the distance, or even more climactically, the empty horizon on which the Teutonic Knights, not yet present, impend."[8] *Looking for Langston* resembles Jameson's delineation of "montage" in that the film attempts to represent, make visible, and even champion at least a few different histories that have, by the strong arm of "official histories," been cloaked.

It would be reductive to account for the dynamic transhistorical referents in the film solely within the terms of the inner working of the formalistic montage paradigm. In the end, this runs too high a risk of reifying history and the present. I myself am in a position of discussing binaries (as the reader will soon see) that flirt with this problematic. In an attempt to resist this trap, I will offer another structural model that considers the interplay of transhistorical elements in this text. Another mode of understanding the interchange between elements corresponding to different historical moments would be the idea of a dialectical interchange between present and past tenses. This seems right in that it speaks to the fact that, as a particular kind of avant-garde film, *Looking for Langston* is grounded in a complex relation of fragments to a whole. For heuristic purposes here, I would like to associate the first pole with a historical black homosexual "tradition" that closes around the images of male Harlem Renaissance queers such as Hughes, Countee Cullen, Alain Locke, Wallace Thurman, Bruce Nugent, and Claude McKay, and I will associate the other pole with contemporary cultural activists such as Essex Hemphill, Marlon Riggs, and Assotto Saint. It would be worthwhile to consider these texts as tangled within a complicated transhistorical dialogue—something akin to Gayl Jones's definition of a traditional African-American oral trope known as "call-and-response," the "antiphonal back-and-forth pattern which exists in many African American oral traditional forms, from sermon to interjective folk tale to blues, jazz and spirituals and so on. In the sermonic tradition, the preacher calls in a fixed or improvised refrain, while the congregation responds, in either fixed and formulaic or spontaneous words and phrases."[9] With this pattern in mind, one can hear Essex Hemphill's impassioned poetic voice crying out from one of these historical poles, "Now we think while we fuck," and actually speaking across time to a "forgotten" or "lost" black queer identity painfully embodied in the hushed tones of Langston Hughes's simple, sorrowful epitaph-like text "Poem":

> I loved my friend
> He went away from me
> There is nothing more to say
> This poem ends
> As softly as it began
> I loved my friend.[10]

By pointing to this cross-time dialogue between black gay males, I am suggesting that Julien makes use of call-and-response to historicize black gay male history and contextualize recent queer African-American cultural production. This technique is rooted in a black vernacular tradition while being a new and innovative approach to filmic production. The positing of this model as a tool for understanding the transhistorical narrative economy in the film does not completely eclipse the notion of the film as a montage. They are at least provisionally compatible paradigms that may melt into one another.

In general terms, I have discussed the situation of the nontraditional fabrics juxtaposed on one another in this "montage" or "call-and-response" weave. Many of these transhistorical pairings are of interest. For example, in a powerful early moment in the film, the voice of bisexual blues singer Bessie Smith is set off by and then briefly mingles with a contemporary song, "Blues for Langston," sung by the songwriter/vocalist Blackberri. There is something uncanny about these voices resonating; the resonance produces a smooth superimposition that is visually impossible. In an interview, British filmmaker Julien commented on his need to turn to America to unearth a queer black history—there was no historical icon as provocative as Hughes on his side of the diaspora. The "American" element that factors into the film's hybrid model can be best understood as a "blues aesthetic." In his seminal study on this American aesthetic form, Houston Baker Jr. describes the blues as a "matrix": "The matrix is a point of ceaseless input and output, a web of intersecting, crisscrossing impulses always in productive transit. Afro-American blues constitute such a vibrant network."[11] *Looking for Langston* incorporates the "matrix" function into its own hybridized aesthetic.

While recognizing this matrix function, it is important to note that the syncretic incorporation of the blues aesthetic does not overshadow the contemporary black British aesthetic that fills out much of the film. Julien wished to assert his own national identity; hence, British locales, actors, and voices are called on to establish a black British cultural presence that shares a certain symmetry with the African-American presence. Coterminous with this American blues aesthetic is the black British diaspora aesthetic of the Black Arts Movement. One can view the film as being very much a part of this British aesthetic movement, which attempts to negotiate representation from a productive space of hybridity, situated between postmodernism and what Paul Gilroy has termed "populist modernism." Gilroy describes the black British film movement (a movement central to the Black Arts Movement) as enacting a Du Boisian double consciousness: on the one hand, its representatives identify as cultural producers who are located *in* modernity and are clearly defenders, producers, and critics of modernism, but, on the other hand, they feel a moral responsibility to act as the "gravediggers of modernity"—to never forget that they are also the "stepchildren of the West" whose task it is to transform modernity and the aesthetics of modernism into vernacular forms that are "populist," expressive, and not elitist. *Looking for Langston*'s cinematic structure as a transhistorical and transnational "weavelike" texture can be understood as a product of the discomfort caused by traditional Western genre constraints that Gilroy locates in popular modernism: "The problem of genre is there in the desire to transcend key Western categories: narrative, documentary, history and literature, ethics and politics."[12]

The remainder of this chapter will focus on what I see as the central binary of the film: a binary of photographic images. The juxtapositions and tensions of the photographic binary bear primary responsibility for shaping the film both visually and thematically. The two most crucial and structuring photographic presences in this film text are those of Harlem Renaissance portrait photographer James Van DerZee and New York avant-garde portrait photographer Robert Mapplethorpe.

The Picture of Melancholia

Before discussing mourning and the functions of the photo texts in Julien's work, I would like to fill in my consideration of *Looking for Langston* as both a photocentric text and a mythotext. This populist modernist mode of "writing" history challenges and confounds traditional historiographies. This point becomes salient when one reads a passage that considers the relation of the photograph to history from Roland Barthes's exquisite book *Camera Lucida*: "A paradox: the same century invented History and Photography. But History is a memory fabricated according to positive formulas, a pure intellectual discourse which abolishes mythic Time; and the Photograph is a certain but fugitive testimony."[13] Although the foundation of Barthes's binary may be somewhat shaky, it serves to illuminate the unique relationship of the photographic document (producing the effect he calls "that-has-been") and the "pure" intellectual discourse of history. The photographs of Hughes and James Baldwin, held up by beautiful queer putti during the film's opening panoramic shots, serve as a fleeting yet powerful testimony to black queer presences within histories that often neglect them. The viewer is left in the position both of reading these vital mythologies and of spinning more narratives around them. The photograph in *Looking for Langston* is a charm that wards off "official histories" and reinscribes necessary mythologies. These mythologies are open spaces of inquiry rather than monolithic narratives full of, for many, identity-denying silences.

In 1915, Freud introduced a theory of mourning that is, like much of Freud, implicitly heterosexist yet riddled with queer possibilities. He writes: "Mourning is regularly the reaction to the loss of a loved one, or to the loss of some abstraction which has taken the place of one such as one's country, liberty, an ideal, and so on."[14] Mourning, unlike melancholia, which he marks as pathological, is a process in which an object or abstraction becomes absent and the withdrawal of libido from the object becomes necessary. But these demands cannot be enacted at once; libido detaches bit by bit, perpetuating a mode of unreality, because, while the process of libido removal is transpiring, the lost object/abstraction persists. It is, in its simplest formulation, a gradual letting go. This process becomes the work of mourning. Van DerZee's and Mapplethorpe's pictures, for radically different reasons, symbolically represent and

Isaac Julien's *Looking for Langston*. Photo by Sunil Gupta. Copyright 1989 Sankofa Film and Video and Sunil Gupta. Courtesy of Third World Newsreel.

stand in as "works" of mourning. In Freud's initial definition, melancholia spills into the realm of the pathological because it resembles a mourning that does not know when to stop.[15]

In his first account of mourning, Freud used the idea as a sort of foil to talk about the psychopathology of melancholia. In *The Ego and the Id,* he begins to deconstruct his previous binary when he realizes that the identification with the lost object that he at first described as happening in melancholia is also a crucial part of the work of mourning. The line between mourning and melancholia in this work of cinematic grieving is amazingly thin; it is a fiction that offers itself readily for deconstructing.

Through a highly formalistic route, Van DerZee's and Mapplethorpe's projects are heavily valanced as works of mourning. Van DerZee and Mapplethorpe are known as master portraitists, and the practice of portraiture suggests another interrelation. Jacques Derrida makes a crucial connection between the work of mourning and prosopopeia, the trope of mourning that Paul de Man wrote about extensively. Prosopopeia was understood by de Man as the trope of autobiography, the giving of names, the giving of face: "the fiction of an apostrophe to an absent, deceased, or voiceless entity, which posits the possibility of the latter's reply and confers upon it the power of speech."[16] The autobiography and the portrait do the work of giving voice to the face from beyond the grave; prosopopeia is also a way of remembering, holding on to, letting go of "the absent, the deceased, the voiceless." Thus, in the same way that she who writes in a biographical vein is summoning up the dead, by the deployment of prosopopeia, she who mourns a friend summons her up through elaborate ventriloquism. This contributes to an understanding of how the trans-historical call-and-response that I proposed earlier might function: a portrait of Hughes, with his less than perfect mouth smiling a characteristically disarming smile, enacts a strategic flexing of the autobiography trope that summons back a dead Hughes, gives him voice, and permits him to engage in a dialogue with the currently living black gay male body of Essex Hemphill. The photographic portrait first gives face, then gives voice.

This giving face and subsequently voice should also be understood as a component of the performative aspect of portrait photography. The portrait photograph is a two-sided performance, one having to do with the photographer who manipulates technology, models, props, and backgrounds behind the camera, and the other with the model who performs "self" especially and uniquely for the camera.[17] Mourning, in all of its ritualized gestures and conventions, is also performative insofar as the mourner plays a very specific role on a culturally prescribed stage. Viewing both portrait photography and mourning as performative practices, one understands the unique linkage between the two practices—in the case of portraiture a lost object is captured and (re)produced, and in melancholic mourning the object is resurrected and retained. Funeral photography, which grew out of the colonial American tradition of "mourning paintings," is situated at the moment in which both performances blur into each and take on a crucial role in each other's theater.

In many cultures, mourning is highly aestheticized. The scenes of mourning that are enacted in James Van DerZee's *The Harlem Book of the Dead* are lush and disquieting. In a morbid grammar (that is in no way devoid of wit), he spells out some of the issues that surface when considering mourning and melancholia. The painful attachments that refuse to diminish quickly during the actual process of mourning and the subsequent inability to check in properly with the reality principle are displayed in the section depicting children titled "Children & the Mystery of Birth." In a gesture that might seem macabre today, Van DerZee posed dead babies with their parents. Asked about this artistic strategy, Van DerZee replied: "It was my suggestion to have them hold the child while the picture was being taken to make it look more natural."[18] This posing of the dead child with the parents succinctly performs the melancholic and gives it a visual presence. This can also be easily read in the photograph of the man buried with his newspaper because his family wished to imagine that he was not actually dead but instead had once again just fallen asleep reading the paper.

Another photo in the "Children & the Mystery of Birth" section employs a different strategy in its attempt to visualize the process of African-American mourning. In this photo, an older child is lying in the casket and a figure that can be presumed to be the father looks on. The child's Boy Scout uniform is laid over the coffin. The twist that Van DerZee achieves in this photograph is enacted through the technology of superimposition. "Ghosted" over the coffin hovers a family portrait. The portrait shows the lost object in question, the assembled nuclear family. The superimposition includes the lost mother, who is absent from the "main" image of the photograph. The viewer wonders where the mother exists in the "real time" of the funeral scene. Was she lost before the boy? Did she pass on with the child? Is her grief so great that she could not pose? This image clearly revolves around the subjectivity of the male figure mourning. The act of mourning in this photo frames no single one lost object (a child, a mother, a uniform) but rather posits a lost concept, an ego ideal that was contained within the fiction of the nuclear family. The work this photograph does involves the revelation of the status of the lost object in this African-American imaginary. The lost and dead are not altogether absent. Not only do they exist within the drama of African-American life, but they help formulate it.

A mortuary portrait of a young man in uniform uses the technology of combination printing to tell its story. The portrait is simply one example of the narrative impulse in Van DerZee's production. In this image, one counts at least four negatives in play. A poem is printed over the image. The poem recounts the sad story of burying a beloved soldier boy. Opposite the text one finds an odd battlefield image. The subject who most closely resembles the corpse holds a pistol during a battlefield scene on the top left side of the image. In this almost cinematic pose one encounters the defeated soldier drawing his weapon to protect an African-American nurse and her dying patient on the battlefield. The melodramatic image is bridged with the equally emotional poem through a smaller battlefield image of two medics transferring an injured soldier across a battlefield. The imaginary that Van DerZee weaves in this image is interested in telling the story of a lost noble soldier. The politics of staging this kind of image betrays one of the political projects of Van DerZee's photography. This image of the exemplary soldier, beautifully enveloped in a U.S. flag, posits an image of a black male as a war hero in a culture that at the time of its fashioning would not acknowledge him as such. The iconography in this instance is clearly uninterested in mourning one individual; rather, the move is to address the needs, aesthetics, and suffering of a larger community.

I first encountered a Van DerZee photo in Barthes's book on photography. On a certain level, both men's work is strongly associated for me: they are both cultural workers who revel in the most gilded and delicious hypersentimentality, both always realizing the influence and limits of the parodic in their work. Granted, this connection is highly unstable, in ways both literal and metaphoric, because these men could never really "speak" to each other. Van DerZee was never in any position to read Barthes's stylized locutions and the commentary that Barthes offers on Van DerZee is flawed by a petty racism. When Barthes wrote about Van DerZee, he contented himself with making a few snide racist remarks about the middle-class subjects (a traditional-looking African-American family) attempting to, in Barthes's own words, "assume the white man's attributes."[19] Van DerZee's aesthetic utterly undercuts Barthes's writing about photography. Van DerZee, I would suggest, disrupts the hypersubjective Barthesian approach to the photographic image. His pictures are never only the anticipation/potential occasion for mourning, like the Barthes Wintergarden picture discussed shortly, but are also a phantasmic illusion that starts from the "end" (death and a communal witnessing of death) and hopes to bring back the dead by a very self-conscious act of prosopopeia. In a strange, yet significant, way, *The Harlem Book of the Dead* beats *Camera Lucida* at its own game.

The photographic text itself, as Barthes has suggested, is already dead; therefore, as a work of art, the photograph is always already a text of mourning. But if death, as in the case of Van DerZee, is the obvious or surface subject of the picture, what might be the role of prosopopeia when considering these pictures? Barthes cathects a photo of his mother as a little girl in the Wintergarden. What fascinates him most about this old photo is the depiction of the time "right before he lived," the historical moment that most interests him because that is when his mother lived without him. This formula, if expanded to consider group identification as opposed to highly intersubjective histories, would account for the power of Van DerZee's photos within the frame of the film. For a generation of black gay men engrossed in the project of excavating deeply buried histories (as far as "official" historical registers are concerned), these pictures depicting everyday life and death during the (queer) Harlem Renaissance show a very crucial moment: a "right before *we* lived" moment that is as important to this community as the moment in his mother's life before his own birth is for Barthes.

We can understand the importance of this move from the intersubjective to the communal moment of mourning by turning to Michael Moon's "Memorial Rags, Memorial Rages." Here Moon completes the task of theorizing the significance and crucial differences in collective mourning begun by Freud in *Group Psychology and Ego Formation.* Both Julien and Moon are keyed in to the power of collective mourning and both understand the need to play with potent queer energies that have changed the face of mourning in ways that are paradigm shaking; the following sentence from Moon's essay illuminates just what kind of tropological revision is at play in Julien's signifying on Van DerZee: "I invoke the social in the face of a predominantly privatized, heterosexualized, teleologized and "task-oriented" conception of grieving and mourning because I want to insist on the specifically queer energies at play—or potentially in play—in our experiences of grief and our practices of mourning in the midst of the continuing desolation of our lives by AIDS."[20] Moon calls attention to the characteristic of a dominant cultural logic of mourning that is, by its very premise and foundational principles, heterosexist. *Looking for Langston* works to undermine hegemonic constructions of mourning and instead prop up an alternate structure that is not pinioned by "privatized . . . and 'task-oriented'" biases but instead posits the necessity for communal practices that speak to the current genocidal crises affecting black and queer communities globally. Julien explains this communal practice as an aesthetic process, relating in an interview that he "played with the surface" of Van DerZee's photos so they would forge an "important relationship" between a contemporary gay scene and a "historical look."[21] A subject is not locating her or his essential history by researching a "racial" or cultural past. More nearly, and most specifically in the case of *Looking for Langston*'s appropriation and reclamations of Van DerZee's photographs and photographic aesthetic, what is transpiring is an insertion of contemporary "self" into a fiction of the past that generates in the communal and individual subject an imaginary coherence within the experience of homophobic representational elisions and a general historical "experience of dispersal and fragmentation, which is the history of all enforced diasporas."[22] Van DerZee's photos help the queer spectator visualize a past and thus enable an "imaginary" coherence that make the visualizing of a present and a future possible.

Disidentifying and Desire in Mapplethorpe

Tony Fischer, in an article on *Looking for Langston,* completely misreads what he calls the "AIDS subplot."[23] The hierarchizing gesture of assigning main plots and subplots in this film shows a profound misunderstanding of the film's structural and political formation. The moment of mourning in which we live informs Julien's film in urgent and compelling ways. The best example of the centrality of AIDS mourning in the film would be a consideration of the influence of Robert Mapplethorpe. Mapplethorpe's pictures cannot, after the grim carnival of controversy around them, be seen any longer without a deep consideration of AIDS and both the gay and black communities' current crisis of mourning. In a *Vanity Fair* interview right before his own death, Mapplethorpe commented that most of the black men who appeared in *Black Book* are now dead because of their poverty, lack of insurance, and the very high price of health care and medications such as AZT.[24] Although Julien's project is, on one level, obviously the reappropriation of the black gay male body from Mapplethorpe, it is difficult to "read" these images and not be reminded of the terrible plague that robbed us of both the beautiful black men in front of the lens and the troublesome white patron/photographer behind the lens.

In considering the film's aesthetic, one cannot miss the compositional influence of Mapplethorpe's photography. Along with the dramatic and elegant Mapplethorpe lighting, the use and celebration of nude black gay male bodies makes visible the dialectical relationship between Mapplethorpe's and Julien's text. Perfectly chiseled black male bodies, framed in striking black-and-white monochromes, occupy the central dream sequences of the film. In his signifying on Mapplethorpe, Julien introduces a crucial tropological revision: he displays black bodies and black bodies together as well as black bodies and white bodies together. In this instance he is rewriting the Mapplethorpe scene by letting these men relate to each other's bodies and not just the viewer's penetrating gaze. Julien and Kobena Mercer's essay "True Confessions" can be read as the "written" theoretical accompaniment to the praxis that is *Looking for Langston.* In it the subject of black gay male pornography is dis-

Isaac Julien's *Looking for Langston.* Photo by Sunil Gupta. Copyright 1989 Sankofa Film and Video and Sunil Gupta. Courtesy of Third World Newsreel.

cussed in the following manner: "The convention in porn is to show single models in solo frames to enable the construction of one-to-one fantasy: Sometimes, when porn models pose in couples or groups, other connotations—friendship, solidarities, collective identities—can struggle to the surface for our recognition."[25] This "accidental" positive identity-affirming effect that takes place in black male porn is being "pushed" and performed in Julien's film;[26] and this is only possible through the playing with form, convention, and even frame that Julien accomplishes through his cinematic practice. This reading by Julien and Mercer casts Mapplethorpe as the exploitative author who sees these black bodies only as meat. But these charges were made early in a debate that, like the current moment of AIDS mourning, has no facile end in sight. Mercer, in a large part as a result of the homophobic right-wing attacks on Mapplethorpe, has reconsidered the images he once denounced as simply reproducing a colonial fantasy: "[T]extual ambivalence of the black nude photograph is strictly undecidable because Mapplethorpe's photographs do not provide an unequivocal yes/no answer to the question of whether they reinforce or undermine commonplace racist stereotypes—rather, he throws the binary structure of the question back at the spectator, where it is torn apart in the disruptive 'shock effect.'"[27] The ambivalence Mercer speaks about recalls an earlier point I posited regarding the ambivalence toward a lost object bringing about melancholia. Melancholia is brought

Isaac Julien's *Looking for Langston*. Photo by Sunil Gupta. Copyright 1989 Sankofa Film and Video and Sunil Gupta. Courtesy of Third World Newsreel.

about by the subject's inability to immediately work out the problems or contradictions that the object and its loss produce. Hence, the ambivalence brings about a certain "shock effect" that Mercer describes, which is, in a striking way, structurally akin to the inner workings of melancholia.

I wish to suggest that the pleasure that Mercer, Julien, and other gay men of color experience when consuming Mapplethorpe's images is a disidentificatory pleasure, one that acknowledges what is disturbing about the familiar practices of black male objectification that Mapplethorpe participated in, while at the same time it understands that this pleasure can not easily be dismissed even though it is politically dangerous.[28] Like melancholia, disidentification is an ambivalent structure of feeling that works to retain the problematic object and tap into the energies that are produced by contradictions and ambivalences. Mercer, Julien, and Jane Gaines have all explicated the ways in which the ambivalence that a spectator encounters when interfacing with these images is not only a racist exploitation of, but simultaneously a powerful validation of, the black male body. Disidentification, as a conceptual model for understanding the "shock effect" produced by these images, acknowledges what is indeed turbulent and troublesome about such images. Peggy Phelan has explained the way

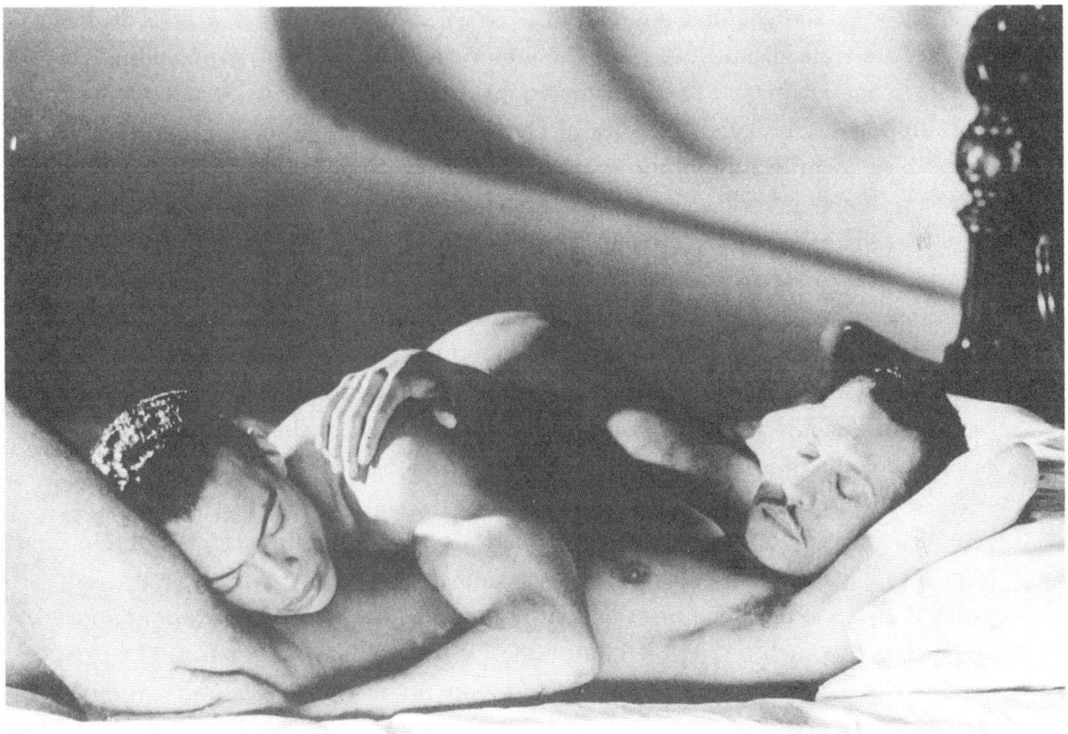

Isaac Julien's *Looking for Langston*. Photo by Sunil Gupta. Copyright 1989 Sankofa Film and Video and Sunil Gupta. Courtesy of Third World Newsreel.

in which "objectification" should not be the last word in any appraisal of Mapplethorpe's work:

> Mapplethorpe's photography does "objectify" men, but what is astonishing about his work is how much room there is for dignity despite this objectification. His photography demonstrates that love and understanding of a body, while always involving objectification, precisely because it is made over in the mind and eye of the other, do not have to eliminate the private grace and power of the model.[29]

The "making over" in the eye and the mind is a transfiguration. The object that is desired is reformatted so that dignity and grace are not eclipsed by racist exploitation. Disidentification is this "making over"; it is the way a subject looks at an image that has been constructed to exploit and deny identity and instead finds pleasure, both erotic and self-affirming. Disidentification happens on the level of both production and reception. The glance that cultural critics and workers such as Mercer and Julien direct at a text such as Mapplethorpe starts out a disidentificatory transfiguration on the level of reception, and later, when the images are incorporated into different cultural texts (Mercer's cultural critique or Julien's cinematic production), a disidentification is enacted that is linked to artistic process and production.

In the same way that one holds on to a lost object until the inner feelings of ambivalence are worked out, Julien sees the importance of our collectively holding on to Mapplethorpe's images. These images are invaluable because they directly speak to the complicated circulation of colonial fantasies in gay communities, both white and of color. Identification in the fantasy narrative (colonial or otherwise), as Judith Butler has shown in her own essay on Mapplethorpe, is never fixed; one can identify not only with characters (occupying either the colonized or colonizer positions), but also with verbs or "acts."[30] This identification, in Mapplethorpe, can perhaps be better understood as a disidentification that refuses to follow the identificatory protocols of the dominant culture. This brings to mind the scene in the film in which the white character takes a tour through the pages of *Black Book* that are projected on the walls of a darkly lit room. Can people who identify as belonging to a once or currently colonized group simply identify with *Black Book* images projected on the wall of the white "patrons'" misty room, or must they, as Mercer suggests, confront their own identification with the white man, or even with the act of thumbing through this "dangerous" book and taking scopic delight in such images? I am suggesting that, for some spectators, this confrontation with whiteness does not occlude the pleasure that such images offer, but rather, that such confrontations can be part of a disidentificatory project that manages to partially recycle and hold on to these representations.

What binds these very different photographic presences in the text for me is a certain quality of mourning intrinsic both to the genre of portraiture and to the specific photographs of Van DerZee and Mapplethorpe used in *Looking for Langston.* Jeff Nunokawa argues that, long before the current epidemic, the history of gay men for mainstream culture has been one of death, doom, and extinction. He explains the ways in which the AIDS epidemic has been figured in the mainstream (straight) imaginary: "AIDS is a gay disease, and it means death, because AIDS has been made the most recent chapter in our culture's history of the gay male, a history which, from its beginning, has read like a book of funerals."[31] Unfortunately, this genocidal wish of the straight mind has been partially fulfilled. Recent queer history, to no small degree, does read like a funeral book. This is equally true of the history of the African-American male, especially the African-American gay male. *The Harlem Book of the Dead* and *Black Book* are both mourning texts that might, on first glance, appear to be such funeral books. There is in fact more to these texts that, when redeployed by cultural producers such as Julien, become meditative texts that decipher the workings of mourning in our culture.

Rethinking Melancholia

I have tried to explicate this quality of mourning in somewhat abstract terms. If one zooms in on certain cinematic moments, a sharper understanding comes into perspective. My argument that *Looking for Langston* is a work of mourning hinges on some specific filmic moments. One of the earliest sound bites heard is the scratchy voice of a late-sixties radio announcer eulogizing Hughes, and the program he announces is called "In Memoriam Langston Hughes." As I pointed out earlier, the film is billed as a meditation on Hughes and the Harlem Renaissance. The next screen that appears, however, reads "dedicated to the memory of James Baldwin." Grief is a precondition to this film. Mourning is never far removed from the "life" in *Looking for Langston.* The scene of mourning and the bar scene that represents the transhistorical space of gay life are separated by a winding staircase. Slow pans up and down show the closeness of these spaces. I do not look at these two scenes, the nightclub and the funeral, as composing a stark binary. This layering of different gay spaces serves to show these different aspects of gay lives as always interlocking and informing each other.

The establishing shot is the lavishly adorned casket surrounded by elegant mourners (a scene that reconstructs various images out of *The Harlem Book of the Dead*). Then there is a slow camera movement from an overhead unmotivated perspective of the filmmaker playing the corpse, body seemingly stiff within the coffin. The connection between looker (Julien conducting his cinematic investigation) and the object of the gaze (the figure of Hughes, who is, in one sense, "invisible," yet very much present under the revisionary gaze) and the audience is radically disrupted and destabilized. This destabilizing of traditional cinematic positionalities is a mirroring of the destabilization and ambivalence of identification that are to be found at the center of the communal mourning scene.

Communal mourning, by its very nature, is an immensely complicated text to read, for we do not mourn just one lost object or other, but we also mourn as a "whole"—or, put another way, as a contingent and temporary collection of fragments that is experiencing a loss of its parts. In this context, mourning Hughes, Baldwin, Mapplethorpe, or the beautiful men in *Black Book* is about mourning for oneself, for one's community, for one's very history. It is not the basically linear line that Freud traces, but a response to the heterosexist and corporate "task-oriented" mourning that Moon describes. Whereas lives that are either/or/and black and queer remain on the line, there is no "normal" teleological end in sight for mourning. Mercer has described the achievement of *Looking for Langston* as working

> precisely in the way it shows how desire and despair run together, and thus how desire always entails rituals of mourning for what is lost and cannot be recovered. There is a sense of mourning not just for Langston, buried in the past under the repressive weight of homophobic and [E]urocentric narratives, but mourning for friends, lovers and others lost to AIDS here and now, in the present. There is mourning but not melancholia: as Langston himself says at the end of the film, "Why should I be blue? I've been blue all night through."[32]

I agree with many of the conclusions of Mercer's essay. I wish here to add a corrective to that reading by depathologizing melancholia and understanding it as a "structure of feeling" that is necessary and not always counterproductive and negative. I am proposing that melancholia, for blacks, queers, or any queers of color, is not a pathology but an integral part of everyday lives. The melancholia that occupies the minds of the communities under siege in this film can be envisioned as the revised version of melancholia that Freud wrote about in his later years. It is this melancholia that is part of our process of dealing with all the catastrophes that occur in the lives of people of color, lesbians, and gay men. I have proposed a different understanding of melancholia that does not see it as a pathology or as a self-absorbed mood that inhibits activism. Rather, it is a mechanism that helps us (re)construct identity and take our dead with us to the various battles we must wage in their names—and in our names. In the end, this analysis does not dismiss the need for and uses of different activist militancies, but instead helps inform a better understanding of them. Douglas Crimp ends his manifesto "Mourning and Militancy" with this stirring sentence: "Militancy, of course, then, but mourning too: mourning *and* militancy."[33]

Julien's melancholic signifying on these two different photographies of mourning supplies a necessary history to a collective struggle. This history comes in the form of identity-affirming "melancholia," a melancholia that individual subjects and different communities in crisis can use to map the ambivalences of identification and the conditions of (im)possibility that shape the minority identities under consideration here. Finally, this melancholia is a productive space of hybridization that uniquely exists between a necessary militancy and indispensable mourning.

Part II

Remaking Genres: Porn, Punk, and Ethnography

Chapter 3

The Autoethnographic Performance: Reading Richard Fung's Queer Hybridity

In the Caribbean we are all performers.
—Antonio Benítez-Rojo

The Queen's English, Too: Queer Hybridity and the Autoethnographic Performance

Are queens born or made? The royal visit sequence of Richard Fung's *My Mother's Place* (1991) undoes the "either/or" bind that such a question produces. A sequence from the film's beginning narrates the moment when the pasty specter of a monarch born to the throne helps to formulate an entirely different type of queen. A flickering sound and image connotes an 8mm camera, the technology used before the advent of amateur video cameras. A long black car leads a procession as schoolchildren, mostly black girls and boys wearing white or light blue uniforms, look on. At the center of the procession, we can easily identify the British queen. The voice-over narration sets the scene:

> Under the watchful eyes of the priests we stand for ages on the sidewalk, burning up in our school uniforms. Then quickly they pass, and all you see is a long white glove making a slow choppy motion. We wave the little flags we were given and fall back into class. White socks on our arms, my sister and I practice the royal wave at home. After Trinidad and Tobago got our independence in 1962, Senghor, Salessi, and Indira Gandhi also made visits. We were given school holidays just like we got for the queen and Princess Margaret, but my mother never took pictures of them.

The young Chinese Trinidadian's identification with the queen is extremely complicated. Practicing the royal wave, in this instance, is an important example of a brand of dissidence that Homi Bhabha has defined as "colonial mimicry": "Mimicry emerges as the representation of a difference that is itself a process of disavowal. Mimicry is thus the sign of the double articulation; a complex strategy of reform, regulation, and discipline, which 'appropriates' the other as it visualizes power."[1] The modalities of difference that inform this royal gesture are structured not only around the colonized/colonizer divide, but also a gay/straight one. This moment of proto-drag "flaunting" not only displays an ambivalence to empire and the protocols of colonial pedagogy, but also reacts against the forced gender prescriptions that such systems reproduce. This mode of mimicry is theatrical inasmuch as it mimes and renders hyperbolic the symbolic ritual that it is signifying upon. This brief "visualization" of power is representative of Fung's cultural performance. Fung's video "visualizes" the workings of power in ethnographic and pornographic films, two discourses that assign subjects such as Fung, colonized, colored, and queer, the status of terminally "other" object. Many of the performances that Fung produces are powerful disidentifications with these othering discourses.

Eve Kosofsky Sedgwick has defined the term *queer* as a *practice* that develops for queer children as

> the ability to attach intently to a few cultural objects, objects of high or popular culture or both, objects whose meaning seemed mysterious, excessive or oblique in relation to the codes most readily available to us, [which] became a prime resource for survival. We needed for there to be sites where meanings didn't line up tidily with each other, and we learn to invest these sites with fascination and love.[2]

Thus, to perform queerness is to constantly disidentify, to constantly find oneself thriving on sites where meaning does not properly "line up." This is equally true of hybridity, another modality where meaning or identifications do not properly line up. The postcolonial hybrid is a subject whose identity practices are structured around an ambivalent relationship to the signs of empire and the signs of the "native," a subject who occupies a space between the West and the rest.

This is not to say that the terms *hybridity* and *queerness* are free of problems. Ella Shohat attempts to temper the celebratory aura that currently envelops the word *hybridity*: "As a descriptive catch-all term, 'hybridity' *per se* fails to discriminate between diverse modalities of hybridity, for example, forced assimilation, internalized self-rejection, political co-optation, social conformism, cultural mimicry, and creative transcendence."[3] It would be dangerous to collapse the different modalities of hybridity we encounter in the First World and its neocolonial territories, and in the various diasporas to which the diversity of ethnically marked people belong. Queerness, too, has the capacity to flatten difference in the name of coalition. Scholars working with these antiessentialist models of identity need to resist the urge to give in to crypto-essentialist understandings of these terms that eventually position them as universal identificatory sites of struggle. Despite some of the more problematic uses of the terms *hybridity* and *queerness,* I take the risk of melding them when discussing the work of cultural producers such as Fung because hybridity helps one understand how queer lives are fragmented into various identity bits: some of them adjacent, some of them complementary, some of them antagonistic. The hybrid—and terms that can be roughly theorized as equivalents, such as the Creole or the mestizo—are paradigms that help account for the complexities and impossibilities of identity, but, except for a certain degree of dependence on institutional frames, what a subject can do from her or his position of hybridity is, basically, open-ended. The important point is that identity practices such as queerness and hybridity are not a priori sites of contestation but, instead, spaces of productivity where identity's fragmentary nature is accepted and negotiated. It is my understanding that these practices of identification inform the reflexivity of Fung's work.

The concept of hybridity has also been engaged by theorists outside of the field of postcolonial or critical race studies. Bruno Latour, the French philosopher of science, has argued that the hybrid is a concept that must be understood as central to the story of modernity. Latour contends that the moderns, the denizens and builders of modernity, are known not for individual breakthroughs such as the invention of humanism, the emergence of the sciences, the secularization and modernization of the world, but instead with the conjoined structure of these historical movements. Latour writes:

> The essential point of the modern constitution is that it renders the work of mediation that assembles hybrids invisible, unthinkable, unrepresentable. Does this lack of representation limit the work of mediation in any way? No, for the modern world would immediately cease to function. Like all other collectives it lives on that blending. On the contrary (and here the beauty of the mechanism comes to light), *the modern constitution allows the expanded proliferation of the hybrids whose existence, whose very possibility, it denies.*[4]

Latour's formulation explains the way in which modern culture produces hybrids while at the same time attempting to elide or erase the representation or signs of hybridity. I want to suggest that Latour's formulation might also give us further insight into empire's panicked response to the hybrids it continuously produces. Empire's institutions, such as colonial pedagogy, are in no small part responsible for the proliferation of hybrid identities, but it is in colonialism's very nature to delineate clearly between the West and the rest. Its terms do not allow for the in-between status of hybridity. The work of hybrid cultural producers such as Fung might thus be understood as a making visible of the mediations that attempt to render hybridity invisible and unthinkable: in both *My Mother's Place* and *Chinese Characters* (1986), Fung works to make hybridity and its process comprehensible and visible.

Fredric Jameson has contended that "The visual is essentially pornographic, which is to say it has its end in rapt, mindless fascination."[5] But some visuals are more pornographic than others. The epistemological affinity of ethnography and pornography has been explained in Bill Nichols, Christian Hansen, and Catherine

Needham's "Ethnography, Pornography and the Discourses of Power," which maps various ways in which the two regimes of ethnography and pornography share a similar discourse of dominance.[6] Both discourses are teleologically cognate insofar as they both strive for the achievement of epistemological utopias where the "Other" and knowledge of the "Other" can be mastered and contained. Ethnotopia can be characterized as a world of limitless observation, where "we know them," whereas pornotopia is a world where "we have them," "a world of lust unlimited."[7] At the end of that essay, the writers are unable to imagine a new symbolic regime or practice where these genres can be reformulated differently, in ways that actively attempt to avoid the imperialist or exploitative vicissitudes of these cinematic genres. My project here is to explicate the ways in which Richard Fung's work invites the viewer to push this imagining further. Fung challenges the formal protocols of such genres through the repetition and radical reinterpretation of such stock characters as the "native informant"[8] and the racialized body in porn. I will consider two of Fung's videos, *My Mother's Place* and *Chinese Characters*. The former traces the Fung family's migratory history in the Asian diaspora through a series of interviews with Rita Fung, the artist's mother; the latter considers the role of the eroticized Asian Other in the discourse of gay male pornography.

A consideration of the performativity of Fung's production sheds valuable light on his project. Reiteration and citation are the most easily identifiable characteristics of this mode of performativity. I will suggest that by its use of such strategies as voice-over monologues, found familial objects such as home-movie footage, and the technique of video keying, Fung's work deploys a practice of performativity that repeats and cites, *with a difference*, the generic fictions of the native Other in ethnography and the Asian "bottom"[9] in fetishizing, North American, specialty porn. The definition of "performative" that I am producing is not meant as an overarching one, but as a working definition designed to deal with the specificity of Fung's productions. This operative understanding of performativity is informed, to some degree, by the work of Judith Butler. In *Bodies That Matter: On the Discursive Limits of Sex*, Butler explains that if a performative succeeds, "that action echoes prior actions, and accumulates the force of authority through the repetition or citation of a prior, authoritative set of practices. What this means, then, is that a performativc 'works' to the extent that it draws on and covers over the constitutive conventions by which it is mobilized."[10] In this quotation, Butler is answering a rhetorical question put forward by Jacques Derrida when he considers whether or not a performative would work if it did not "repeat a 'coded' or iterable utterance . . . if it were not identifiable in some way as a 'citation.'"[11] Butler, in her analysis, is in agreement with Derrida as she understands a performative as working only if it taps into the force of its site of citation, the original that is being repeated, while it draws on and, in time, covers the conventions that it will ultimately undermine. Although Butler's essay is concerned specifically with the performative charge of queerness, its ability to redo and challenge the conventions of heterosexual normativity, it can also explicate the workings of *various* "minority" identifications. Homi Bhabha defines the power of performance in the postcolonial world as the "'sign of the present,' the performativity of discursive practice, the *récits* of the everyday, the repetition of the empirical, the ethics of self-enactment."[12] The repetition of the quotidian in Bhabha, like citation and repetition in Butler, elucidates Fung's own ethics of self-enactment.

Fung's performances work as "autoethnography," inserting a subjective, performative, often combative, "native I" into ethnographic film's detached discourse and gay male pornography's colonizing use of the Asian male body. I will be suggesting that through acts like postcolonial mimicry and the emergence of a hybridized and queerly reflexive performance practice, the social and symbolic economy that regulates otherness can be offset.

The movement of personal histories into a public sphere is typical of autoethnography. Françoise Lionnet describes the way in which autoethnography functions in written cultural production as a "skepticism about writing the self, the autobiography, turning it into the allegory of the ethnographic project that self-consciously moves from the general to the particular to the general."[13] These movements from general to specific, and various shades in between, punctuate Fung's work. Lionnet, in her study of folk anthropologist and novelist Zora Neale Hurston, conceives of autoethnography as a mode of cultural performance. She explains that autoethnography is a "text/performance" and "transcends pedestrian notions of referentiality, for the staging of the event is part of the process of 'passing on,' elaborating cultural forms, which are not static and inviolable but dynamically involved in the creation of culture itself."[14] The creation of culture in this style of performance is always already braided to the production of self in autoethnography insofar as culture itself is the field in which this "figural anthropology" of the self comes to pass.[15] Mary Louise Pratt also employed the term *autoethnography* in her study of travel writing on the imperial frontier. In this study, Pratt lucidly outlines the differences between ethnography and autoethnography:

> I use these terms [*autoethnography* and *autoethnographic expression*] to refer to instances in which colonized subjects undertake to represent themselves in ways which engage with the colonizer's own terms. If ethnographic texts are a means in which Europeans represent to themselves their (usually subjugated) others, autoethnographic texts are those the others construct in response to or in dialogue with those metropolitan representations.[16]

Conventional video and documentary style can, in the case of Fung and in the light of Pratt's definition, be understood as the "colonizer's terms" that are being used to address the metropolitan form. But in Fung's case these terms work to address more than just the metropolitan form and the colonizer. The terms are also meant to speak to the colonized in a voice that is doubly authorized, by both the metropolitan form and subaltern speech. I am not proposing an explanation where form and content are disentangled; more accurately, I mean to imply that the metropolitan form is inflected by the power of subaltern speech, and the same is equally true in reverse. Fung's cultural work elucidates a certain imbrication—that the metropolitan form needs the colonial "other" to function. Autoethnography is a strategy that seeks to disrupt the hierarchical economy of colonial images and representations by making visible the presence of subaltern energies and urgencies *in* metropolitan culture. Autoethnography worries easy binarisms such as colonized and the colonizer or subaltern and metropolitan by presenting subaltern speech through the channels and pathways of metropolitan representational systems.

Lionnet's and Pratt's theorizations are useful tools in understanding the tradition of autobiographical film that has flourished in North America since 1968.[17] The practice of combining evidentiary sound/image cinema with narratives of personal history has been especially prevalent in video documentary production since the advent of widespread independent video production in the late 1960s. Video technology provided disenfranchised sectors of the public sphere with inexpensive and mobile means to produce alternative media. Video documentary practices were adopted by many different minority communities that might be understood as counterpublics. Native Americans, African-Americans, Asians, Latina/os, feminists, gay men, and lesbians all made considerable contributions to the field of documentary video. In the 1980s, AIDS/HIV activist groups such as ACT-UP made use of this technology and the practices of documentary in politically adroit ways.[18]

We might consider this modality as an intensification of what Jim Lane has called the "personal as political trend" in post-1960s autobiographical film.[19] Lane registers a diminishing production of overtly political cinema in the face of what he understands as the more privatized identity politics of the 1970s and 1980s. Such a dichotomy would be of little use when considering trends in video production, a medium that has always found political relevance precisely in the politics of identity and different minority communities.

This strain of autobiographical documentary is best illustrated in recent work by numerous queer video artists. Fung's practice shares an autoethnographic impulse with the work of Sadie Benning and the late Marlon Riggs, to identify only two examples from a larger field. Riggs excavated an African-American gay male image that has been elided in the history of both black communities and queer communities.[20] Benning's confessional experimental videos produce an interesting ethnography of white queer youth culture.[21] In both these examples, the artists inhabit their videos as subjects who articulate their cultural location through their own subcultural performances as others: poetic teen angst monologues in the case of Benning, and, from Riggs, vibrant snap diva virtuosity that includes, but is not limited to, dance, music, and monologues.

The queer trend that I am identifying is in many ways an effort to reclaim the past and put it in direct relationship with the present. Autoethnography is not inter-

My Mother's Place (1991). Courtesy of Richard Fung.

ested in searching for some lost and essential experience, because it understands the relationship that subjects have with their own pasts as complicated yet necessary fictions. Stuart Hall provides a formulation that addresses this complicated relationship between one's identity and one's past:

> Far from being eternally fixed in some essentialized past, they [identities] are subject to the continuous play of history, culture and power. Far from being grounded in a mere "recovery" of the past, which is waiting to be found and which, when found, will secure our sense of ourselves into eternity, identities are the names we give to the different ways in which we are positioned by, and position ourselves within, narratives of the past.[22]

A subject is not locating her or his essential history by researching a racial or cultural past; what is to be located is in fact just one more identity bit that constitutes the matrix that is hybridity. This relationship between a past and a present identity is articulated through a voice-over near the end of *My Mother's Place,* when Fung explains that his mother "connects me to a past I would have no other way of knowing. And in this sea of whiteness, of friends, enemies and strangers, I look at her and know who I am." The past that Rita makes available to Richard is not an essentialized racial past, but instead a necessary fiction of the past that grounds the video artist in the present.

Fung's relationship with and love for his mother are at the center of *My Mother's Place.* The video paints an endearing portrait of Rita Fung as a woman who came of age during colonialism and took her identifications with the colonial paradigm with her to the moment of decolonization. It is shot in Canada and Trinidad and is composed of a series of "interviews" and recollections that form a decidedly personal register. This video portrait of his mother is a queer son's attempt to reconstruct and better understand his identity formation through equally powerful identifications, counteridentifications, and disidentifications with his mother and her own unique relationship to the signs of colonization. The tape relies on its documentary subject's ability to tell her own story in a witty and captivating fashion.

The opening of *My Mother's Place* includes a section subtitled "Reading Instructions." This depicts a sequence of women, mostly academics and activists, mostly women of color, sitting in a chair in front of a black background on which photographs of different women's faces are projected. After the women pronounce on various critical issues including imperialism, gender, political action, and exile, the screen is filled with captions that loosely define the cluster of talking heads on the screen. The descriptions include: teacher, writer, sociologist, arts administrator, feminist, poet, Jamaican, English, Indian, friends. The visual text is accompanied by Fung's voice-over saying "these women have never met my mother." This "not lining up" of sound and image is not meant to undermine any of the women's interviews. More nearly it speaks to the ways in which identification with neither his mother nor his academic friends and colleagues suffices. This moment where things do not line up is a moment of reflexivity that is informed by and through the process of queerness *and* hybridity. It is a moment where hybridity is not a fixed positionality but a survival strategy that is essential for both queers and postcolonial subjects who are subject to the violence that institutional structures reproduce.

This skepticism and ambivalence that Lionnet identifies as being characteristic of autoethnography can be located throughout Fung's project. Fung employs various tactics to complicate and undermine his own discourse. During a sequence toward the middle of the video, the artist once again employs home-movie footage. The 8mm home video instantly achieves a texture reminiscent of childhood. In viewing the section from the tape, the spectator becomes aware of the ways in which the videographer supplies contradictory information on three different levels: the visual image, the voice-over, and the written text that appears on the screen. The visual image shows a young Rita Fung strolling the garden in her 1950s-style *Good Housekeeping* dress and red pillbox hat. She does not look directly at the camera. Her stride is calm and relaxed. There is a cut and Rita Fung reappears, her back to the camera as she walks off, holding the hand of a little boy. The little boy is wearing a white button-down oxford and black slacks. He holds on tightly to his mother's hand. The next cut shows both mother and son smiling and walking toward the

My Mother's Place (1991). Courtesy of Richard Fung.

camera. This is the first view the spectator has of the narrator. The voice-over scene matches the image by narrating a family history:

> It's Sunday after Mass. Dressed in satin, she looks like the woman in the *Good Housekeeping* magazine that arrives from the States. During the week she is off to work while I go to school. She wears a pencil behind her right ear and her desk is near the Coke machine. When she is not at the shop she is washing clothes, cooking, sitting on a box in the garden, cutters in hand, weeding. In the evening she is making poppy sauce or making cookies to sell. We dropped six cookies at a time in a plastic bag while we watched *Gunsmoke* on TV. When I bring home forms from school she puts "housewife" down as occupation. The women in *Good Housekeeping* are housewives. In the afternoon they wait at home to serve cookies and milk to their children. Mom was never home when I got home from school.

When this segment of narration concludes, the flickering sound of home projector fades and is replaced by the film's nondiegetic score. Text appears over the image of young Richard and Rita Fung. It reads: "These pictures show more about my family's desire than how we actually lived." The voice-over narration then continues: "But in all the family pictures this is the only shot that shows what I remember." The image that follows this statement is of a young Richard wearing shorts and a T-shirt, still holding on to his mother's hand as they both dance. A new title is superimposed over the image and this text responds to the last bit of narration by explaining: "We're doing the twist." The next image shows an uncoordinated little Richard dancing and jumping barefoot in his backyard. He looks directly at the camera and sticks his tongue out. His manner is wild and effeminate. The narrator then introduces the last installment of text in this segment by saying: "And me, well, you can see from these pictures that I was just an ordinary boy doing ordinary boy things." The screen is then once again covered with text. The story superimposed over the image is one that is familiar to many children who showed cross-dressing tendencies in early childhood: "One day Mom caught me in one of her dresses and threatened to put me out in the street. . . . I was scared but it didn't stop me." When Fung betrays the visual image as a totally imaginary ideal that was more about his parents' fantasy life than about what really happened, he is disavowing the colonial fantasy of assimilation that his family's home movies articulated. In this scene, and throughout *My Mother's Place,* the "Queen's English" is spoken by a mimic man, a subject who has interpolated the mark of colonial power into his discourse but through repetition is able to disarticulate these traditional discourses of authority. The term coined by Bhabha to describe the condition of the colonized subject, "not quite/not white," aptly depicts the overall effect of the "all-American" home-movie footage. The statements disseminated through the visual text are directly connected with Fung's then protoqueer identity as an effeminate boy, the type of queer child whom Sedgwick describes as a subject for whom meaning does not neatly line up. He was not, as his voice-over suggested, "an ordinary boy doing ordinary boy things"; he was, in fact, a wonderfully swishy little boy who, among other things, liked to dress in his mother's *Good Housekeeping*-style dresses, liked the fictional moms on television who baked cookies for their children. I would also suggest that we might understand the actual storytelling practice of the film, the not lining up of image, sound, and text, as something that is decidedly queer about Fung's production. This not lining up of image and sound is a deviation from traditional documentary, which is chiefly concerned with sound and image marching together as a tool of authorization. The not-lining-up strategy was employed in different ways in Fung's earlier videotape *Chinese Characters,* achieving similar disidentificatory effects. Although the two tapes deal with vastly different subjects, they nonetheless, on the level of process and practice, share significant strategical maneuvers that once again are indebted to a predominantly queer wave in documentary production.

Transfiguring the Pornographic

The reassertions of agency that Fung displays in *My Mother's Place,* the way in which he asserts the natives' authority in the ethnographic project, are not entirely different from those that are achieved in *Chinese Characters.* This videotape performs an intervention in the field of mainstream pornography by adding an Asian male presence where it has routinely been excluded. This experimental documentary interviews gay

Asian men about their relationships to pornography. The documentary subjects reflect on the way in which pornography helped mold them as desiring subjects. The tape also includes a narrative sequence in which a young Asian man penetrates the white gay male field of pornography by being video-keyed into an early porn loop.

The mainstream gay pornography that has dominated the market, produced by California-based companies such as Catalina, Falcon, and Vivid Video, has contributed to a somewhat standardized image of the porn performer. It is paradoxical that the promise of pornotopia, the promise of lust unlimited, desire without restriction, is performed by a model who generally conforms to a certain rigid set of physical and racial characteristics. This standardized porn model is a paler shade of white, hairless, and he is usually young and muscled. He is the blueprint that is later visualized infinitely at gay male identity hubs such as gyms and dance clubs. The mainstream porn image, throughout the late 1980s and early 1990s, continued to evolve into an all-too-familiar clean-shaven Anglo twenty-something clone. Although the pornography with which Fung interacts in his interventionist video performances is not quite as homogenized as today's pornography, the porn loops he riffs on still display the trace of this white normative sex clone. The point here is not to moralize about how such an image might be harmful, for it is my belief that it is a futile project to deliberate on the negativity or positivity of images within representational fields.[23] Instead, it is far more useful to note the ways in which Fung transfigures porn through his practices. His video production illuminates the normative logics of porn productions by deploying, through an act of postcolonial mimicry, a disidentification with a popularized ideal: the Asian gay male body. Fung's disidentification with the generic and racially inflected protocols of porn opens up a space that breaks down the coherence of white domination in the gay male erotic imaginary. This disidentification accesses possibilities, through the unlikely vehicle of the orientalized body, that are ultimately sex- and pornography-positive, but nonetheless rooted in a struggle to free up the ethnocentric conceit that dominates the category of the erotic in the pornographic imaginary. By "ethnocentric conceit" I mean the troubling propensity of representing standardized white male beauty as a norm, and the tendency in erotic representation to figure nonwhite men as exotic kink.

It is important to note here the powerful connection between gay male porn and gay male culture. Richard Dyer, in an often-cited essay on gay male pornographic production, has pointed out that gay male pornography is analogous to gay male sexuality in more general terms.[24] Understanding pornography as an analog to broader aspects of gay male culture makes even more sense today, as pornography, during the AIDS pandemic, is one of the few completely safe and sex-positive, identity-affirming spaces/practices left to gay men. Fung's critique of porn, or the one that is being offered here, should not be understood as antipornographic; rather, by unveiling the ethnocentric bias at work in the pornographic imaginary that is collectively produced by the porn industry, one can better understand the larger problem of white normativity and racism within North American gay male culture.

In her essay "The She-Man: Postmodern Bi-Sexed Performance in Film and Video," Chris Straayer described the process of this reenacting of historically denied agency in Fung's work. "Fung uses technology to intervene in conventional positioning," she explains. "First he video-keys himself into a pornographic film where he then poses as the lure for a desiring 'stud.'"[25] Straayer's description is evocative of the way in which the terrain of pornography becomes a contact zone,[26] one in which the ideological (visualized in Fung's technological reinsertion into the representational field) and the epistemological (pornography's need to carnally know the Other) collide.

The ideological effect is visible in a scene from *Chinese Characters* where an actual Chinese character is video-keyed into an exclusively white gay male porn film. The Asian male body, after being keyed into the grainy seventies porn loop, proceeds to take what seems like a leisurely stroll in an outdoor sex scene. The act of taking a leisurely walk is designed to connote casual tourism. The touristic pose taken here is quite different from the usual options available to gay men of color in the pornography industry. This performatively reappropriates the position of the white male subject who can touristically gaze at minority bodies in such tapes as *Orient Express* (1990), *Latin from Manhattan* (1992), or *Blackshaft* (1993).[27] The newly subjectivized Other who has been walking through this scene then comes face to face with a character from this porn loop. The white male reaches out to the Asian male who, by the particular generic protocols of this vanilla porn subgenre, would be excluded from that symbolic field. Donning a "traditional" dome-shaped Asian field-worker's hat, the Asian male subject plays with his own nipples as he then materializes in a California poolside orgy. Such a performance of autoeroticism, within a symbolic field such as the 1970s white male porn loop, realigns and disrupts the dominant stereotype insofar as it portrays the Asian male body not as the perpetually passive bottom who depends on the white male top, but instead as a subject who can enjoy scopic pleasure in white objects while at the same time producing his own pleasure.

Fung later, in a print essay, deals with the marginal genre of interracial porn, especially tapes featuring Asian men.[28] In this essay, Fung explains that the Asian male body in interracial videotapes is almost always cast as the passive bottom who depends on the white male top to get off. I find it significant that this inquiry into interracial porn follows an initial engagement with porn's exclusionary and racially biased image hierarchy (the critique that *Chinese Characters* produces). Within the logic of porn, a subfield such as racially integrated or exclusively nonwhite tapes is roughly equivalent to other modalities of kink such as bondage, sadomasochism, shaving, and so on. The point here is that, because of white normativity of the pornotopic field, race *counts* as a different sexual practice (that is, doing sadomasochism, doing Asians). Thus, race, like sadomasochism, is essentially a performance. An observation of Fung's practices reveals that the Asian men in his tapes essentially repeat orientalized performances with a difference through the video insertions and interviews they perform in the tape.

Chinese Characters narrates another cultural collision through different representational strategies. What seems like a traditional Chinese folktale is first heard as the camera lyrically surveys what appears to be a Chinese garden. When the visual image abruptly cuts to a full body shot of an Asian man trying on different outfits, the nondiegetic "traditional" Chinese music is replaced by a disco sound track that signifies that one has entered a gay male subculture. For a brief period we continue to hear the folktale with the disco sound track. When the folktale expires, we hear the sound track of a porn trailer that announces the names of recognizable white porn performers/icons, such as Al Parker. The announcer's voice produces a typical raunchy rap that eventually fades as a techno disco beat rises in volume. The Asian man finally chooses his outfit and commences his cruise. The filaments of the artist's hybridized identity, in this brief sequence, are embodied in sound and performance. The gay man's body literally bridges these different sound messages: traditional Chinese music, the heavy accent of a Chinese-American retelling what seems to be an ancient fable, the voice of the white porn announcer as he describes the hot action, and the techno beat that eventually emerges as the score for the gay man's cruise. On the level of the visual, the fact that the subject is dressing during the scene identifies it as a moment of queer hybrid self-*fashioning*. Both the performances of drag and striptease are signified upon during this sequence. Rather than taking off his clothing, as in the traditional striptease, the process of revealing an "authentic" self, the Asian male about to commence his cruise continuously dresses and redresses, enacting a kind of counter-striptease that does not fetishize a material body but instead mediates on the ways in which, through costume and performance, one continuously *makes* self. Each outfit that is tried on displays a different modality of being queer; all the ensembles depict different positions on a gay male subcultural spectrum. All of it is disguise and the sequence itself works as a catalog of various queer modalities of self-presentation.

Of these different disguises, the orientalized body is one of the most important. Fung's critique is not simply aimed at the exclusion of Asians from pornographic video and, in turn, other aspects of a modern gay life-world. It is also, through a mode of mimicry that I understand as disidentificatory, a challenge to the limited and racist understandings of the gay male body in pornography. *Orientalism* is a powerful critical term first coined by Edward Said in his influential study of that name. Said described orientalism as "a style of thought that is based on an ontological and epistemological division made between 'the Orient' and (most of the time) 'the Occident.'"[29] The totalizing implications of Said's theory have been critiqued by many scholars. Bhabha, in perhaps the most famous of these challenges to Said's analysis of orientalism, points to the ambivalence of power in colonial discourse, arguing that Said's narrative of orientalism posited all agency and power on the side of the "Occident," ignoring the ways in which the colonized might gain access to power

My Mother's Place (1991). Courtesy of Richard Fung.

and enact self against and within the colonial paradigm.[30] Lisa Lowe has made a significant contribution to the development of the theoretical discourse on orientalism by further describing the phenomenon with a special attention to its nuanced workings:

> I do not construct a master narrative or a singular history of orientalism, whether of influence or of comparison. Rather, I argue for a conception of orientalism as heterogeneous and contradictory; to this end I observe, on the one hand, that orientalisms consist of uneven orientalist situations across different cultural and historical sites, and on the other, that each of these orientalisms is internally complex and unstable. My textual readings give particular attention to those junctures at which narratives of gendered, racial, national and class differences complicate and interrupt the narrative of orientalism, as well as to the points at which orientalism is refunctioned and rearticulated against itself.[31]

Fung's engagement with orientalism can be understood to operate in a way similar to Lowe's. Orientalism in *Chinese Characters,* like the signs of colonial power in *My Mother's Place,* are refunctioned by Fung's disidentification with these cultural referents. Disidentification is the performative re-citation of the stereotypical Asian bottom in porn, and the trappings of colonial culture. In this instance, we have a useful example of the way in which disidentification engages and recycles popular forms with a difference. Fung's strategy of disidentification reappropriates an ambivalent yet highly charged set of images—those representing the queer Asian body in porn—and remakes them in a fashion that explores and outlines the critical ambivalences that make this image a vexing site of identification and desire for Asian gay men and other spectators/consumers with antiracist political positions. The erotic is not demonized but instead used as a site for critical engagement. Documentary, in the case of Fung's production, is a reflexive practice inasmuch as it aims to rearticulate dominant culture and document a history of the other, an orientalized other that remakes otherness as a strategy of enacting the self that is undermined and limited by orientalist and colonialist discourses.

Finding Fung

Specific scenes, postcolonial or decolonized spaces such as Fung's Trinidad or the Asian community in Toronto, enable these sorts of rearticulations by functioning as contact zones, locations of hybridity that, because their location is liminal, allow for new social formations that are not as easily available at the empire's center.

The Caribbean basin is an appropriate setting for *My Mother's Place* in that it is a "contact zone," a space where the echoes of colonial encounters still reverberate in the contemporary sound produced by the historically and culturally disjunctive situation of temporal and spatial copresence that is understood as the postcolonial moment.

Pratt elaborates one of the most well developed theories of contact zones. For Pratt, the "contact" component of contact zone is defined as a perspective: "A 'contact' perspective emphasizes how subjects are constituted in and by their relations to each other. It treats the relations among colonizers and colonized, or travelers and 'travelees,' not in terms of separateness or apartheid, but in terms of copresence, interaction, interlocking understanding and practices, often within radically asymmetrical relations of power."[32]

For Pratt, a contact zone is both a location and a different path to thinking about asymmetries of power and the workings of the colonizer/colonized mechanism. Both videotapes I have analyzed in this chapter stage copresences that are essentially instances of contact: the contact between a colonized queer boy (and his mother) with the signs of empire and imperialism like the queen, *Good Housekeeping* magazine, and *Gunsmoke* in *My Mother's Place,* and, in the case of *Chinese Characters,* the contact between the Asian male body in pornotopia and the whiteness of the industry that either relegates him to the status of perpetual bottom or excludes him altogether.

It would also be important to situate the artist's own geography in this study of contact zones. Fung's Trinidad is considered a contact zone par excellence in part because its colonial struggle has been well documented by postcolonial thinkers such as C. L. R. James who have written famous accounts of the island's history of colonization.[33] Fung's status as Asian in a primarily black and white colonial situation further contributes to Fung's postcolonial identity. An Asian in such a setting, like an Asian in the already subcultural field of (white-dominated) gay male culture, is at least doubly a minority and doubly fragmented from the vantage point of dominant culture. Canada, on the other hand, has not received extensive consideration as a postcolonial space.[34] A settler colony, Canada's status as not quite First World and not quite Second World positions it as a somewhat ambiguous postcolonial site. Canada, for example, is an importer of U.S. pornography. It is, therefore, on the level of the erotic imaginary, colonized by a U.S. erotic image hierarchy.[35] The geographic location of Fung's production is significant when considering the hybridity of his representational strategies. Fung's *place,* in both Canada, Trinidad, gay male culture, documentary practice, ethnography, pornography, the Caribbean and Asian diasporas, is not quite fixed; thus, this work is uniquely concentrated on issues of place and displacement.

Furthermore, these zones are all productive spaces of hybridization where complex and ambivalent *American* identities are produced. The process by which these hybrid identity practices are manufactured is one that can be understood as syncretism. Many Latin American and U.S. Latino critics have used the term not only to explicate a complex system of cultural expressions, but also to describe the general character of the Caribbean. The Cuban theorist of postmodernism, Antonio Benítez-Rojo, uses the term *supersyncretism,* which for him arises from the collision of European, African, and Asian components within the plantation. For Benítez-Rojo, the phenomenon of supersyncretism is at its most visible when one considers performance:

> If I were to have to put it in a word I would say performance. But performance not only in terms of scenic interpretation but also in terms of the execution of a ritual. That is the "certain way" in which two Negro women who conjured away the apocalypse were walking. In this "certain kind of way" there is expressed the mystic or magical (if you like) loam of civilizations that contributed to the formation of Caribbean culture.[36]

Benítez-Rojo's description is disturbing insofar as it reproduces its own form of orientalism by fetishizing the conjuring culture of Cuban Santeria and its mostly black and often female practitioners in a passing lyrical mention. There is, nonetheless, a useful refunctioning of this formulation. Instead of Benítez-Rojo's example, consider the acts that Fung narrates: the way in which a protoqueer Chinese Trinidadian boy with a sock on his hand mimics the queen's wave, a gesture that is quite literally the hailing call of empire. Fung's videos are especially significant in that through such acts and performances they index, reflect on, and are reflexive of some of the most energized topics and debates confronting various discourses, such as cultural studies, anthropology, queer theory, and performance studies. In the end, white sock sheathed over his hybrid's hand like a magical prophylactic, protecting him from the disciplinary effect of colonial power, the queer gesture of Fung's wave deconstructs and ruptures the white mythologies of ethnotopia and pornotopia.[37]

Chapter 4

"The White to Be Angry": Vaginal Creme Davis's Terrorist Drag

The year 1980 saw the debut of one of the L.A. punk scene's most critically acclaimed albums, the band X's *Los Angeles.* X was fronted by John Doe and Exene Cervenka, who were described by one writer as "poetry workshop types,"[1] who had recently migrated to Los Angeles from the East Coast. They used the occasion of their first album to describe the effect that city had on its white denizens. The album's title track, "Los Angeles," narrates the story of a white female protagonist who had to leave Los Angeles because she started to hate "every nigger and Jew, every Mexican who gave her a lot of shit, every homosexual and the idle rich." Today, the song reads for me like a fairly standard tale of white flight from the multiethnic metropolis. Yet, I would be kidding myself if I pretended to have had access to such a reading back then, for I had no contexts or reading skills for any such interpretation.

When I contemplate these lyrics today, I am left with a disturbed feeling. When I was a teenager growing up in South Florida, X occupied the hallowed position of favorite band. When I attempt to situate my relation to this song and my own developmental history, I remember what X meant to me back then. Within the hermetic Cuban-American community I came of age in, punk rock was not yet the almost routine route of individuation and resistance that it is today. Back then it was the only avant-garde that I knew; it was the only cultural critique of normative aesthetics available to me. Yet, there was a way in which I was able to escape the song's interpellating call. Although queerness was already a powerful polarity in my life and the hissing pronunciation of "Mexican" that the song produced felt very much like the epithet "spic" that I had a great deal of experience with, I somehow found a way to resist these identifications. The luxury of hindsight lets me understand that I needed X and the possibility of subculture they promised at that moment to withstand the identity-eroding effects of normativity. I was thus able to enact a certain misrecognition that

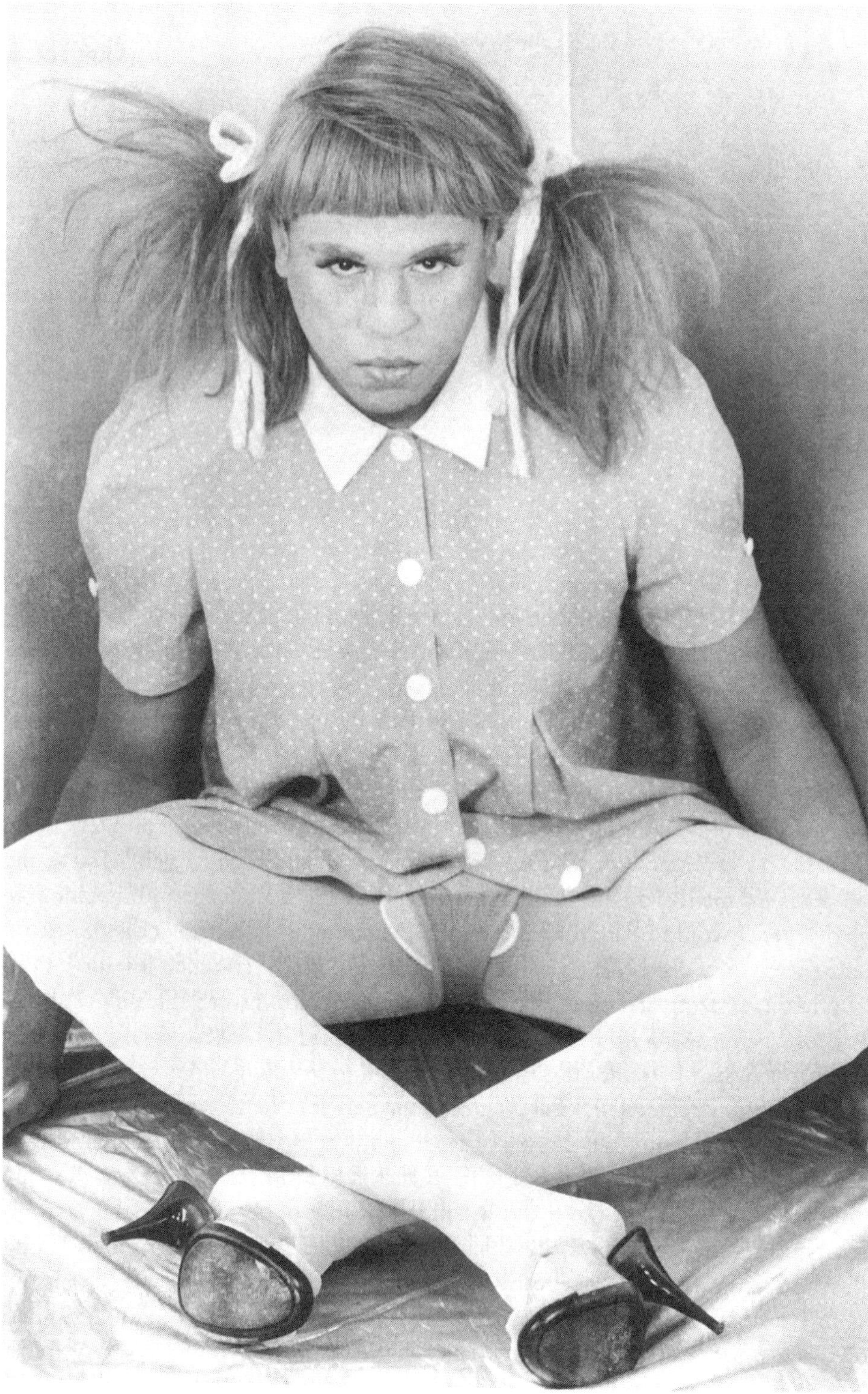

Vaginal Davis as the bad seed. Photo by Rick Castro.

let me imagine myself as something other than queer or racialized. But such a misrecognition takes a certain toll. The toll is one that subjects who attempt to identify with and assimilate to dominant ideologies pay every day of their lives. The price of the ticket is this: to find self within the dominant public sphere, we need to deny self. The contradictory subjectivity one is left with is not just the fragmentary subjectivity of some unspecified postmodern condition; it is instead the story of the minoritarian subject within the majoritarian public sphere. Fortunately, this story does not end at this difficult point, this juncture of painful contradiction. Sometimes misrecognition can be *tactical.* Identification itself can also be manipulated and worked in ways that promise narratives of self that surpass the limits prescribed by the dominant culture.

In this chapter, I will discuss the cultural work of an artist who came of age within the very same L.A. punk scene that produced X. The L.A. punk scene worked very hard to whitewash and straighten its image. Although many people of color and queers were part of this cultural movement, they often remained closeted in the scene's early days. The artist whose work I will be discussing came of age in that scene and managed to resist its whitewashing and heteronormative protocols.

The work of drag superstar Vaginal Creme Davis, or, as she sometimes prefers to be called, Dr. Davis, spans several cultural production genres. It also appropriates, terroristically, both dominant culture and different subcultural movements. Davis first rose to prominence in the Los Angeles punk scene through her infamous 'zine *Fertile La Toyah Jackson* and her performances at punk shows with her Supremes-like backup singers, the Afro Sisters. *Fertile La Toyah Jackson*'s first incarnation was as a print 'zine that presented scandalous celebrity gossip. The 'zine was reminiscent of *Hollywood Babylon,* Kenneth Anger's two-volume tell-all history of the movie industry and the star system's degeneracy. The hand-stapled 'zine eventually evolved into a video magazine. At the same time, as the 'zine became a global subcultural happening, Davis's performances in and around the L.A. punk scene, with the Afro Sisters and solo, became semilegendary. She went on to translate her performance madness to video, starring in various productions that include *Dot* (1994), her tribute to Dorothy Parker's acerbic wit and alcoholism, *VooDoo Williamson—The Doña of Dance* (1995), her celebration of modern dance and its doyennes, and *Designy Living* (1995), a tribute to Noël Coward's *Design for Living* and Jean-Luc Godard's *Masculin et féminin.*

According to Davis's own self-generated legend, her existence is the result of an illicit encounter between her then forty-five-year-old African-American mother and her father, who was, at the time, a twenty-one-year-old Mexican-American. Davis has often reported that her parents only met once, when she was conceived under a table during a Ray Charles concert at the Hollywood Palladium in the early 1960s.

Although the work with the Afro Sisters and much of her 'zine work deals with issues of blackness, she explores her Chicana heritage with one of her musical groups, ¡Cholita!—a band that is billed as the female Menudo. This band consists of both

Vaginal Davis. Photo by Rick Castro.

men and women in teenage Chicana drag who sing Latin American bubblegum pop songs with titles like "Chicas de hoy" (Girls of today). ¡Cholita! and Davis's other bands all produce socially interrogative performances that complicate any easy understanding of race or ethnicity within the social matrix. Performance is used by these theatrical musical groups to, borrowing a phrase from George Lipsitz, "rehearse identities"[2] that have been rendered toxic within the dominant public sphere but are, through Davis's fantastic and farcical performance, restructured (yet not cleansed) so that they present newly imagined notions of the self and the social. This chapter focuses on the performance work done through *The White to Be Angry,* a live show and a CD produced by one of Davis's other subculturally acclaimed musical groups, Pedro, Muriel, and Esther. (Often referred to as PME, the band is named after a cross section of people that Davis met when waiting for the bus. Pedro was a young Latino who worked at a fast-food chain and Muriel and Esther were two senior citizens.) This chapter's first section will consider both the compact disc and the live performance. The next section interrogates questions of "passing," and its specific relation to what I am calling the cultural politics of *disidentification.* I will pursue this thread, "passing," in relation to both mainstream drag and a queerer modality of performance that I call Davis's "terrorist drag." The final section considers Davis's relation to the discourse of "antigay."

Who's That Girl?

Disidentification is a performative mode of tactical recognition that various minoritarian subjects employ in an effort to resist the oppressive and normalizing discourse of dominant ideology. Disidentification resists the interpellating call of ideology that fixes a subject within the state power apparatus. It is a reformatting of self within the social. It is a third term that resists the binary of identification and counteridentification. Counteridentification often, through the very routinized workings of its denouncement of dominant discourse, reinstates that same discourse. In an interview in the magazine *aRude,* Davis offers one of the most lucid explications of a modality of performance that I call disidentificatory. Davis responds to the question "How did you acquire the name Vaginal Davis?" with a particularly elucidating rant.

> It came from Angela Davis—I named myself as a salute to her because I was really into the whole late '60's and early '70's militant Black era. When you come home from the inner city and you're Black you go through a stage when you try to fit the dominant culture, you kinda want to be white at first—it would be easier if you were white. Everything that's negrified or Black—you don't want to be associated with that. That's what I call the snow period—I just felt like if I had some cheap white boyfriend, my life could be perfect and I could be some treasured thing. I could feel myself projected through some white person, and have all the privileges that white people get—validation through association.[3]

The "snow period" Davis describes corresponds to the assimilationist option that minoritarian subjects often choose. Although sanctioned and encouraged by the

Vaginal Davis as a lovelorn dominatrix. Photo by Rick Castro.

dominant culture, the "snow period" is not a viable option for people of color. More often than not, for the person of color, snow melts in the hands of the subject who attempts to acquire privilege through associations (be they erotic, emotional, or both) with whites. Davis goes on to describe her next phase.

> Then there was a conscious shift, being that I was the first one in my family to go to college—I got militant. That's when I started reading about Angela and the Panthers, and that's when Vaginal emerged as a filtering of Angela through humor. That led to my early 1980's a capella performance entity, Vaginal Davis and the Afro Sisters (who were two white girls with Afro wigs). We did a show called "we're taking over" where we portrayed the Sexualese Liberation Front which decides to kidnap all the heads of white corporate America so we could put big black dildos up their lily white buttholes and hold them for ransom. It really freaked out a lot of the middle-class post-punk crowd—they didn't get the campy element of it but I didn't really care.[4]

Thus the punk-rock drag diva elucidates a stage or temporal space where the person of color's consciousness turns to her or his community after an immersion in white culture and education. The ultramilitant phase that Davis describes is typically a powerful counteridentification with the dominant culture. At the same time, though, Davis's queer sexuality, her queerness *and* effeminacy, kept her from fully accessing

Black Power militancy. Unable to pass as heterosexual black militant through simple counteridentification, Vaginal Davis instead disidentified with Black Power by selecting Angela and *not* the Panthers as a site of self-fashioning and political formation. Davis's deployment of disidentification demonstrates that it is, to employ Kimberele William Crenshaw's term, an *intersectional strategy*.[5] Intersectionality insists on critical hermeneutics that register the copresence of sexuality, race, class, gender, and other identity differentials as particular components that exist simultaneously with one another. Vintage Black Power discourse contained many homophobic and masculinist elements that were toxic to queer and feminist subjects. Davis used parody and pastiche to remake Black Power, opening it up via disidentification to a self that is simultaneously black and queer. (With her group ¡Cholita! she performs a similar disidentification with Latina/o popular culture. As Graciela Grejalva, she is not an oversexed songstress, but instead a teenage Latina singing sappy bubblegum pop.)

Davis productively extends her disidentificatory strategy to her engagement with the performative practice of drag. With the advent of the mass commercialization of drag evident in suburban multiplexes that program such films as *To Wong Foo, Thanks for Everything! Julie Newmar* and *The Bird Cage,* or VH-1's broadcasts of RuPaul's talk show, it seems especially important at this point to distinguish different modalities of drag. Commercial drag presents a sanitized and desexualized queer subject for mass consumption. Such drag represents a certain strand of integrationist liberal pluralism. The sanitized queen is meant to be enjoyed as an entertainer who will hopefully lead to social understanding and tolerance. Unfortunately, this boom in filmic and televisual drag has had no impact on hate legislation put forth by the New Right or on homophobic violence on the nation's streets. Indeed, this "boom" in drag helps one understand that a liberal-pluralist mode of political strategizing only eventuates a certain absorption and nothing like a productive engagement with difference. Thus, although RuPaul, for example, hosts a talk show on VH-1, one only need click the remote control and hear about new defenses of marriage legislation that "protect" the family by outlawing gay marriage. Indeed, the erosion of gay civil rights is simultaneous with the advent of higher degrees of queer visibility in the mainstream media.

But while corporate-sponsored drag has to some degree become incorporated within the dominant culture, there is also a queerer modality of drag that is performed by queer-identified drag artists in spaces of queer consumption. Félix Guattari, in a discussion of the theatrical group the Mirabelles, explains the potential political power of drag:

> The Mirabelles are experimenting with a new type of militant theater, a theater separate from an explanatory language and long tirades of good intentions, for example, on gay liberation. They resort to drag, song, mime, dance, etc., not as different ways of illustrating a theme, to "change the ideas" of spectators, but in order to trouble them, to stir up uncertain desire-zones that they always more or

> less refuse to explore. The question is no longer to know whether one will play feminine against masculine or the reverse, but to make bodies, all bodies, break away from the representations and restraints on the "social body."[6]

Guattari's take on the Mirabelles, specifically his appraisal of the political performance of drag, assists in the project of further evaluating the effects of queer drag. I do not simply want to assign one set of drag strategies and practices the title of "bad" drag and the other "good." But I do wish to emphasize the ways in which Davis's *terroristic drag* "stirs up desires" and enables subjects to imagine a way of "break[ing] away from the restraint of the 'social body,'" while sanitized corporate drag and even traditional gay drag are unable to achieve such effects. Davis's political drag is about creating an uneasiness, an uneasiness in desire, which works to confound and subvert the social fabric. The "social body" that Guattari discusses is amazingly elastic and it is able to accommodate scripts on gay liberation. Drag like Davis's, however, is not easily enfolded in that social fabric because of the complexity of its intersectional nature.

There is a great diversity within drag performance. Julian Fleisher's *The Drag Queens of New York: An Illustrated Field Guide to Drag,* surveys underground drag and differentiates two dominant styles of drag, "glamour" and "clown."[7] New York drag queens such as Candis Cayne or Girlina, whose drag is relatively "real," rate high on the glamour meter.[8] Other queens, such as Varla Jean Merman (who bills herself as the love child of Ethel Merman and Ernest Borgnine) and Miss Understood, are representative of the over-the-top parody style of drag known as "clown." Many famous queens, such as Wigstock impresario and mad genius The "Lady" Bunny, appear squarely in the middle of Fleisher's scale.[9] On first glance, Vaginal, who is in no way invoking glamour or "realness," and most certainly does not *pass* (in a direct sense of the word), seems to be on the side of clown drag. I want to complicate this system of evaluation and attempt a more nuanced appraisal of Vaginal Davis's style.

Vaginal Davis's drag, while comic and even hilarious, should not be dismissed as just clowning around. Her uses of humor and parody function as disidentificatory strategies whose effect on the dominant public sphere is that of a counterpublic terrorism. At the center of all of Davis's cultural productions is a radical impulse toward cultural critique. It is a critique that, according to the artist, has often escaped two groups who compose some of drag's most avid supporters: academics and other drag queens.

> I was parodying a lot of different things. But it wasn't an intellectual type of thing—it was innate. A lot of academics and intellectuals dismissed it because it wasn't smart enough—it was too homey, a little too country. And gay drag queens hated me. They didn't understand it. I wasn't really trying to alter myself to look like a real woman. I didn't wear false eyelashes or fake breasts. It wasn't about the realness of traditional drag—the perfect flawless makeup. I just put on a little lipstick, a little eye shadow and a wig and went out there.[10]

Vaginal Davis. Photo by Rick Castro.

It is the "innateness," the "homeyness," and the "countryness" of Davis's style that draws this particular academic to the artist's work. I understand these characteristics as components of the artist's guerrilla style, a style that functions as a ground-level cultural terrorism that fiercely skewers both straight culture and reactionary components of gay culture. I would also like to link these key words, *innateness, homeyness,* and *countryness,* that Vaginal calls on with a key word from the work of Antonio Gramsci that seems to be a partial cognate of these other terms: *organic.*

Gramsci attempted to both demystify the role of the intellectual and reassert the significance of the intellectual's role to a social movement. He explained that "Every social group, coming into existence on the original terrain of an essential function, creates together with itself, organically, one or more strata of intellectuals which give it homogeneity and an awareness of its own function not only in the economic but also in the social and political fields."[11] Davis certainly worked to bolster and cohere the L.A. punk scene, giving it a more significant "homogeneity" and "awareness."[12] At the same time, her work constituted a critique of that community's whiteness. In this way, it participated in Gramsci's project of extending the scope of Marxist analysis to look beyond class as the ultimate social division and consider *blocs.* Blocs are, in the words of John Fiske, "alliance[s] of social forces formed to promote common social interests as they can be brought together in particular historical conditions."[13] The Gramscian notion of bloc formation emphasizes the centrality of class relations in any critical analysis, while not diminishing the importance of other cultural struggles. In the life-world of mostly straight white punks, Davis had, as a black gay man, a strongly disidentificatory role within that community. I suggest that her disidentifications with social blocs are productive interventions in which politics are destabilized, permitting her to come into the role of "organic intellectual." Vaginal Davis did and did not belong to the scene but nonetheless did forge a place for herself that is not *a* place, but instead the still important *position* of intellectual.

A reading of one of Davis's spin-off projects, a CD and live show by her hard-core/speed metal band Pedro, Muriel, and Esther, *The White to Be Angry,* will ground this consideration of Vaginal Davis as organic intellectual. Although I focus on this one aspect of her oeuvre, it should nonetheless be noted that my claim for her as organic intellectual has a great deal to do with the wide variety of public performances and discourses she employs. Davis disseminates her cultural critique through multiple channels of publicity: independent video, 'zines, public-access programming, performance art, anthologized short fiction, bar drag, the weekly L.A. punk-rock club Sucker, for which she is a hostess and impresario, and three different bands (the aforementioned PME and ¡Cholita! as well as the semimythical Black Fag, a group that parodies the famous North American punk band Black Flag). In the PME project, she employs a modality of drag that is neither glamorous nor strictly comedic. Her drag is a terroristic send-up of masculinity and white supremacy. Its focus and pitch are political parody and critique, anchored in her very particular homey/organic style and humor.

The White to Be Angry and "Passing"

It is about 1:30 in the morning at Squeezebox, a modish queercore night at a bar in lower Manhattan. It was a warm June evening. PME's show was supposed to start at midnight. I noticed the band's easily identifiable lead singer rush in at about 12:30, so I had no illusion that the show was going to begin before 1:00 A.M. I have whiled away the time by watching thin and pale go-go boys and girls dancing on the bars. The boys are not the beefy pumped-up white and Latino muscle boys of Chelsea. This, after all, is way downtown, where queer style is decidedly different from the ultramasculine muscle drag of Chelsea. Still, the crowd here is extremely white and Vaginal Davis's black six-foot-six-inch frame towers over the sea of white post-punk clubgoers.

Before I know it Miss Guy, a drag performer who exudes the visual style of the "white trash" southern California punk waif, stops spinning her classic eighties retro-rock, punk, and new-wave discs.[14] Then the Mistress Formika, the striking leather-clad Latina drag queen and hostess of the club, announces the band. I am positioned in the front row, to the left of the stage. I watch a figure whom I identify as Davis rush by me and mount the stage.

At this point, a clarification is necessary. Vaginal is the central performance persona of the artist I am discussing, but she is certainly not the only one. She is also the Most High Rev'rend Saint Salicia Tate, an evangelical churchwoman who preaches "Fornication, no! Theocracy, yes!"; Buster Butone, one of her boy drag numbers, who is a bit of a gangsta and womanizer; and Kayle Hilliard, a professional pseudonym that the artist employed when she worked as an administrator at UCLA.[15] These are just a few of the artist's identities (I have yet to catalog them all).

The identity I will see tonight is a new one for me. Davis is once again in boy drag, standing on stage in military fatigues, including camouflage pants, jacket, T-shirt, and hat. The look is capped off by a long gray beard, reminiscent of the beard worn by the 1980s Texas rocker band ZZ Top. Clarence introduces himself. During the monologue we hear Vaginal's high-pitched voice explain how she finds white supremacist militiamen to be "really hot," so hot that she herself has had a race and gender reassignment and is now Clarence. Clarence is the artist's own object of affection. Her voice drops as she inhabits the site of her object of desire and identifications. She imitates and becomes the object of her desire. The ambivalent circuits of cross-racial desire are thematized and contained in one body. This particular star-crossed coupling, black queen and white supremacist, might suggest masochism on the part of the person of color, yet such a reading would be too facile. Instead, the work done by this performance of illicit desire for the "bad" object, the toxic force, should be considered as an active disidentification with strictures against cross-racial

Vaginal Davis as Clarence. Courtesy of Vaginal Davis.

desire in communities of color and the specters of miscegenation that haunt white sexuality. The parodic performance works on Freudian distinctions between desire and identification; the "to be or to have" binary is queered and disrupted.

When the performer's voice drops and thickens, it is clear that Clarence now has the mike. He congratulates himself on his own woodsy militiaman masculinity, boasting about how great it feels to be white, male, and straight. He launches into his first number, a cut off the CD, "Sawed-Off Shotgun." The song is Clarence's theme:

> I don't need a 'zooka
> Or a Ms. 38
> I feel safer in New York
> Than I do in L.A.
>
> You keep your flamethrower
> My shotgun is prettier
>
> Sawed-off shotgun
> Sawed-off
> Shotgun
>
> My shotgun is so warm it
> Keeps me safe in the city
> I need it at the ATM
> Or when I'm looking purdy
> In its convenient carrying case
> Graven, initialed on the face
> Sawed-off shotgun
>
> Sawed-off
> Shotgun
> Yeah . . . wow!

The singer adopts what is a typical butch hard-core stance while performing the song. The microphone is pulled close to his face and he bellows into it. This performance of butch masculinity complements the performance of militiaman identity. The song functions as an illustration of a particular mode of white male anxiety that feeds ultraright-wing movements such as militias and that are endemic to embattled straight white masculinity in urban multiethnic spaces such as Los Angeles. The fear of an urban landscape populated by undesirable minorities is especially pronounced at privileged sites of consumerist interaction such as the ATM, a public site where elites in the cityscape access capital as the lower classes stand witnesses to these interactions, mechanical transactions that punctuate class hierarchies. Through her performance of Clarence, Vaginal inhabits the image, this picture of paranoid and embattled white male identity in the multiethnic city. The performer begins to subtly undermine the gender cohesion of this cultural type (a gender archetype that is always figured as heteronormative), the embattled white man in the multiethnic metropolis, by alluding to the love of "purdy" and "prettier" weapons. The eroticizing of the weapon in so overt a fashion reveals the queer specter that haunts such "impenetrable" heterosexualities. Clarence needs his gun because it "is so warm" that it keeps him "safe in the city" that he no longer feels safe in, a city where growing populations of Asians, African-Americans, and Latinos pose a threat to the white majority.

Clarence is a disidentification with militiaman masculinity—not merely a counteridentification that rejects the militiaman—but a *tactical misrecognition* that consciously views the self as a militiaman. This performance is also obviously not about passing inasmuch as the white face makeup that the artist uses looks nothing like real white skin. Clarence has as much of a chance to pass as white as Vaginal has to pass

Vaginal Davis as Clarence. Courtesy of Vaginal Davis.

as female. Rather, this disidentification works as an *interiorized passing.* The interior pass is a disidentification and tactical misrecognition of self. Aspects of the self that are toxic to the militiaman—blackness, gayness, and transvestism—are grafted onto this particularly militaristic script of masculinity. The performer, through the role of Clarence, inhabits and undermines the militiaman with a fierce sense of parody.

But Davis's disidentifications are not limited to engagements with figures of white supremacy. In a similar style, Clarence, during one of his other live numbers, disidentifies with the popular press image of the pathological homosexual killer. The song "Homosexual Is Criminal" tells this story:

A homosexual
Is a criminal
I'm a sociopath, a pathological liar
Bring your children near me
I'll make them walk through the fire

I have killed before and I will kill again
You can tell my friend by my Satanic grin
A homosexual is a criminal
A homosexual is a criminal

I'll eat you limb from limb
I'll tear your heart apart
Open the Frigidaire
There'll be your body parts
I'm gonna slit your click
Though you don't want me to
Bite it off real quick
Salt 'n' Peppa it too.

At this point in the live performance, about halfway through the number, Davis has removed the long gray beard, the jacket, and the cap. A striptease has begun. At this point, Clarence starts to be undone and Davis begins to reappear. She has begun to interact lasciviously with the other members of her band. She gropes her guitarist and bass players as she cruises the audience. She is becoming queer and, as she does so, she begins to perform homophobia. This public performance of homophobia indexes the specters of Jeffrey Dahmer, John Wayne Gacy, and a pantheon of homosexual killers. The performance magnifies images from the homophobic popular imaginary. Davis is once again inhabiting phobic images with a parodic and cutting difference. Thus, although many gay people eschew negative images, Davis conversely explodes them by inhabiting them with a difference. By becoming the serial killer, whose psychological profile is almost always white, Vaginal Davis disarticulates not only the onus of performing the positive image that is generally borne by minoritarian subjects, but also the Dahmer paradigm in which the white cannibal slaughters gay men of color. The performance of "*becoming* Dahmer" is another mode of hijacking and lampooning whiteness. Drag and minstrelsy are dramatically reconfigured; performance genres that seemed somewhat exhausted and limited are powerfully reinvigorated through Davis's "homey"-style politics.

By the last number, Vaginal Davis has fully reemerged and she is wearing a military fatigue baby-doll nightie. She is still screaming and writhing on the stage and she is soaked in rock-and-roll sweat. The Clarence persona has disintegrated. *Long live the queen!* During an interview, Davis explained to me that her actual birth name is Clarence.[16] What does it mean that the artist who negotiates various performance personas and uses Vaginal Creme Davis as a sort of base identity reserves her "birth name" for a character who suggests the nation's current state of siege? Davis's drag, this reconfigured cross-sex, cross-race minstrelsy, can best be understood as *terrorist drag*—terrorist in that she is performing the nation's internal terrors around race, gender, and sexuality. It is also an aesthetic terrorism: Davis uses ground-level guerrilla representational strategies to portray some of the nation's most salient popular fantasies. The fantasies she acts out involve cultural anxieties surrounding miscegenation, communities of color, and the queer body. Her dress does not attempt to index outmoded ideals of female glamour. She instead dresses like white supremacist militiamen and black welfare queen hookers. In other words, her drag mimesis is not concerned with the masquerade of womanliness, but instead with conjuring the nation's most dangerous citizens. She is quite literally in "terrorist drag."

Although Davis's terrorist drag performance does not engage the project of passing, as traditional drag at least partially does, it is useful to recognize how passing and what I am describing as disidentification resemble each other—or, more accurately, how the passing entailed in traditional drag implicates elements of the disidentificatory process. Passing is often not about bold-faced opposition to a dominant paradigm or a wholesale selling out to that form. Like disidentification itself, passing can be a third modality where a dominant structure is co-opted, worked on and against. The subject who passes can be simultaneously identifying with and rejecting a dominant form. In traditional male-to-female drag, "woman" is performed, but one would be naive and deeply ensconced in heteronormative culture to consider such a performance, no matter how "real," as an actual performance of "woman." Drag performance strives to perform femininity and femininity is not exclusively the domain of biological women. Furthermore, the drag queen is disidentifying, sometimes critically and sometimes not, with not only the ideal of woman but the a priori relationship of woman and femininity that is a tenet of gender-normative thinking. The "woman" produced in drag is not a woman, but instead a public disidentification with woman. Some of the best drag that I have encountered in my research challenges the universalizing rhetorics of femininity.

Both modalities of performing the self, disidentification and passing, are often strategies of survival. (As the case of Davis and others suggests, often these modes of performance allow much more than mere survival, and subjects fully come into subjectivity in ways that are both ennobling and fierce.) Davis's work is a survival strategy on a more symbolic register than that of everyday practice. She is not passing to escape social injustice and structural racism in the way that some people of color might. Nor is she passing in the way in which "straight-acting queers" do. Her disidentification with drag plays with its prescriptive mandate to enact femininity through (often white) standards of glamour. Consider her militiaman drag. Her dark brown skin does not permit her to pass as white, the beard is obviously fake, and the fatigues look inauthentic. Realness is neither achieved nor the actual goal of such a project. Instead, her performance as Clarence functions as an intervention in the history of cross-race desire that saturates the phenomenon of passing. Passing is parodied and this parody becomes a site where interracial desire is interrogated.

Davis's biting social critique phantasmatically projects the age-old threat of miscegenation, one of the phenomena that white supremacist groups fear the most, onto the image of a white supremacist. Cross-race desire spoils the militiaman's image.[17] It challenges the coherence of his identity, his essentialized whiteness, by invading its sense of essentialized white purity. The militiaman becomes a caricature of himself, sullied and degraded within his own logic.

Furthermore, blackface minstrelsy, the performance genre of whites performing blackness, is powerfully recycled through disidentification. The image of the fat-lipped Sambo is replaced by the image of the ludicrous white militiaman. The photographer Lyle Ashton Harris has produced a series of elegant portraits of himself in whiteface. Considered alongside Davis's work, Harris's version of whiteface is an almost *too literal* photo negative reversal. By figuring the militiaman through the vehicle of the black queen's body, Davis's whiteface interrogates white hysteria, miscegenation anxiety, and supremacy at its very core. Eric Lott, in his influential study of minstrelsy in the dominant white imagination, suggests that "[t]he black mask offered a way to play with collective fears of a degraded and threatening—and male—Other while at the same time maintaining some symbolic control over them."[18] Harris's photography replicates traditional whiteface so as to challenge its tenets in a different fashion than that of Davis. Harris's technique addresses the issue of "symbolic control" but does so in the form of a straightforward counteridentification; and although counteridentification is certainly not a strategy without merits, Davis's disidentification with minstrelsy offers a more polyvalent response to this history. Davis's disidentificatory take on whiteface both reveals the degraded character of the white supremacist and wrests "symbolic controls" from white people. The white supremacist is forced to cohabit in one body with a black queen in such a way that the image loses its symbolic force. A figure that is potentially threatening to people of color is revealed as a joke.

The dual residency in Davis's persona of both the drag queen and the white supremacist is displayed in the CD's cover art. The illustration features Clarence cleaning his gun. Occupying the background is a television set broadcasting a ranting white man reminiscent of right-wing media pundit Rush Limbaugh, a monster truck poster titled "Pigfoot," a Confederate flag, a crucifix, assorted pornography, beer bottles, and a knife stuck in the wall. Standing out in this scene is the framed photo of a black drag queen: Vaginal Davis. The flip side of the image is part of the CD's interior artwork. Vaginal sits in front of a dressing mirror wearing a showgirl outfit. She is crying on the telephone as she cooks heroin on a spoon and prepares to shoot up. A picture of Vaginal in boy drag is taped to the mirror. Among the scattered vibrators, perfume bottles, and razors is a picture of Clarence in a Marine uniform. These images represent a version of cross-racial desire (in this instance the reciprocated desire between a black hooker/showgirl and a white supremacist gun nut militiaman) that echoes what Vaginal, in the 1995 interview in *aRude,* called the "snow period" when "some cheap white boyfriend" could make one's life perfect, permitting the queen of color to feel like "some treasured thing" who hopes for "the privileges that white people get—validation through association." The image of the snow queen, a gay man of color who desires white men, is exaggerated and exploded within these performances. It is important to note that this humor is not calibrated to police or moralize against cross-racial desire. Instead, it renders a picture of this desire, in its most fantastic and extreme form. By doing so it disturbs the coherence of the white militiaman's sexual and racial identity, an identity that locates itself as racially "pure." Concomitantly, sanitized understandings of a gay identity, an identity that is often universalized as white, are called into question.

Davis has remarked that academics and intellectuals have dismissed her work as "homey" or "country." I have attempted to point to the ways in which Davis's low-budget performances intervene in different circuits of publicity: predominantly white post-punk queercore spaces such as Squeezebox and, further, the spaces of predominately white masculinity that are associated with hard-core and speed metal music. Davis's signature "homeyness," which I have already linked to an *organic* and terroristic politics, also permits us to further understand her as an "organic intellectual," that is, an intellectual who possesses a "fundamental connection to social groups."[19] These social groups include, but are certainly not limited to, various subcultural sectors: punks, queers, certain communities of color. In the wake of deconstruction, the word *organic* has become a suspect term that implies a slew of essentialist and holistic presuppositions. By linking *organic* to Davis's notion of *homey* and *country,* I wish to take some of the edge off the word. My invocation of organic intellectual is meant to foreground the importance of cultural workers to ground-level politics of the self, while avoiding the fetishizing of the minoritarian intellectual.

Furthermore, Gramsci's work offers a view of Davis as *philosopher.* Gramsci contended that philosophy was

> a conception of the world and that philosophical activity is not to be conceived solely as the "individual" elaboration of systematically coherent concepts, but also and above all as a cultural battle to transform the popular "mentality" and to diffuse the philosophical innovations which will demonstrate themselves to be "historically true" to the extent that they become concretely—i.e., historically and socially—universal.[20]

Davis's work fits in with this Gramscian model of philosophy insofar as her cultural production attempts to dismantle universals within both the dominant public sphere and various subcultures, both of which are predominantly white. The Gramscian notion of "a philosophy of praxis" helps transcend a more traditional Marxian binary between praxis and philosophy.[21] Vaginal Davis's performance attempts to unsettle the hegemonic order through performance of praxis (a performance that imagines itself as praxis). The performances that are produced are rooted within a deep critique of universalism and the dominant power bloc.

The cultural battle that Davis wages is fought with the darkest sense of humor and the sharpest sense of parody imaginable. Her performances represent multiple counterpublics and subjects who are liminal within those very counterpublics. She shrewdly employs performance as a modality of counterpublicity. Performance engenders, sponsors, and even *makes* worlds. The scene of speed metal and post-punk music is one that Davis ambivalently inhabits. Her blackness and queerness render her a freak among freaks. Rather than be alienated by her freakiness, she exploits its energies and its potential to enact cultural critique.

Antigay?

A close friend of mine and I have a joke that we return to every June. On the occasion of gay pride celebrations of lesbian and gay visibility and empowerment held early in the summer in many major North American cities, we propose a *gay shame day parade*. This parade, unlike the sunny gay pride march, would be held in February. Participants would have to deal with certain restrictions if they were to properly engage the spirit of gay shame day: Loud colors would be discouraged; gay men and lesbians would instead be asked to wear drab browns and grays. Shame marchers would also be asked to carry signs no bigger than a business card. Chanting would be prohibited. Parade participants would be asked to parade single file. Finally, the parade would not be held on a central city street but on some backstreet, preferably by the river. We have gotten a lot of laughs when we narrate this scenario. Like many gags, it is rooted in some serious concerns. Although we cannot help but take part in some aspects of pride day, we recoil at its commercialism and hack representations of gay identity. When most of the easily available and visible gay world is a predominantly white and male commercialized zone (the mall of contemporary gay culture), we find little reason to be "proud."

Some of these sentiments are taken up in an anthology edited by Mark Simpson titled *Anti-Gay*.[22] With its minimalist black courier print on a plain safety yellow cover, the book makes a very low-key visual statement that would be appropriate for our aforementioned gay shame day. Simpson's Introduction focuses on the failure of "queer's grandiose ambitions." He claims that "[b]y focusing on the shortcomings of gay and refusing to be distracted by how terrible heterosexuality is supposed to be, *Anti-Gay* may even offer the beginnings of a new dialectic, a new conversation with the world, one that is rather more interesting than the current ones."[23] I agree with some of Simpson's remarks. The gay communities we live in are often incapable of enacting any autocritique that would engage the politics of gender, racial diversity, and class. But rather than being critical about the *politics* of the mainstream gay community, Simpson seems merely to be bored by a conversation that he feels has ceased to be "interesting."

At one point in his discussion, Simpson mentions the homogeneity of the book's contributors: "It [*Anti-Gay*] doesn't promise to be more inclusive than gay (contributions by only two women, only one bisexual and none from people of colour)."[24] Simpson's attack on *gay* is not concerned with its exclusivity, its white normativity, or its unwillingness to form coalitions with other counterpublics, including feminist (both lesbian and straight) and other minoritized groups. My own playful critique of the gay community manifested in the gay shame day joke emanates from a deep frustration on my part with what I call mainstream or corporate homosexuality. By contrast, to be "antigay" in Simpson's sense of the word is to offer criticism in a "been-there-done-that" style whose main purpose is to register tedium.

The forms of "antigay" thinking put forward in Vaginal Davis's work are vastly different in origin and effect than Simpson's *Anti-Gay.* Davis's brand of antigay critique offers something more than a listless complaint. This additional something is a sustained critique of white gay male normativity and its concomitant corporate ethos.

"Closet Case," another track on PME's album is, at first glance, a critique of closeted homosexuality. Further analysis also reveals that the song critiques an aesthetic rather than a type of individual. The song's lyrics depict a mode of living that is recognizable (especially from Davis's perspective as a working-class gay man of color) as a bourgeois southern California brand of urban gay male style.

Closet Case

She drives a Trans Am
And she lives in the Valley
Every night she cruises
Gasoline alley

Salon tan
Ray Ban
All buff
Acts tuff
Big Dick, heavy balls
Nice pecs, that ain't all

Y'know she's a closet case

Got blow-dried hair, wears a lot of cologne
Call her own condo on her cellular phone

She's 38 but thinks she's 21
Covers those wrinkles in collagen
Old enough to be Richard Harris
Facial Scrub: plaster of Paris

You know she's a closet case
(Salon tan!)
You know she a closet case
(Ray-Ban!)

The closet here is not necessarily the one inhabited by those who engage in homosexual acts but deny a gay identification. Instead, the queen depicted in this song is more recognizably in the closet about his age, appearance, and quotidian habits. Davis satirizes the closet queen whose style is easily recognizable on a map of urban southern California homosexualities. A quick review of the particular type of queen being delineated is useful here. Brand names like Ray-Ban and Trans Am, as well as cellular phones and condos, and the price tags associated with these commodities, are integral to this queen's identity. Equally important are the leisure-time salon tan, facial scrubs, and collagen injections. Most important of all is the "buff" gym-built body. Davis's song offers the anatomy (physical, behavioral, and socioeconomic) of the normative and corporate homosexual. The closet case of the song is an elite within a larger spectrum of gay communities. Davis's satirical parody does the work of atomizing this cultural type. Humor is used to mock and degrade this mode of apolitical gayness, disrupting its primacy as a universal mold or pattern. Antigayness here is used as a way of lampooning and ultimately disrupting a modality of white gay male hegemony.

This same renunciation of elite gay male style is narrated in "No Thank You Please," in which Davis recants the snow queen's desire for elite white gay males. The song's narrator manifests her displeasure for these gay elites by employing the raunchiest of vernaculars:

No Thank You Please

So you want to lick my pussy?
Well you can't cuz you're a sissy
Can't get into my bed
I won't give you head
Say, no thank you please
I don't eat head cheese

I can't get involved
Bang your head against the wall
Take me to the king of hearts
There they have bigger parts
Chandelier hanging
Sexy gangbanging
Say no thank you please
I don't eat head cheese

You better take me to the rack
I'm looking for my bladder snack

He feels on my crotch
It's not worth the notch
Say no thank you please
I don't eat head cheese

LA water polo team
All the men are hot and lean
Get into your tub
A rub-a-dub-dub
A splishing a splashing
A urine reaction
I can't get involved
Bang your head against the wall.

The one-minute-and-five-second song's tempo is relentlessly fast. Davis/Clarence snarls the lyrics. Her deep and husky voice booms in the tradition of classic punk-rock rants. There is a powerful juxtaposition between lyrics that indicate that she will not let the sissy addressee "lick her pussy" and the actual butch vocal style. The lyrics themselves map out the snow queen's desire ("LA water polo team / All the men are hot and lean") and then resist that desire ("I can't get involved"). The last line of the song, "Bang your head against the wall," does the work of performing butch masculinity and, at the same time, the general frustration that characterizes the snow queen's desire—the desire for white men who almost exclusively desire other white men.

This reading and its emphasis on Davis's snow queen disidentification are not meant to dismiss the song's antigayness. Indeed, the snow queen herself, or at least a snow queen with some degree of reflexivity, understands the "antigay" position from the vantage point of a gay man who has been locked out of the elite white gay male sphere of influence.

According to Stuart Hall, who has adapted Gramsci's theorizations for race analysis, the notion of the *war of positions* (as opposed to an outdated orthodox Marxian *war of maneuver*) "recognizes the 'plurality' of selves or identities of which the so-called 'subject' of thought and ideas is composed."[25] Michael Omi and Howard Winant describe a war of maneuver as "a situation in which subordinate groups seek to preserve and extend a definite territory, to ward off violent assault, and to develop an internal society as an alternative to the repressive social system."[26] In contrast, a war of positions is predicated on the understanding that diverse sites of institutional and cultural antagonism must be engaged to enact transformative politics. Whereas the war of maneuver was a necessary modality of resistance at a moment when minoritarian groups were directly subjugated within hegemony, the more multilayered and tactical war of positions represents better possibilities of resistance today, when discriminatory ideologies are less naked and more intricate.

Gramsci offers an expanded understanding of both the individual subject and the collective subject. He does not permit any pat definitions of group identity or the role of any individual within such a collective matrix. Within Gramsci's writing on the ideological field we come to glimpse that subordinated ideologies are often rife with contradictory impulses, that "subordinated ideologies are necessarily and inevitably contradictory."[27] Thus, Gramsci lets us understand not only working-class racism, but also gay racism or homophobia within communities of color.

Cornel West has also turned to Gramsci's work in emphasizing the need to forge a microstructural analysis of African-American oppression where traditional Marxian hermeneutics can only offer macrostructural analysis.[28] Readings that posit subordinate groups as unified entities fail to enact a multivalent and intersectional understanding of the various contingencies and divergencies within a class or group. Thus, Gramsci offers an extremely appropriate optic through which to evaluate the disidentificatory work that Davis performs within subordinated classes such as "gays" and liminal groups like the hard-core/punk-rock community. Hall explains that Gramsci

> shows how the so-called "self" which underpins these ideological formations is not a unified but a contradictory subject and a social construction. He thus helps us understand one of the most common, least explained features of "racism": the "subjection" of the victims of racism to the mystifications of the very racist ideologies which imprison and define them. He shows how different, often contradictory elements can be woven into and integrated within different ideological discourse; but also, the nature and value of ideological struggle which seeks to transform popular ideas and the "common sense" of the masses.[29]

"Queerness" and "blackness" need to be read as ideological discourses that contain contradictory impulses within them—some liberatory, others reactionary. These discourses also require hermeneutics that appraise the intersectional and differential crosscutting currents with individual ideological scripts. Davis's work is positioned at a point of intersection between various discourses (where they are woven together), and from this point she is able to enact a parodic and comedic demystification; the potential for subversion is planted.

Disidentification, as a mode of analysis, registers subjects as constructed and contradictory. Davis's body, her performances, all her myriad texts, labor to create critical uneasiness, and, furthermore, to create desire within uneasiness. This desire unsettles the strictures of class, race, and gender prescribed by what Guattari calls the "social body." A disidentificatory hermeneutic permits a reading and narration of the way in which Davis clears out a space, deterritorializing it and then reoccupying it with queer and black bodies. The lens of disidentification allows us to discern seams and contradictions and ultimately understand the need for a war of positions.

Part III

Critical *Cubanía*

Chapter 5

Sister Acts: Ela Troyano and Carmelita Tropicana

This chapter tells the story of two sisters. Ela Troyano and Alina Troyano are Cuban-American queer feminist performers who have been working in New York City since the early 1980s. Ela Troyano is a filmmaker as well as a performer. Alina Troyano, known better by her stage name Carmelita Tropicana, identifies as a lesbian and started by performing at the now-famous lesbian feminist performance space known as the WOW Café. Both sisters played prominent roles in the New York avant-garde film and theater movements of the 1980s. Although some commentators have discussed their cultural productions and performances, no more than passing references have been made to their identities as U.S. Latinas.[1] I take this opportunity to discuss the specificity of their identities and the ways in which their identity practices inflect and shape their work.

I am especially interested in analyzing two modes of cultural critique that the artists employ. Camp and *choteo* are both styles of performance and reception that rely on humor to examine social and cultural forms. The bulk of this chapter will consider the ways Ela Troyano signifies upon an established tradition of camp avant-garde filmmaking and the way Carmelita Tropicana uses the Cuban style of *burla* (which roughly translates as joking or exaggerated comedic performance). Both performance styles have usually been described as specifically male practices.[2] I will explore how two sisters dereify these modes of self-enactment.

Both camp and *choteo* are, within the terms of this study, disidentificatory practices. These two modes of self-enactment, or style politics, differ from the other modes of disidentification that I outline in this study primarily in their strategic and disarming use of humor. Comedic disidentification accomplishes important cultural critique while at the same time providing cover from, and enabling the avoidance itself of, scenarios of direct confrontation with phobic and reactionary ideologies.

Finally, this essay will consider the question of hybridity and the role it plays within U.S. identity. Although I discuss camp alongside my reading of Troyano's filmic production and *choteo* as it is discernible through Carmelita Tropicana's skits, monologues, and stand-up comedy, both disidentificatory strategies are present in the work of each sister. Hybridity is one way to discuss the crossfire of influences, affiliations, and politics that happen between a lesbian identity, as well as in or in between the intersection of Cuban and North American traditions of performance.

The heuristic impulse that propels this chapter is concerned with a distinctly lesbian and Latina camp sensibility. There is some question as to whether or not "camp" is camp when it happens outside of its usual cultural parameters. The discourse on camp has been—at least since Susan Sontag's infamous notes from the 1960s—a discourse of middle- to upper-class white gay male sensibilities.[3] The notion of camp I mine in this chapter is one in which "camp" is understood not only as a strategy of representation, but also as a mode of enacting self against the pressures of the dominant culture's identity-denying protocols. *Carmelita Tropicana* (1993), a short film by Ela Troyano, clearly articulates an ironic system of signs that, while still being very campy, is decidedly not employing the same referents as white male camp. The humor that Carmelita Tropicana produces represents a life-world that we can understand, according to the film's eponymous performance artist star, as "Loisaida."[4] The Lower East Side of *Carmelita Tropicana* is a queer and Latina life-world where the dominant culture makes only one appearance in the form of over-the-top send-ups of abortion rights counterprotesters. Beyond that, the queer life-world that the film depicts is one of Latinas and lesbians, political activities, and performance artists.

Before I delve into my reading of *Carmelita Tropicana* and the specificities of *cubana* lesbian camp, I want to mention the one piece of cultural-studies writing that has in some way loosely interrogated the issue of Latino kitsch: Celeste Olalquiaga's *Megalopolis: Contemporary Cultural Sensibilities.*[5] Olalquiaga's book delineates three degrees of kitsch sensibility in New York and its relation to Latino religious objects. The first degree constitutes a fascination with these objects because they represent a model of spirituality that is not available to the aficionado. They are representations of powerful emotions that help the first-degree kitsch follower grasp these higher emotions. The second degree of kitsch is the untangling of the icon from its religious/emotional context. Its representation is dislodged from its cultural referent, the empty icon or gaudy bauble that can be found at Little Ricky's on the Lower East Side.[6] The third degree of kitsch is a true postmodern hybrid, the recycling of a past cultural construct for a present tense. Here Olalquiaga's primary example is the *altares* produced by Chicano, Nuyorican, and some white artists. In this final degree of kitsch, the kitsch object is recycled and recontextualized in a high-art setting. The recycling is, I will argue, central to any understanding of *Carmelita Tropicana.* The importance of this pioneering study is indicated in the film as the actual book appears at Carmelita's bedside in her own kitschy bedroom. Interestingly enough, the book itself, within this frame and recontextualization, becomes a bit of "Loisaida" kitsch.

What Olalquiaga's book fails to do, however, is factor the unique relation of sexual minorities to the kitsch object. We might also tease out her use of the word *kitsch* instead of *camp,* a word that resonates as the way in which a minority culture reappropriates the dominant culture. Olalquiaga's word choice underplays, and potentially erases, the roles of queers in the production and consumption of kitsch objects and/or sensibilities. One of the difficulties in writing about kitsch and camp is that the two words are often confused with each other. This interchangeability is, of course, wrong, because both words have ontologically distinct (though not entirely separate) lives. Andrew Ross makes a distinction between the two by describing kitsch as having more "high"-art pretensions and a higher degree of self-seriousness, whereas camp seems to be more ironic and playful.[7] Eve Kosofsky Sedgwick defines camp as being more spacious and "out" than kitsch.[8] Indeed, the word *camp* is integral to what Esther Newton calls the "gay world" of homosexuality, whereas kitsch's usage seems to be less tied to any specific group.[9] More recent accounts of aesthetics that relish the "tacky" are the works of Sontag, Ross, and Sedgwick. This itself is not a rule, as the example of Sedgwick, in *The Epistemology of the Closet,* deliminating the binary of art/kitsch makes evident. Kitsch is most definitely on the queer side of the binary in that text. But in *Megalopolis,* kitsch is not a survivalist mode of identity enactment within a phobic public sphere. Instead, it is a nostalgic postmodern aesthetic that is basically a longing for a lost emotional intensity. Like Olalquiaga, I identify a certain mode of cross-generational, cross-cultural recycling in U.S. Latino culture, but, unlike her, I name it "camp" because I am interested in considering its convergences, alignments, and reverberations with the camp produced by sexual minorities. My reading suggests that *Carmelita Tropicana* and its star's performance disrupt the stability of the camp = queer/kitsch = ethnic protocol.

Beyond the synthesis of the Latino and the campy, *Carmelita Tropicana* articulates a distinctly lesbian camp. There is no doubt that camp has been overwhelmingly associated with the gay male subculture, but the work of some lesbian and feminist theorists has begun to suggest a powerful tradition of female and lesbian camp. Pamela Robertson, for example, has undertaken a project to "de-essentialize" the link between gay men and camp, a link that, in Robertson's estimation, "reifies both camp and gay male taste."[10] Robertson suggests that

> camp as a structural activity has an affinity with feminist discussions of gender construction, performance, and enactment; and that, as such, we can examine a form of camp as a feminist practice. In taking on camp for women, I reclaim a form of female aestheticism, related to female masquerade, that articulates and subverts the image- and culture-making process to which women have traditionally been given access.[11]

Following Robertson, I see Troyano's film and its star performance as producing a mode of camp that subverts dominant image- and culture-making apparatuses (especially Hollywood film) that have either rendered invisible or grossly caricaturized lesbians, Latinas, and especially Latina lesbians. An important by-product of this mode of camp is the dislodging of the discourse of camp from male dominance.

But, if the discourse of camp has been male-dominated, the social and aesthetic history itself suggests more complex and complicated dynamics. Although Ela Troyano's first film, *Bubble People* (1982), has not been widely seen, it both situates and comments on her work in relationship to that of Jack Smith. *Village Voice* journalist C. Carr provides a valuable account of an interaction between the director and her famous star, Jack Smith:

> There is a scene in Bubble People where the spectral Jack Smith, looking like a drag biker, has a little encounter with the filmmaker Ela Troyano. "I am the Bubble Goddess," he intones, then pauses. "Tell me the truth. Has the camera started?" Close-up on his beads and beard and wraparound orange shades. "We can get better results if we're honest with each other, and you tell me the camera has started. Depicting what a great actor I must be."[12]

Within the campy moment, one sees a serious instant where filmmaker and performer check in with each other, collaborating as equals; it is ultimately an instant where, in the tradition of the North American avant-garde of the 1960s, the film's artifice is stripped away. This was one of many collaborations between Smith and Troyano. According to Carr, Troyano began taking pictures because she wanted to work with Smith, a performer she had admired, and he needed someone to take the photographs for his slide shows.[13] It is my belief that reading Troyano's film as also influenced by Smith makes available a more comprehensive understanding of her production.

Smith, the now-legendary avant-garde filmmaker and performance artist who died of AIDS complications in 1989, pioneered an image of a hilarious and hyperactive gay male subjectivity that had not only not existed in representation before him, but was essentially unimaginable to queer spectators. Smith's project in his various underground acting jobs during the 1960s, his own films, which included the censored underground classic *Flaming Creatures* (1963), and his various stage performances during the almost three decades that his career spanned, were described by Michael Moon as "a fiercely unsentimental project of reclaiming his own and other people's queer energies (all kinds of queer people, including gay ones) from the myriad forms of human wreckage into which our society has tended to channel it."[14] In the same way that Olalquiaga's third degree of kitsch recaptures a lost presence, Smith's performances and film reclaim lost queer energies.

Carmelita Tropicana features four very different versions of the Latina: Carmelita, Orcchidia, Sophia, and Dee. In the film, the Carmelita character is a Loisaida performance artist and lesbian activist. Her sidekick and constant companion is the flaky

Orcchidia, also a member of the fictional direct-action group GIA and a practitioner of postmodern dance, holistic medicine, and the Afro-Cuban religion of Santeria. Although these women differ from each other in their varying levels of spaciness and neurosis, Carmelita's sister Sophia is nothing like the other Latina women in the film. Sophia is desperately trying to make it in the corporate business world and tries her best to dress for success. The film suggests that Sophia, despite her aspirations to be a conservative and upwardly mobile Latina, is often embroiled in Carmelita's life. Dee, a woman who first mugs Carmelita on her way home from a performance and later meets up with her victim in jail after the other women are arrested in a demonstration, is a *hermana sandunguera.* Of all these women, Dee is perhaps the greatest challenge to the dominant culture's understanding of just what constitutes a Latina. Dee is, by ancestry, a North American Anglo, but she was inducted into a Puerto Rican women's gang in prison. Dee's identification as Latina undermines the misconception of Latinos as a racially homogeneous group. Her place in the film serves to destabilize any reductive understanding of Latina/o status. Dee's HIV-positive status also offers a representation of the ways in which the virus does not discriminate and affects women (especially women of color) with equal brutality.

The film's very first scene, in which the lesbian performance artist emerges from a backdrop of flashy colored curtains and proceeds to feign a thick Cuban accent as she launches into her opening monologue, establishes the film's narrative space. During that monologue, Carmelita speaks of the mixing of cultures in Loisaida:

> Loisaida is the place to be. That's right. It's multi-cultural, multi-generational, mucho multi, multi-lingual. And like myself you gotta be multi-lingual. I am very good with the tongue. As a matter of fact the first language I learned when got to New York was Jewish. I learned from my girlfriend Sharon. She is Jewish. She teach me and I write poem for her in Jewish. Title of the poem is "Oy-Vay Number One": Oy-vay / I schlep and schlep / I hurt my tuchas / I feel meshuggeneh / Oy-vay. Thank you very much.

In this scene, Cuban identity is recycled and remade. Carmelita's thick accent during the monologue is obviously fake. The artist's name harks back to the famous nightclub that signifies the excessive opulence of prerevolution Cuba. The garish, sparkling red dress that she wears signifies a lost notion of glamour that is associated with the Cuba of the 1950s. There is also a campification of the present that occurs when Carmelita describes the Lower East Side as "multi-cultural, multi-generational, mucho multi, multi-lingual." This last reference to the multilingual sets Carmelita up to purr "I am very good with the tongue," a double-entendre quip that is reminiscent of Mae West. Carmelita's Yiddish joke also aligns her with an earlier tradition of ethnic comics who were Jewish. All of what transpires in this scene is a recycling that I identify as the film's camp practice. The recycling encompasses a distant Cuban past (the Club Tropicana of the 1950s, Ricky Ricardo's exaggerated accent, a showgirl's sparkly red dress), an American past (the very history of stand-up comedy and the formidable influence of Jews in this North American tradition), and the recent U.S. past (in the form of a reference to the already exhausted wars over multiculturalism in the academy and popular culture).

Carr has explained that "if Jack Smith has been her [Troyano's] greatest influence as a filmmaker—along with Jacques Rivette and Russ Meyer—she's been informed just as much by Smith's performance."[15] The centrality of performance art to Troyano's work is apparent in *Carmelita Tropicana*. Carmelita Tropicana's performance—the very fact that she is clearly performing during the film's opening scene—connotes the importance of performance within both the film and the mode of cultural enactment that I am calling *cubana* dyke camp. As the film's narrative proceeds from this space of performative enunciation, the spectator is left with the residual understanding that this narrative is not only about a performance artist, but also about performance itself, particularly performance that is campy in its negotiations between Latina identity practices, queer/lesbian humor, and the dominant culture.

After Carmelita describes the Lower East Side world as "the place to be," the film's next two scenes depict a different version of Loisaida. Walking home from her performance, Carmelita is mugged by a female assailant who later turns out to be Dee. The sequence depicts the reality of urban crime and violence that many U.S. Latinas cope with on a day-to-day basis. Nonetheless, the film's camp valence takes the edge off this incident when it is revealed that the mugger's only weapon is a pen. Here Troyano's film both achieves a realist representation and then, with its last twist, spins into absurdist dimensions first explored by Smith and other 1960s filmmakers, such as Ron Rice and Ken Jacobs. An establishing shot of a street sign that reads "Ave C" and "Loisaida" concretely locates the film's settings.

A tracking shot moves from the street sign to a large movie poster in Carmelita's bedroom. The poster is for a Latin American melodrama titled *La Estrella Vacía* (The empty star). The poster, and other aspects of the mise-en-scène, demarcate Carmelita's personal space as being as thoroughly campy as her performance. Carmelita's bedcover is decorated with extravagant roses. Her bed itself is draped with a white mesh netting that gives it an almost Victorian look. The room's walls are painted a bright pink. The aforementioned copy of *Megalopolis* is thrown on Carmelita's bed. Her phone is an old black dial phone that looks as though it is out of a 1940s film noir. Carmelita is awakened from her slumber by the ringing phone. The caller is a butch lesbian Latina known as the "Dictator," the leader of a feminist organization called the GIA, a parodic representation of organizations such as the Lesbian Avengers or Queer Nation. The Dictator orders the star to rendezvous with other members of GIA at Tompkins Square Park. As the Dictator barks her orders, the call-waiting signal clicks on the phone line. As she code-switches from English to Spanish, the brief conversation with her father reveals that she has a seven-year-old brother, Pepito, and her father is having his prostate operated on.[16] She switches back to the now-enraged Dictator, who quotes World Health Organization statistics on HIV infection in women and children. She follows this statement with a command to "never put me on hold." The phone conversation, like Carmelita's room, depicts the mixing of cultures and historical moments. The room's deco ambiance is offset by the postmodern theory book that is casually tossed on the bed. The old-fashioned phone has the ultramodern feature of call waiting. Her conversation with her lesbian activist mentor is cut up with a conversation with her Cuban father. Troyano employs this mixing across time and cultures to achieve a radical camp effect that reveals, in exaggerated terms, the *mestizaje* of contemporary U.S. Latino culture and politics.

Although Orcchidia and Carmelita are space cadets in the eyes of the over-the-top butch character the Dictator, they work, within the film's comedic frame, as important social factors. Their trendy apparel—Carmelita's ridiculously high-heeled tennis shoes and Orcchidia's multicolored beanie hat, and the standard issue of New York activist leather jackets that both women wear—both lampoons and represents the lifestyle of the "Loisaida" dyke activist.

Fashion is important elsewhere in the film. Sophia, Carmelita's darker-skinned sister, is in "Dressed for Success Hispanic Corporate Woman" garb. The camera surveys Sophia piece by piece as she reads a magazine article that explains the various "don'ts" for Latinas in the corporate machine. Sophia, with steak tartare lipstick, fuschia nail polish, excessively high heels, and gold door-knocker earrings, embodies all of these "don'ts" that the article warns against. In the next scene she appears in, Sophia's whole body fills the screen, displaying her amalgamation of fashion "mistakes." In this scene she is harassed by a bodega clerk who, through the lens of the usual racist assumptions of what a Latina looks like, presumes that Sophia is a monolingual African-American. Sophia snaps back sharply that "Latinas come in all colors, *nena.*" This scene is significant in that it humorously challenges racist depictions of Latinas within and outside of the Latina/o community.

To get what is powerful and potentially socially destabilizing about the *cubana* dyke camp I am describing, one must have some access to the queer life-world that is being signified upon. The fact that most of the film is set in a women's prison needs to be understood as a campy metacommentary on one of Hollywood's most common depictions of Latinas as tough bull dykes in the B movie "women in prison" genre. Part of the camp effect is the biting commentary about the treatment of Latina bodies within Hollywood's prescribed operating procedures. What is also relevant about the recycling of this site is the juxtaposition of seeing these particular Latinas, characters who are quirkier and more complicated than any image that Hollywood has been able to invent when trying to represent Latinas, within this standardized backdrop. Jean Carlomusto's video *L Is for the Way You Look* (1991) is another experimentation with the uses of lesbian camp. In that project, an actual clip from a women's prison movie is shown, dubbed over with lines from lesbian theorists Monique Wittig and Audre Lorde. The scene concluded with the prisoners rallying together and chanting "Let's get Zsa Zsa," a reference to Zsa Zsa Gabor's insistence that she could not go to jail for slapping a Beverly Hills police officer because she was afraid of lesbians. Moments like these in Troyano's and Carlomusto's films take back the negative image and resuscitate it with the powerful charge of dyke camp.

In *Carmelita Tropicana,* Troyano uses the prison scene for a movie within a movie through a flashback sequence that depicts the story that Carmelita tells her sister Sophia about the tragedy of their great-aunt Cukita. Whereas the prison scene itself mimics a B movie, the flashback is shot in black and white and is silent with musical accompaniment and subtitles. Great-aunt Cukita's husband is a refined *habanero* electrical engineer. After killing the woman whom he blindly fell in love with, he

Carmelita Tropicana: Your Kunst *Is Your* Waffen. Photo by Paula Court.

commits suicide by ingesting poison. The widowed aunt is then seduced by a lowly delivery boy who, presumably knowing that he can never really have Cukita, kills her after dancing a passionate tango with her. The black-and-white sequence recasts the entire film in terms of prerevolution Cuba and assigns two of the characters (the butch players in the main narrative) the roles of men. This (fe)male drag is, in a way, akin to a tradition of campy male drag that we might associate with venues such as Jack Smith's performances and Charles Ludlam's Ridiculous Theatrical Company. Carmelita's transformation into the "ugly man," a rough, pockmarked, and unshaven proletarian deliveryman (and her new character, Pingalito, in her stage show *Milk of Amnesia*), is a campy reappropriation of the drag used in the rich tradition of North

American avant-garde theater and drag revues. The male character in this sequence is supposed to register both outside of and inside of the erotics of "butch/femme." This depiction of a lost exilic homeland—with its politics replaced by a drag performance of an ill-fated heterosexual, class-defined romance—enables an opulent scene of cross-identification that is, in one manner of speaking, *queer.* Cross-identifications, as Sedgwick and others have forcefully argued, are standard operating procedures for queers. Sedgwick has explained that queer is a moment of perpetual flux, a movement that is eddying and turbulent. The word *queer* itself, in its origins in the German *quer,* means "across"; the concept itself can only be understood as connoting a mode of identifications that is as relational as it is oblique.[17] There is something distinctly queer about the lesbian cross-dressing in *Carmelita Tropicana;* it reproduces various identifications across a range of experiences—cultural, racial, political, sexual . . .

The flashback posits a historical condition—"always the same story . . . *violencia y amor*"—that unites the four women across their differences. It is at this point that the women in prison sequence transmutes into a send-up of a Hollywood musical. All the prison cells automatically click open and the four female protagonists emerge in *rumbera* outfits made out of what appear to be military fatigues. The musical number that ensues is a Mexican *ranchera* titled "Prisioneras del amor." The choice of a Mexican *ranchera* is indicative of Latina camp's ability to index and reclaim clichéd and sentimental moments and tropes across *latinidad.* East Coast Latinas performing a West Coast musical genre with a Mexican song comments on the ways in which Hollywood cinema, along with other aspects of dominant culture, such as census taking, collapse the diversity of the U.S. Latino community into one set of shallow cultural stereotypes. Troyano's film, in this instance, plays with the dominant mode of storytelling. The lyrics themselves, "Prisioneras del amor / prisioneras de la vida," could be the title of a Mexican melodrama. The song speaks in lavish terms as to how love offers both great warmth and great pain ("el amor lo da calor y también gran dolor"). The song unites the four women who had previously been squabbling with one another in the cell. The women speak of their commonality as prisoners of love and life. The song calls for the throwing off of habits of incarcerated nuns and making liberation their new religion.[18] Although this musical number is extravagant and brilliantly over the top, it should not be dismissed as nothing more than campy fun. The metaphor of Latinas as prisoners is a poignant one when discussing the status of the Latina and lesbian image within representation. The idea of liberation that is invoked in this song is also a more serious and political call for liberation from a dominant culture that reduces such identities to hollowed-out stereotypes. Troyano's strategic use of camp allows her film and its characters to reinhabit these stereotypes, both calling attention to the inaccuracy of these representations and "fixing" such representation from the inside by filling in these representational husks with complicated, antiessentialist, emotionally compelling characters.

Carmelita Tropicana is a film that refigures camp and rescues it from a position as fetishized white queer sensibility. Camp is a form of artificial respiration; it breathes new life into old situations. Camp is, then, more than a worldview; it is a strategic response to the breakdown of representation that occurs when a queer, ethnically marked, or other subject encounters his or her inability to fit within the majoritarian representational regime. It is a measured response to the forced evacuation from dominant culture that the minority subject experiences. Camp is a practice of suturing different lives, of reanimating, through repetition with a difference, a lost country or moment that is relished and loved. Although not innately politically valenced, it is a strategy that can do positive identity- and community-affirming work. *Carmelita Tropicana* represents *cubana* camp and at the same time returns to the island itself with a highly melodramatic story, a story that has been lost for the two sisters (described earlier).

Such a deployment of camp styles and practices is, at its core, a performative move. Reiteration and citation are the most easily identifiable characteristics of this mode of camp performativity. According to Judith Butler, a performative provisionally succeeds if its action echoes prior actions, and accumulates the force of authority through the repetition or citation of a prior, authoritative set of practices. For Butler, a performative draws on and covers over the constitutive conventions by which it is mobilized.[19] Butler is concerned specifically with the performative charge of queerness, and it is my contention that this theory is also applicable to the workings of various minority groups. The repetition of the quotidian is precisely what the *cubana* kitsch and Lower East Side lesbian style in *Carmelita Tropicana* is enacting.

The repetition that Butler outlines, like the reclaiming in Jack Smith's work that Michael Moon outlines and the recycling that Olalquiaga discusses, can all contribute to a potential understanding of the camp project that is *Carmelita Tropicana.* The larger than life (i.e., Hollywood icon) takes on aspects of the everyday; the exotic is "de-exoticized" and brought into the subject's sphere of the ordinary; artifacts from the past that have been discarded as "trashy" (the word *kitsch* comes from a German phrase loosely meaning "street rubbish") are recuperated and become a different "new" thing. With this in mind, I argue that lesbian camp and also *cubana* camp are materialized in *Carmelita Tropicana,* whose star works as the ultimate campy dyke, whose filmmaker and star bridge lost countries with contemporary urban life, queer politics with Latina aesthetics, and which, in general, elevates the trashy to blissful heights.

Camping like a Butch: The Female-to-Male Drag

One of the most powerfully argued cases for the existence of lesbian camp is Sue-Ellen Case's "Towards a Butch-Femme Aesthetic."[20] Case takes to task a trend in feminist theory that has stigmatized the butch in the butch/femme dyad as a male-identified subject suffering from a form of false consciousness. Kate Davy has challenged Case's formulations by contending that camp is not a useful strategy of resis-

Carmelita Tropicana. Photo by Dona Ann McAdams.

tance for female subjects in the same way that it is for gay males. Davy addresses Case's theoretical maneuver:

> She invokes Camp as a "discourse," instead of merely using its salient elements, the baggage of Camp discourse is imbricated in her argument. The result is that the subject position she constructs does not walk out of the hom(m)osexual frame of reference as effectively as it could, for Camp as a discourse is both ironically and paradoxically of hom(m)osexuality, that is, male sexuality. . . . In Case's scheme, Camp is a neutral, nonideologically bound discourse in that it is produced by both Gay Men and Lesbians out of the condition of being closeted.[21]

For Davy, camp is a discourse that provides certain tools that she catalogs as artifice, wit, irony, and exaggeration, and these tools are available to butch-femme gender play separate from the ways in which they are inscribed by camp as a historically marked phenomenon. Although I find myself agreeing with much of Davy's critique of Case, I worry about what seems a too easy equivalence between Irigarayan hom(m)osexuality and gay male sexuality. Although I do not doubt that the historicity of camp has been historically "marked" as Davy describes, I see in certain modes of lesbian performance, to borrow a phrase from experimental filmmaker Barbara Hammer, a "dyketactics" that dislodges the discourse of camp from certain traditions of male dominance.

Carmelita's female-to-male drag, and its specifically campy cultural critique, function as a dyketactics that avoids the pitfalls that Davy describes. Davy, paraphrasing Wayne Dynes's *Encyclopedia of Homosexuality*,[22] asserts:

> Camp is always represented with an invisible wink. But instead of realizing the promise and threat of its subversive potential for imagining and inscribing an "elsewhere" for alternative social and sexual realities, the wink of Camp (re)assures its audiences of the ultimate harmlessness of its play, its palatability for bourgeois sensibilities. . . .
>
> Camp is neither good nor bad, it is just more or less effectively deployed. In the context of gay male theater and its venues, Camp is indeed a means of signaling through the flames, while in lesbian performance it tends to fuel and fan the fire.[23]

I partially agree with Davy's point that camp is neither intrinsically good or bad. What is perplexing about this passage is her need to follow this statement with the generalization that camp is useful for gay men but counterproductive for lesbians. After disavowing any understandings of camp as having an a priori ideological charge (neither good nor bad), she proceeds to reinscribe an understanding of it as being a politically viable strategy only for gay men. I take issue with this turn in Davy's argument because I see it as undervaluing lesbian camp as a valuable disidentificatory strategy of enacting identity through the powerful rhetorics of parody and pastiche. I am also weary of one of the most significant repercussions of Davy's argument: the reification of camp as an exclusively gay male practice. Finally, I see some dangers in dismissing the ideological and survivalist dimensions for all queers. Cathy Griggers has contended that the description of camp as "prepolitical" is a common miscomprehension of the straight mind:

> Take camp struggles over straight semiosis, for example, which *gay and lesbian* subcultures have always understood as a style of everyday cultural politics and survival and not as prepolitical, a reading produced by straight "politicized subjects." If we premise that the body is not outside textuality, that the body itself is a field of significations, a site for the production of cultural meanings and ideological ramifications, then we admit that we play the game this way or that, we can choose to pass or not within the scene and the next, but we can't choose to stop playing with signs, with our own *material* cultural production as a cultural (i.e., visibly signifying) body.[24]

Griggers succinctly describes my problems with Davy's understanding of lesbian camp as an unproductive site of resistance. To limit or foreclose the possibility of lesbian camp is to circumscribe both lesbian and queer identifications.

Carmelita Tropicana's camp exceeds Davy's formulations, contests the bourgeois conventions within the Cuban exile community, and undermines the patriarchal character of most representations of Cuban and Cuban-American identity. A section of her performance *Milk of Amnesia* stars Pingalito—a name that sounds like a diminutive of the Cuban slang for penis—a character she plays in drag as a stereotypically loud Cuban man. Carmelita's drag performance operates on an axis concerned with more than biological gender difference. In this instance, the drag is calibrated also to represent and parody identities across class, national, and generational lines. Pingalito's monologue represents a national character that is recognizable as a Cuban form of masculine jingoism. A skit from the 1990 play *Memorias de la revolución* has Pingalito breaking away from the diegesis of the play and addressing the audience in his capacity as tour guide and authority on *cubanidad.* Pingalito wears the national dress of a Cuban male, the guayabera shirt. He also wears a brown fedora hat and dark fifties-style glasses that are held together at the nose bridge with tape. He punctuates his every locution with a wave of or a puff on his large cigar. Pingalito comments on the play's diegesis and then proceeds to give the spectator a context for understanding the play, a lecture on Cuba. As a visual prop he pulls out a paper place mat from his pocket. He explains that the place mat is from the restaurant Las Lillas, a popular Cuban steak house in Miami. The reference to Las Lillas is a manifestation of a certain mode of Cuban-American camp—it recalls a bit of middle-class Cuban-American family-life culture within the context of lesbian performance art. The camp speech-act references the elusive yet powerful binds between a past life in a typical homophobic middle-class emigrant family in Miami and the bohemian art world of New York avant-garde lesbian Lower East Side performance spaces such as the Club Chandelier and the WOW Café. The place mat has a picture of Cuba on it and it is titled "Facts about Cuba." The first fact read by Pingalito is that "Cuba is the

Carmelita Tropicana. Photo by Dona Ann McAdams.

Pearl of the Antilles." The character, speaking in a ridiculously exaggerated accent, proceeds to wax romantic about the beauty of the landscape. The monologue concludes with Pingalito performing a familiar form of Latino machismo as he describes the showgirls at the famous club Tropicana as possibly the most impressive feature of this landscape. Pingalito is incensed when he reads the next fact, an assertion that Cuba is slightly smaller than Pennsylvania. Pingalito warns the audience not to believe everything they read because he has been to Pennsylvania, and furthermore, he has a cousin who lives in Pennsylvania, and he knows for a fact that Cuba is bigger. With these first two facts, Carmelita establishes Pingalito's overzealousness by his ludicrous nationalism. The performance is especially poignant for second-generation Cuban-Americans who have never seen the island and have had to depend on similarly hyperbolic renditions of their lost homeland. When Pingalito warns the audience not to believe everything they read, he signifies upon the condition of second-generation Cuban Americans who have to juggle, decipher, and translate propaganda and anecdotal evidence in order to "know" their native land.

The third fact is that Spanish is Cuba's national language. Pingalito comments that it is a very beautiful language that Cubans speak with their mouths and hands. This reminds Pingalito of one of his favorite Cuban sayings: "¿Oye mano, adónde está tu abuela?" (Hey, brother, where is your grandmother?), which leads him to the fourth fact: "Three-fourths of all Cubans are white and of European descent." Pingalito adds that of this three-fourths, most have dark tans all year. He explains that when asked about the location of his grandmother he responds "dark and proud." This last bit of *cubana* kitsch makes a joke that challenges predictable racisms within the European Cuban population. Pingalito's quip speaks to the hypocrisy of Cubans who can trace their European roots to Spain but are nonetheless unable to pin down that missing grandmother who is, more often than not, of African descent.

Davy and other critics do not recognize the ability of lesbian camp to imagine new realities. The routine I have transcribed here is one in which camp not only accesses a new reality, but also lodges, through auspices of humor, a pointed social critique. Absent from Pingalito's monologue is the "wink" that Davy writes about. No one is let off the hook; the ironic and sharp attacks on Cuban and Cuban-American racism, sexism, and general hypocrisy are *not* retracted. Homi K. Bhabha's description of colonial mimicry as a form of imitation that resembles, but never quite succeeds in reproducing, the colonizer's image functions to describe the mimicry that is at the center of Carmelita's drag performances. This style of mimicry reproduces a facsimile that misses because it is "not quite/not white."[25] The effect of this image is not assimilation, but rather menace to the colonial/dominant paradigm. Carmelita's mimicry of the Cuban national character, and her decision to personify him as a machista, is a funny, yet nonetheless serious, examination and exploration of *cubanidad.*

Carmelita's performance ultimately proves that camp and lesbian drag are spacious

Carmelita Tropicana. Photo by Paula Court.

modes of self-authorization and self-enactment. Drag's elasticity extends to depict various subjectivities that traverse not only gender identification, but also national, class, and geographic identity coordinates. (Pingalito in "*Memorias de la revolución,* for example, is an older Miami-based Cuban exile who is sheltered within that city's right-wing Cuban power base while he pines for a mythical lost Cuba.) Her performance as Pingalito helps her access aspects of *cubanidad* and her mimicry of such aspects lodges critical readings of these identities and the systems of power and entitlement that fuel them. Carmelita's drag does not wink at the jingoistic Cuban nationalist and reassure him that everything is satisfactory; rather, it renders visible the mechanisms of privilege that such subjectivities attempt to occlude.

The Importance of Being *Choteo*

The great Cuban anthropologist and ethnographer Fernando Ortiz defined the word *choteo* in his lexicon of *cubanismos* as follows:

> In spite of the foregoing, the Africanist thesis is more versimilar, founded as it is on the *locumí* or *yoruba* term *soh* or *chot,* which means "to speak, to say," and, besides, "to throw," "to tear," "to cast out," all of which harmonizes with the respective sense of our *choteo.* From the root *cho* or *soh* are derived *sohroh,* "to converse," *sohrohelin,* "to speak to someone behind his back," *sohwerewere,* "to speak without rhyme or reason."
>
> Likewise, *porpongué chota* is "act of spying," "to pry," and *lucumí cho* is, also, "to keep watch," "to spy" which avoids the gypsy etymology of *chota,* as well as that of *choteo.*[26]

Ortiz's definition of *choteo* is central to this reading. The etymology he presents suggests that *choteo* is imported from African culture as a mode of being, a style of performance, a practice of everyday life. It signifies upon a range of activities that include tearing, talking, throwing, maligning, spying, and playing. All these verbs help to partially translate the practice of *choteo.*

Gustavo Pérez Firmat questions the validity of Ortiz's claims and suggests that there might be more to some of the European origins of the word. At one point he describes Ortiz's text itself as being "untidy." This critic does not explain, however, that *choteo* is, by its very foundations, a creolization, a cross-cultural mix that often resembles a cross-cultural mess. Ultimately, Pérez Firmat extols the text's virtues as being a work of high modernism, virtually "*The Wasteland* of modern dictionaries."[27] Its fragmentation should not be confused with traditional modernism's characteristics because it offers a glimpse at the operations of creolization in the specific form of the practice of *choteo.*

I propose *choteo* as another optic, one that is perhaps aligned with a camp reading, and, at other times, perhaps out of sync with such a hermeneutic, in order to decipher Carmelita's performances and production. *Choteo* is like camp in that it *can be* a fierce send-up of dominant cultural formations. *Choteo,* again, like camp, can be a style of colonial mimicry that is simultaneously a form of resemblance *and* menace. Both strategies possess a disidentificatory potential insofar as they mediate between a space of identification with and total disavowal of the dominant culture's normative identificatory nodes.

Cuban essayist Jorge Mañach also made an important contribution to the delineation of *choteo*. For Mañach, *choteo* was a performance style about the "cubano de la calle" (the average Cuban on the street). His book *Indignación del choteo* is concerned with describing the Cuban national character and a particular strain of this character that is *choteo*. For Mañach, *choteo* is a pathological weak spot in the Cuban composition, a shortcoming, a lack of seriousness, a fault. This chapter aims, in part, to depathologize this aspect of *cubanidad* and reconsider it as a strategy of self-enactment that helps a colonized or otherwise dispossessed subject enact a self through a critique of the normative culture. A practitioner of *choteo* is known as a *choteador*. Mañach describes *choteo* as "una actitud erigida en hábito, y esta habitualidad es su característica más importante" (an attitude hardened into a habit, and this habitualness is its most important characteristic).[28] It is so habitual it becomes systematic. *Choteo* is a form of mockery and joking that systematically undermines all authority. It is a practice that perpetuates disarray, mixture, and general confusion.[29]

The character of Pingalito offers a powerful example of *choteo* in action. Pingalito is *choteador* par excellence. His monologue on race on the island and his citation of a cryptic racist question are an instance where the *choteador*, through mockery and exaggeration, lampoons the polite racisms of everyday Cuban life. One should remember that this transpires within a camp performance that attempts to mimic and menace these phobic national identifications.

A performance by Carmelita in *The 1990 Decade Show* at the Studio Museum of Harlem contained sketches and bits that also serve as examples of Carmelita as *choteadora*. During one of her routines, the performance artist explains how she is not just a beauty queen but is always thinking, which makes her an intellectual. She thinks about origins. She wonders out loud where she, Carmelita, learned her famous brand of Cuban-Japanese cooking, her well-known chicken sushi. She then wonders how she, Carmelita, heard her calling to start her church of the born-again virgins, which is based in the heart of the Lower East Side. Finally, Carmelita explains that her calling came to her from the Virgin Mary. Taking her fresh-fruit boa and putting it on her head like a heavenly shroud, Carmelita channels visions of the holy Virgin that appeared to her at sea in 1955. This apparition is a *choteo* retelling of the Virgen de la Cobre, Cuba's patron saint, a Virgin who appeared to sailors lost at sea. Carmelita is in a rowboat, starving and knowing that the only food she has is one little Milky Way. With the fruit boa/shroud, Carmelita deploys a booming voice, still retaining the same thick and exaggerated Cuban accent, to retell her divine vision. The Virgin announces herself as Mary and explains that the goddess herself has chosen her to be the next hottest Latin superstar. She qualifies this by explaining that she has to wait until Robert Redford discovers Latinos in *The Milagro Beanfield War.* Carmelita takes off the boa, assuming her usual persona, and jumps up and down exclaiming, "I knew it, I knew it!" The Virgin continues to illustrate her future, calling, "Listen, Carmelita, Cuba will no longer be your home, her revolution will not be your revolution. Yours will be an international revolution to give dignity to Third World women everywhere. Carmelita, the *Kunst* is your *Waffen.*" Carmelita drops the fruit boa and responds to the Virgin with some skepticism, "I don't know about this *Kunst* thing, it sounds a little homoerotic." The Virgin explains that *Kunst* is German for art and *Waffen* means weapon, your art is your weapon. Carmelita accepts the Virgin's prophecy, and at that very moment she decides to make art her life.

There is much to unpack from this skit. Performing Virgen de la Cobre drag is perhaps that ultimate *choteo* of "authority" for a pious Catholic Cuban or the syncretic practitioner of Santeria. That authority in this instance is not only the Virgin but also a national symbol. The Cuban Revolution is also satirized in this monologue when Carmelita is told that it is not her revolution. I suggest that this statement connotes, through the extravagant mockery of *choteo,* a powerful disidentification with the Cuban revolution. The situation for left-leaning Cuban-Americans in the United States is a difficult one. Any critique of the Cuban Revolution instantly opens up Cuban-Americans to the charge that they are exactly like the right-wing anticommunist groups that dominate U.S. Cuban-American politics. Carmelita's realization (what some would call an abandonment) that this is not her revolution, and that she is instead fighting a revolutionary struggle for the recognition of the dignity of Third World women everywhere, is the sober political kernel at the center of the *choteo* joke. Carmelita is disidentifying with the revolution, not rejecting it and not embracing it without reservations. Instead, she sees her progressive politics anchored in gender struggles across the Third World. In asserting this agenda, Carmelita resists the pull of programmatic Cuban exile politics. She wishes to transcend the murky politics around the island and instead embrace issues of gender and identity that have been given secondary status by the revolution. It should be stressed that the prioritizing of gender politics does not mean the total abandonment of the revolution's politics and achievements in overturning class hierarchies.

The remark that she will only become an international superstar after Robert Redford discovers Latinos in *The Milagro Beanfield War* indicates the ways in which U.S. Latinas and Latinos are "discovered" by mainstream culture. That Latinas can only ascend to superstardom after having the road paved for them by aging Hollywood stars like Redford and vehicles like *The Milagro Beanfield War* is the everyday reality of U.S. Latinas/os in the media. Carmelita's quip is a *choteo* attack on this reality, exposing the racist working of the entertainment industry and the way in which performers of color are contained, limited, and exploited within that industry.

Once the performance artist adopts her mantra "your *Kunst* is your *Waffen,*" she then proceeds to do a trilingual medley that weaves German and Cuban songs together. Her repertoire includes the folk classic "Guantanamera," "Qué será, será," and "Oh, Tannenbaum." This musical number is a *choteo* of multiculturalism, internationalism, and hybridity, topics that are treated with deadly seriousness elsewhere. Carmelita's cracking voice and bogus accent point out the incoherency of such politics. *Choteo* revels in the chaotic, the ambivalent, the "untidy." In this case, *choteo* elucidates the ambivalent, complicated, mixed-up, and jumbled nature of the hybrid self through this comical medley.

Carmelita's performance can be read alongside Gloria Anzaldúa's description of the culture-crossing new mestiza. For Anzaldúa, the queer is the "supreme crosser of cultures," because

> homosexuals have strong bonds with the queer white, Black, Asian, Native American and with the queer in Italy, Australia and the rest of the planet. We come in all colors, classes and races, all time periods. Our role is to link people with each other—the Blacks with Jews and Indians with Asians with whites with extraterrestrials. It is to transfer ideas from one culture to another. Colored homosexuals have more knowledge of other cultures; have always been at the forefront (although sometimes in the closet) of all liberation struggles and have survived them despite all odds.[30]

I hesitate to fully embrace Anzaldúa's formulation because I worry that it contains the potential for being too celebratory of queer diversity, and in doing so elides the recalcitrant racisms and phobias that are still present throughout queer culture. I see Carmelita's border-crossing medley as understanding these risks and, through *choteo,* both celebrating what can be emancipatory about crossing borders and identifications and mocking this very practice, foregrounding what can be potentially disastrous, ridiculous, and even toxic about these connecting strategies.

Performing the Hybrid Self

In this chapter, I have risked setting up a dichotomy where the intractable connections between lesbian identity and Cuban ethnicity are discussed in wildly divergent terms, thus setting up a false divide between the two identity coordinates. My intention has not been to consign camp style to lesbian subjectivity and suggest that *choteo* functions only as a strategy to read Cuban identity. Instead, I want to suggest how Carmelita's is a hybrid self; by better understanding her via her performance of this hybridized self, we can begin to make inroads toward an understanding of the survivalist practice of dyke self-fabrication. Her *choteo* style is campy and *choteo* is inflected in her campiness. Carmelita does not hesitate to remind her audience of her various identity markers: she lists nightclub performer, beauty queen, intellectual, political activist, superintendent, and performance *artiste.* To this we can add camp queen, diva, *choteadora,* female impersonator, male impersonator, lesbian, *cubana en exilio,* off-key songstress, and Carmen Miranda clone. All of these roles, identifications, and routines compose Carmelita Tropicana's hybrid self.

It is important to specify that the mode of hybridity that Carmelita is representative of is a survivalist strain of self-production. Carmelita's work is not a celebration of a fixed hybrid identity. It is not a style of internationalism or cosmopolitanism. Carmelita's hybridity is enacted through performance in much the same way that Ella Shohat and Robert Stam describe the hybrid subject's theatricality: "The Hybrid diasporic subject is confronted with the 'theatrical' challenge of moving, as it were, among the diverse performative modes of sharply contrasting cultural and ideological worlds."[31]

Griggers reminds us that

> [c]ultural mappings of lesbian bodies will also have to include intermingling among minorities. These specific sites of mixing and transformation will shape the political stakes and the political strategies for lesbian-feminist-queer-nation alliance and any possible alliance between that configuration and ethnic minorities. Take the case, from the 1950's to the present, of lesbians becoming only with much difficulty lesbian-feminists and then becoming, after even more struggle, lesbian-feminists of color (these hybridities were always present, of course, but for years remained invisible within the minority social bodies of feminism or African-Americanism or Hispanic-Americanism). The history of this particular struggle over the intermingling of minoritarian social bodies is entirely representative of the dilemmas facing the traditional political notion of identity politics grounded in a totalized, stable, fixed subject.[32]

Lesbians of color have complicated reductionist and antiracist understandings of what lesbian identity might be.[33] Carmelita, who is a cultural production herself, always appearing in character, defies notions of a fixed subjectivity. Her queer and *cubana* body is unstable and fragmented; it registers on its surface the intermingling of the identity bits that make up her performances and persona, because she appears and participates in various forms of media (film, theater, more experimental performances) always within character, undermining notions of authenticity and realness in favor of queer self-making practices. This self is not limited to the one performance persona. Drag identities such as Pingalito, who is a persona that is layered over the already fictional construct of Carmelita, contribute to her queerly fabricated self. Through the character of Pingalito, Carmelita assimilates and appropriates theatrical and performance practices from the world of gay male subcultures.

Troyano's film, as I have argued, is also a hodgepodge of different styles, influences, and genre. Its hybridity is a queer one that lets it crisscross from genres like the women in prison film to the Latina American melodrama, from scenes like the lesbian activist protest to a nightclub cabaret. It ultimately reasserts through the three siblings of different races the diversity and complexity of U.S. Latina/o identities. The sharp contrast between Sophia's gold door-knocker earrings and Carmelita's super high-heel sneakers reminds one of the multiplicity of personal styles that also fall under the hybrid category of the U.S. Latina.

Carmelita Tropicana. Photo by Dona Ann McAdams.

Troyano's film and the piece of (cultural) work that is Carmelita are instances in which dominant culture is mimicked, mocked, and finally worked until its raw material can be recyled to ends that are female, Latina, and queer-affirmative. Popular forms are disidentified with, which means parodied with campy extravagance or heckled by this mode of dissidence for majoritarian culture. The spectator is left with a gaudy spectacle that affirms self-subjectivities that are both Latina and queer. These productions, in turn, remind us that identity politics does not need only to be rooted in essentialized notions of the self and simplistic understanding of resistance, but rather that it is essentially a politics of hybridity that works within and outside the dominant public sphere, and in doing so contests the ascendant racial, sexual, and class strictures.

Chapter 6

Pedro Zamora's *Real World* of Counterpublicity: Performing an Ethics of the Self

Pedro Zamora died on November 11, 1994. He was twenty-two. The day after his death, a cover story appeared in the *Wall Street Journal.* The article explained that Pedro received thousands of fan letters a week. It quoted one from a South Carolina woman, who wrote: "I never thought anyone could change my opinion of homosexuals and AIDS. Because of you I saw the human side of something that once seemed so unreal to me." The letter speaks to Pedro's intervention in the public sphere. It bears witness to the difference this young Latino's life's work made. In this chapter, I will suggest that although these interventions in the majoritarian public sphere were important, one would fail to understand the efficacy of the activist's tactics and the overall success of his life's work if one only considered such letters. Pedro's work enabled the possibility of queer and Latino counterpublics, spheres that stand in opposition to the racism and homophobia of the dominant public sphere. Through this labor one begins to glimpse new horizons of experience.

In what follows, I will outline the activism and cultural interventions of televisual activist Pedro Zamora and describe the way in which he performed what I understand as a Foucauldian ethics of the self. This "working on the self" allowed Zamora to take a *next* step: a leap into the social through the public performance of an ethics of the self. I will also call attention to the ways in which this Cuban-American cultural worker's performances accomplished tasks that enabled the enactment of queer and Latino identity practices in a phobic public sphere. These tasks include the denouncement of the dominant public sphere's publicity that fixes images and understandings of queerness and *latinidad*; the enactment of resistance to the reductive multicultural pluralism that is deployed against them; the production of an intervention within the majoritarian public sphere that confronts phobic ideology; and the production of counterpublicity that allows the *possibility* of subaltern counterpublics.

In *The Care of the Self,* the third volume of his *History of Sexuality,* Michel Foucault elaborated, through a tour of antiquity and its philosophical underpinnings, an ethics of the self—a working on the self for others.[1] *The Care of the Self* emphasizes an ethics around nourishing and sustaining a self within civil society. It is ultimately expedient to cite one of Foucault's more elucidating interviews at some length for the purpose of explicating "the care of the self" and its roots in Hellenistic and Greco-Roman culture:

> What interests me in the Hellenistic culture, in the Greco-Roman culture, starting from the third century BC and continuing until the second or third century after Christ, is a precept for which the Greeks had a specific word, *epimeleia heautou,* which means taking care of oneself. It does not mean simply being interested in oneself, nor does it mean having a certain tendency to self-attachment or self-fascination. *Epimeleia heautou* is a very powerful word in Greek which means "working on" or "being concerned with" something. For example, Xenophon used *epimeleia heautou* to describe agricultural management. The responsibility of a monarch for his fellow citizens was also *epimeleia heautou.* That which a doctor does in the course of caring for the patient is *epimeleia heautou.* It is therefore a very powerful word; it describes a sort of work, an activity; it implies attention, knowledge, technique.[2]

I consider the work of televisual activist Zamora to be just such a sort of "work" that disseminated and "publicized" "attentions, knowledges, and techniques" that are consequential to the project of minoritarian subjectivity. I will suggest that Zamora worked within *The Real World,* which one should never forget is a product of the corporate entity MTV, and yet still managed to find ways to do this work *despite* the corporate ethos that ordered that program. Foucault had, at a later stage in his thinking, decided that our understanding of power could be augmented by richer discourse on the subject. Work on the ethics of self ultimately allows us a new vantage point to consider the larger games of truth that organize the social and the relations of these games to states of domination. Within the structure of MTV, and its corporate structure, Zamora performed his care of the self as truth game that "was for others," letting them see and imagine a resistance to entrenched systems of domination.

It is important to note that Foucault's "care of the self" is based on the lives of citizens and not slaves within antiquity. George Yúdice has pointed out this limit in Foucault's project and has gone on to theorize how an "ethics of marginality" might be extracted from Foucault's project:

> The problem with Foucault's analysis, as I see it, is that the examples are drawn from the aesthetic practices of Greek freeman and, more important, modernist art. In both cases only elites engage in these particular types of self-analysis and self-formation. This does not mean, however, that Foucault's framework prohibits a priori other types of self-formation related to different social groups. On the contrary, insofar as knowledge, politics (power), and ethics mutually condition each other, despite their relative autonomy, the particularities of the group

> that engages in ethical practices (its knowledges, its politics) must be taken into consideration. If Foucault could trace the genealogy for dominant groups, it should be equally possible to trace that of dominated and oppressed peoples.[3]

Yúdice outlines the very specific origins of Foucault's paradigm. He suggests that even though elitist and First Worldist limitations exist within Foucault's paradigm, this does not mean that "Foucault's framework prohibits a priori other types of self-formation related to different social groups." Yúdice uses Rigoberta Menchú's *testimonio, I, Rigoberta Menchú: An Indian Woman in Guatemala,* as an example when unfolding his theory of an ethics of marginality. He uses the case of Menchú to amend Foucault's notion of "an aesthetics of existence" and transform it into an ethics in which practical politics plays a central role. Yúdice explains that "We might say that a 'practical poetics' is the ethical 'self-forming activity' in which the 'self' is practiced in solidarity with others struggling for survival. Menchú, in fact, has turned her identity into a 'poetics of defense.'"[4] The example of Menchú and her *testimonio* potentially elucidates our understanding of the politics that undergirds Zamora's uses of the self, his care of the self for others. *The Real World* employs what it calls "video confessionals." These confessionals have been small rooms within the casts's living space where individual members are encouraged to "confess" to the camera outside the space of social negotiation. These spaces have been used by the cast as sites where they could perform their selves solo and in private. Real Worlders have used these solo performances to argue for themselves and their identities. These spaces of self-formation are, of course, highly mediated by MTV, even more mediated than Menchú's *testimonio,* which was transcribed and heavily edited by Elisabeth Burgos-Debray. Yet, this corporate mediation does not foreclose the counterpublic building possibilities within these video *testimonios.* Whereas his housemates and cast members from other seasons used the video confessionals to weigh in on domestic squabbles, Zamora used them as vehicles to perform the self for others. Zamora's work, these quotidian video performances, function like video *testimonios* that convert identity into a "poetics of defense."

Following Yúdice's lead, I am disidentifying with Foucault's paradigm insofar as I am redeploying it and, to a certain extent, restructuring it, in the service of minoritarian identity. This chapter is interested in imagining an ethic of the minoritarian self. Within a Foucauldian framework recalibrated to consider the minoritarian subject's care of the self, to work on oneself is to veer away from models of the self that correlate with socially prescribed identity narratives. The rejection of these notions of the self is not simply an individualistic rebellion: resisting dominant modes of subjection entails not only contesting dominant modalities of governmental and state power but also opening up a space for new social formations. The performance of Latina/o, queer, and other minoritarian ontologies—which is to say the theatricalization of such ethics of the self—conjures the possibility of social agency within a world bent on the negation of minoritarian subjectivities. My project here is to map and document a minoritarian ethics of the self and, more important, the ways in which representations of and (simultaneously) by that self signal new spaces within the social. I will also suggest that the televisual dissemination of such performances allows for the *possibility of counterpublics*—communities and relational chains of resistance that contest the dominant public sphere. Within radical movements, Zamora's work may not register as progressive enough or may be seen as redundant. The fact that he agreed to work within the tepid multicultural frame of the corporate entity MTV might immediately diminish his significance to already-established activist communities. It is my contention that Zamora's work was not for other activists, queer or Latino, but was instead for a world of *potentially* politicized queers and Latinos; for a mass public that is structured by the cultural forces of homophobia and racism; for those who have no access to more subculturally based cultural production and grassroots activism. Thus, Zamora's activism preaches to the not yet converted, and in doing so may not seem as radical as the work of other activists, but should be acknowledged as frontline struggle and agitation.

My focus on a nexus of identity markers that circulate around queer and Latino is of importance for various reasons. The AIDS emergency has become a painful habit of being for many of us. Those of us who live inside and around Latino communities and queer communities know the ways in which so much has been lost—indeed, that the present and far too many futures have been robbed. The necessity of publicizing such ethics of the self, of moving these ethics beyond the privatized zones of individual identities, is great during our contemporary health crisis.

But AIDS is only one of the reasons why publicizing and performing an ethics of self seems so essential for Latina/o and/or queer politics. The disjunctures between queer and Latino communities are many. The mainstream gay community ignores or exoticizes Latino bodies, while many Latino communities promote homophobia. Yet, as of November 1994, the month Zamora died, the linkages between queerness and *latinidad* have never seemed so poignant. The congressional election, nicknamed the "Republican revolution" by some news media pundits, made the headlines by establishing the New Right's majority status in the U.S. Senate and the House of Representatives. This reactionary tidal wave also included legislation that was calibrated to legislate against certain identities. Although two antigay measures were barely defeated in Idaho and Colorado, California's Proposition 187, which further erodes the nation's civil rights by denying health care and education to immigrants who have been classified as "illegal" by the state apparatus, was passed. The targeted immigrant communities are non-Europeans, especially Latinos. An antilesbian and gay measure passed in Colorado in 1992—which read very much like the barely defeated ordinances in Idaho and Oregon—proposed that lesbians and gay men be stripped of any basic civil rights that would acknowledge and protect their minority status. The 1992 Colorado proposition was eventually overruled by the Supreme Court. Nonetheless, the popularity of such initiatives says something about the national body: homophobia, racism, and xenophobia are being codified in legislation. Certainly, it can be argued that these hate discourses have always been the law of the land, yet there is something particularly disturbing about the fact that the majoritarian public sphere announces these prohibitions and discriminatory practices as sites to rally around. Indeed, homohatred and Latino bashing are two of the New Right's most popular agenda issues. The 1992 Republican convention made all of this quite clear as countless speakers at the podium and delegates interviewed on the floor voiced their anti-immigrant and "pro-family" (which is always antiqueer) rhetoric. The 1996 GOP convention chose to remove ultraright zealots Pat Buchanan and Pat Robertson from roles of visibility, thus allowing much of their politics of exclusion to be relocated right below the surface of the televisual proceedings. Despite this prime-time camouflage and a hollow rhetoric of "inclusion," the New Right's agenda, spelled out in the GOP platform, still promised a repeal of civil-rights legislation, further attacks on immigrants, xenophobic welfare reform, and more family values.

I am interested here in unveiling moments in which the majoritarian public sphere's publicity—its public discourse and reproduction of that discourse—is challenged by performances of counterpublicity that defy its discriminatory ideology. Counterpublicity is disseminated through acts that are representational *and* political interventions in the service of subaltern counterpublics.[5] The philosopher Nancy Fraser, following the work of other writers, has criticized Jürgen Habermas's account of the public sphere for focusing primarily on the constitution of one monolithic bourgeois public sphere at the expense of considering other possibilities for publicity. Even though Habermas's work is essentially a critique of the bourgeois public sphere, his lack of recourse to counterpublics essentially reinscribes the exclusionary logic and universalism of the bourgeois public sphere. Counterpublics, for Fraser, "contest[ed] the exclusionary norms of the 'official' bourgeois public sphere, elaborating alternative styles of political behavior and alternative norms of public speech."[6] Fraser points to the significance of subaltern counterpublics for women, people of color, gay men and lesbians, and other subordinated groups. Oskar Negt and Alexander Kluge describe the public sphere as being composed of various forms of publicity that are connected to different communities and modalities of publicity. Negt and Kluge's work maintains that counterpublics often emerge out of already-existing industrial and commercial channels of publicity, especially the electronic media.[7]

The act of performing counterpublicity in and through electronic/televisual sites dominated by the dominant public sphere is risky. Many representations of counterpublicity are robbed of any force by what Miriam Hansen has called the "marketplace of multicultural pluralism."[8] The practices of queer and Latino counterpublicity—acts that publicize and theatricalize an ethics of the self—that I am mapping present strategies that resist, often through performances that insist on local specificities and historicity, the pull of reductive multicultural pluralism.

The best way we can understand the categories *queer* and Latina/o or *latinidad* is as counterpublics that are in opposition to other social factions. What is primarily at stake is space. The mode of counterpublicity I am discussing makes an intervention in public life that defies the white normativity *and* heteronormativity of the majoritarian public sphere. Thus, I am proposing that these terms be conceptualized as social movements that are contested by and contest the public sphere for the purposes of political efficacy—movements that not only "remap" but also *produce* minoritarian space.

The theoretical schools I am blending here—social theory influenced by Habermas and Foucault's discourse analysis—are more often than not pitted *against* each other. Habermas's thinking appeals to and attempts to reconstruct rationality. Foucault's, in its very premise, is a critique of rationality. The mappings that public-sphere social theory provide are extremely generative ones. Yet, as I leave the work of social theorists such as Negt and Kluge, Hansen, and Fraser and return to the major source of these paradigms, Habermas, I find myself having misgivings with his project's philosophical tenets—namely, his use of and investment in communicative reason.[9] Habermasian communicative reason presupposes that within the framing of all communicative gestures there exists an appeal to an undeniable "good" that would alleviate all disagreements within the social. Foucauldians and others find the category of a universally defined good to be an exceedingly easy target.

My post-Habermasian use of the public sphere is primarily indebted to Negt and Kluge's critique of Habermas, especially their move to critique the underlying concepts of universal reason that they identify in his project. Their critique utilizes Immanuel Kant's critical philosophy to problematize the category of an abstract principle of generality. Their work then opens up space to conceptualize multiple publics, complete with their own particularities.

Jon Simmons has explained that it is indeed difficult to locate Foucault on any map of politics inherited from nineteenth-century philosophy. But he goes on to add that

> Foucault does belong to a "we," though this "we" is not easily classifiable according to traditional categories. How does one define the gay movement, feminism, youth protests, the movements of ethnic and national minorities, and the diffuse discontents of clients of educational, health and welfare systems who are identified as single mothers, unemployed, or delinquent? His transgressive practices of self with writing, drugs, gay friendship and S/M operate in the space opened by these movements. Those whose designated desires, genders, ethnic identities, or welfare categorizations do not seem to fit in this space. It is in this space where some women refuse to be feminine and become feminists; in which black-skinned people refuse to be Negroes and become African-Americans; and in which men who desire other men might refuse to be homosexuals and become gay. Like Foucault, they practice politics of those who refuse to be who they are and strive to become other.[10]

The space that Simmons describes is what I consider the transformative political space of disidentification. Here is where Negt and Kluge function for me as valuable supplements to Foucault's mappings of the social. This space, what Simmons calls Foucault's "we," can be given a new materiality and substance when transcoded as counterpublics. Fredric Jameson, in a fascinating essay on Negt and Kluge, sees this connection between the German writers and Foucault, despite the fact that he is ultimately opposed to Foucault and valorizes Negt and Kluge:

> The originality of Negt and Kluge, therefore, lies in the way in which the hitherto critical and analytical force of what is widely known as "discourse analysis" (as in Foucault's descriptions of the restrictions and exclusions at work in a range of so-called discursive formations) is now augmented, not to say completed, by the utopian effort to create space of a new type.[11]

The definition of counterpublics that I am invoking here is intended to describe different subaltern groupings that are defined as falling outside the majoritarian public sphere; it is influenced by a mode of discourse theory that critiques universalities and favors particularities, yet it insists on a Marxian materialist impulse that *regrids* transgressive subjects and their actions as identifiable social movements. Thus, my notion of a counterpublic resonates alongside Simmons's description of "those whose designated desires, genders, ethnic identities, or welfare categorizations do not seem to fit." The object of my study, Pedro Zamora, was, from the purview of the dominant public sphere, one of those who did not seem to fit. In this way, his work can be understood as a counterpublic response to dominant publicity.

The young Cuban-American activist disidentified with that dominant publicity, working with *and* on one of its "channels," MTV. Habermas, following the example of Frankfurt school predecessor Theodor Adorno, would probably see MTV as the providence of monopoly capitalism, locked into a pattern of sameness that was only calibrated to reproduce the consumer. A strict Habermasian reading could never see MTV as a stage where radical work could be executed. Negt and Kluge understand that, in this postmodern moment, the electronic media is essential to the reproduction of state capitalism and counterpublicity. Zamora also understood this. Using his keen sense of counterpublicity, he spotted *The Real World*'s potential as an exemplary stage. One need only consider the cover letter he sent MTV when he was applying for the show to understand how the young activist immediately saw the political potential of the medium. I will first cite a section of the letter where his pitch challenges the producers to consider the possibility of having a person living with AIDS on the show:

> So why should I be on *The Real World*? Because in the real world there are people living productive lives who just happen to be HIV+. I think it is important for people my age to see a young person who looks and feels healthy, can party and have fun but at the same time needs to take five pills daily to stay healthy.

> On one of your episodes this season [season two] you had an HIV+ guy come in and talk about AIDS/HIV with the group. He was there a few hours and he left. I wonder what kind of issues would have come up if that HIV+ guy would be living with the group, sharing the bathroom, the refrigerator, the bedroom, eating together? Everyday for six months. Things that make you go hmmmm.[12]

Here Zamora describes the dramatic and televisual energy his inclusion in the show would generate. He does not pitch his project in all its political urgencies. He understands that one needs to disidentify with the application process to be given access to the stage that the cable program provided him. He plays up the fact that his inclusion would make for good TV as well as be an important political intervention. He next speaks to his willingness to sacrifice his own privacy for the sake of his activism:

> I know that being on *The Real World* would mean exposing the most intimate details of my life on national television. How comfortable am I with that? Well, I do that through my job every day.
>
> If I can answer the questions of an auditorium full of fifth graders with inquiring minds, I am sure I could do it on national television.[13]

Zamora is willing to sacrifice his right to privacy because he understands that subjects like himself never have full access to privacy. Although the dominant public sphere would like to cast him in the zone of private illness, it is clear that any fantasy of real privacy, as *Bowers v. Hardwick* signals, is always illusory. In this statement, the young activist conveys his understanding that his desires, gender identifications, health, and national and ethnic minority status keep him from having any recourse to the national fantasy of privacy to which other subjects in the public sphere cling.

Magic Johnson, who achieved celebrity before he tested positive for the virus, uses his celebrity and the mass media in ways that are similar to those used by Zamora, who came into celebrity through *The Real World*. Hansen offers a reading of Magic Johnson's case that is so relevant here that it is worth citing at length:

> When basketball player Magic Johnson used his resignation upon having tested positive to advocate safe sex he did more than put his star status in the service of a political cause; he made a connection, albeit a highly personalized one, between the industrial-commercial public sphere of sports, its local reappropriation within the African-American community, and the counterpublic struggle surrounding AIDS. While the latter is by now organized on an international scale, it continues to be marginalized domestically as a "special interest," to be denied public status with reference to its roots in gay subculture. Johnson's gesture not only made public a concern that the neoconservative lobby has been trying to delegitimize as private; it also, if only temporarily, opened up a discursive arena, in both mainstream publicity and within the African-American community, in which sexual practices could be discussed and negotiated, rather than merely sensationalized or rendered taboo. Not least, it provided a way to return sex education to schools from which it had disappeared under Reagan.[14]

Although there is much to say about the vastly divergent strategies of negotiation that Johnson and Zamora employed, it is useful to consider how the two men's examples are similar. Both used the power of celebrity to make counterpublic interventions by way of using the mainstream media, a mode of publicity that is usually hostile to counterpublic politics. Both used their national stages to appear to various publics, including a mass public and the minoritized counterpublics from which they locate their own identities. They also decided to combat the neoconservative strategy of relegating a public health emergency to privatized and individual illness. Practicing a public ethics of the self, both men thematized and theatricalized their illness as public spectacles. The New Right is bent on removing AIDS from the public agenda, nourishing ignorance through the suppression of safe-sex pedagogy, and finally, cutting off federal support to people with AIDS (PWAs) and medical research. To better understand Zamora's example, it is useful to review the show's five-season run, noting shifts in each incarnation of the show.

Since its inception in 1991, MTV's *The Real World* has included queers in its "real-life" ensemble cinema verité-style melodrama. The show's premise is simple: seven videogenic young people, all strangers, are chosen to live in a house together. The twenty-something group is usually racially diverse. Its gender breakdown is usually four men and three women. It has had five different "casts" and five different incarnations, in five different cities: New York, Los Angeles, San Francisco, London, and Miami. Each season has included a gay or lesbian character. The New York cast included Norman, a white man who sometimes identified as bisexual and sometimes as gay. While being rather charismatic, Norman was something of a minor character on the show; most of that season focused on the contrived sexual tension between innocent country girl Julie and Eric, a New Jerseyan Herb Ritts model who was nominally straight and went on to host the illustrious MTV dance-party show *The Grind.* Much steam was lost in the show's second season, in which the queer came as a midseason replacement. Beth was a white lesbian who worked in B horror-movie production. Beth received probably less screen time than any other character in the show's five seasons. Norman and Beth both dated, but their sexual lives were relegated to "special episodes." The way in which these two characters were contained and rendered narratively subordinate to the show's straight characters is a succinct example of the inane multicultural pluralism that Hansen has described. It also clearly displays some of the ways in which queers and the counterpublicity they might be able to disseminate are rendered harmless within the channels of the electronic media and the majoritarian public sphere. Zamora was the third season's house queer. He did not, however, fall into obscurity the way his queer predecessors had. Rather, he managed to offer valuable counterpublicity for various subaltern counterpublics that included U.S. Latinos, queers, and people living with AIDS.

For five months Zamora was one of the few out gay men appearing regularly on television.[15] He was also one of the few Latinos seen regularly on national television. Furthermore, he was one of the few out people living with AIDS on television. There should be no mistake as to MTV's motives in selecting Zamora. He was as handsome as a model and rarely looked "ill" in any way. He was a Cuban-American, a group that comes as close as any Latino community in the United States to qualifying as a "model minority." Although articulate and skilled as a public speaker, he had a thick Cuban accent that must have sounded very "tropical" to North American ears. One could argue, in fact, that he walked a road that was paved by a previous "Latin star," Ricky Ricardo.[16] Zamora was selected because of these features and his agency in this selection process was none. He fit a larger corporate schema as to what MTV wanted for the show and these reasons led to his being represented. Yet, Zamora was more than simply represented; he used MTV as an opportunity to continue his life's work of HIV/AIDS pedagogy, queer education, and human-rights activism. Unlike his queer predecessors, he exploited MTV in politically efficacious ways; he used MTV more than it used him.

The fourth season of the show was set in London. At this point the show broke from its pattern of having an out house queer. *The Real World* London show was less contentious than the San Francisco show. It only included one ethnic minority, a black British jazz singer, and not one out lesbian, gay, bisexual, or transgendered person. It would seem that ethnic, racial, and sexual diversity that characterized the show's first three seasons was put on hold after the explosive San Francisco season (discussed later in this chapter). I will argue that the soft multicultural pluralism that characterized the series was exploited and undermined by Zamora and some of his peers. I am suggesting that the fourth season of *The Real World* can be read as a backlash of sorts; which is to say that it was an escape from North American politics and social tensions to a storybook England, a fantasy Europe that had none of its own ethnic or sexual strife. (The roommates actually lived in a flat that was made up to look like a castle.)

The fifth season, set in Miami, represents a back-to-basics approach in which the tried-and-true formula of nominal racial and sexual diversity was reestablished. The Miami cast included two women of color: Cynthia, an African-American waitress from Oakland, California, and Melissa, "the local girl," a Cuban-American woman from the Miami area. The house queer spot went once again to a white man, as it did in the show's classic first season. Dan, a college student from Rutgers University, was raised in the Midwest, where he grew up watching the show like many queer kids in the United States. In a feature article in *Out* magazine, Dan spoke about the way in which he, as a pre-out youth, marveled at seeing an out Norman in the show's first season. In the article he expresses his understanding that he was now, thanks to the show, going to be the most famous gay man in America. The young Real Worlder's statement testifies to the counterpublic-making properties of the program. Dan aspires to be a model and a writer for flashy fashion magazines. His interviews on the program and in the print media indicate that he was cognizant of a need to be a public "role model" for queers, but his performances fell short of the radical interventions that Zamora produced.

Dan understood the need to perform a positive image; Zamora, on the other hand, was conscious of the need to take the show's title seriously and be radically *real.* A coffee-table fan book that MTV published in 1995 while the fourth season was airing prints "sound bites" by many of the show's stars, producers, and crew; the book's revenues go, in part, to the foundation started in Zamora's name. In that book, story editor Gordon Cassidy comments:

> The one thing I feel best about in this show is what Pedro enabled us to present to the rest of the country, and not just about AIDS, but about who he was as a person, things that networks can't get away with. You think of the problems networks have portraying gay relationships, interracial relationships, and he was all of those.[17]

The fact that Zamora was indeed all of these things is especially important. The "realness" of Pedro and the efficacy and power of his interventions have as much to do with the manner in which he insisted on being a complicated and intersectional subject: not only gay but a sexual person; a person of color actively living with another person of color in an interracial relationship; a person living with AIDS. Although Cassidy's comments could be read as an example of MTV's patting itself on the back, much of what he is saying is accurate. As of this moment, with few exceptions, broadcast network television is unable and unwilling to represent queers who are sexual yet not pathological, interracial relationships, and stories about AIDS that portray the fullness and vibrancy of such a life narrative.

To understand Pedro's intervention one needs to survey the status of homosexuality on television at the time of his death in November 1994. A *Los Angeles Times* feature article cites Richard Jennings, executive director of Hollywood Supports, a group promoting positive gay portrayals in film and television, on the resurgence of gay characters in the media: "As gays have increasingly 'come out,' many viewers have become aware of gay brothers, sisters and friends. Together with gay viewers, they are increasingly asking for sympathetic gay portrayals."[18] This lobbying is opposed by right-wing activists such as the Reverend Louis Sheldon, head of the Orange County–based Traditional Values Coalition. Sheldon is quoted in the same article as saying that "Homosexuals should not be portrayed at all on TV." Sheldon, a bigot who is notorious for "picketing" outside of AIDS memorials and funerals, feels that sympathetic gay role models confuse viewers and contends that "If young males need to identify with someone, they should identify with Clint Eastwood."[19] One might wish to dismiss Sheldon's comments as the demented ravings of an Eastwood groupie, but one cannot underestimate the influence that such zealots continue to exercise over mainstream broadcasting.

Although some advertisers seem to have become more accepting of queer representation—Ellen DeGeneres's very public coming out in the spring of 1997 and the appearance of a black gay supporting character in ABC's *Spin City* are evidence of this—very few queer characters on television have, as of this writing, performed their sexualities on the screen. For example, when producer Darren Star wanted to show his gay character, Matt, kissing another man on the season finale of *Melrose Place* in the spring of 1994, the Fox network balked and asked them not to, afraid that advertisers would withdraw their advertising, as they did for a 1989 episode of ABC's *thirtysomething* that showed two gay men in bed together.

Within this context, Zamora's performance of self, his publicized "care of the self," especially as represented in an episode that featured an exchanging of rings ceremony with boyfriend Sean, can be seen as radical interventions. In that episode, originally broadcast on November 3, 1994, the two men kiss no fewer than seven times in the half-hour program. Zamora's romance was, according to producer John Murray, significant within the history of the show as it was, "probably the deepest we've ever gotten into a relationship in our three seasons."[20] (Since then, Dan dated two men in the show's fifth season, one a closeted white man, the other an out Cuban-American. Although both these relationships seem significant in that they were *real* queer couplings on television, neither bond seemed as serious or ultimately as memorable as Pedro and Sean's.) When I suggest that such performances function as counterpublicity, I am imagining the effect that they might have on a queer child or adult whose access to queer cultures or energies might be limited or nonexistent. These highly mediated images, brought into the fold through the highly mediated channels of corporate broadcasting, still served as a site where children and others could glimpse a queer *and* ethnic life-world. What started out as tokenized representation became something larger, more spacious—a mirror that served as a prop for subjects to imagine and rehearse identity. This, in part, enables the production of counterpublics.

It would be a mistake to elide the representational significance of Zamora's work on the mainstream. Pedro, as Bill Clinton put it, gave AIDS a very "human face." Beyond that, he gave it a vibrant, attractive, politicized, and brown face. He showed an ignorant and phobic national body that within the bourgeois public's fantasy of privacy, the binarism of public health and private illness could no longer hold—that the epidemic was no longer an abstract and privatized concern. He willfully embodied and called attention to all those things that are devastating and ennobling about possessing a minority subjectivity within an epidemic. Although MTV gave Zamora a stage to do this work of education and embodiment, however, it should not be too valorized for this contribution because it often attempted to undercut it. What follows is a brief synopsis of Pedro's role and work on *The Real World*. It focuses on those episodes that are pertinent to Pedro's story or the story I am telling in this chapter. I then consider the show's nineteenth episode in more detail.

The show begins with Cory, a college student from California who rendezvoused with Pedro on a train.[21] The young Anglo woman is very taken with Pedro, and Pedro, for his part, as he explains in a voice-over, was expecting to meet a woman who would be very much like Cory, very "all-American." Soon all of the roommates are assembled: Judd, a Jewish cartoonist from Long Island; Pam, an Asian-American medical student; Mohammed, an African-American Bay Area musician and writer; Puck, a white man who was a bicycle messenger; and Rachel, a Republican Mexican-American from Arizona who is applying to graduate school.[22] (I am aware that the preceding descriptions seem to be somewhat stock, but these were the primary identity accounts that the program offered.) That first episode concluded with Pedro sharing his scrapbook with his roommates. The scrapbook consisted of newspaper clippings from around the nation of his activist work. This outed him to the rest of the cast not only as queer but also as a person living with AIDS. Rachel was put off by this display and proceeded, during an interview in the confessional,[23] to voice her AIDSphobic and homophobic concerns about cohabiting with Pedro. Thus, that first episode began with the "all-American girl" meeting the handsome young stranger on a train and concluded with a conservative Latina expressing a phobic position against the young AIDS educator. This episode framed Pedro as one of the show's "star" presences, unlike the queers from previous seasons.

Episode two presents an early confrontation between Pedro and the show's other star presence, Puck. Pedro objects to Puck's post-punk hygiene in the kitchen and throughout the living space. The show had hoped to frame this confrontation as a sort of odd couple dilemma, but it ignored the fact that Puck's lack of hygiene was nothing short of a medical risk for a person living with a compromised immune system. While Rachel goes to an "Empower America" fund-raiser and meets the New Right's beloved Jack Kemp, one of her personal heroes, Pedro goes on a first date with Sean, an HIV-positive pastry chef with a disarming smile. Sean and Pedro's relationship advances and the couple falls in love by episode six. Puck makes homophobic jokes about Pedro during this episode. According to interviews with the cast after the series was completed, these comments from Puck were a regular household occurrence that was, through editing strategies, downplayed by the producers.

In episode eight, Pedro goes for a medical examination. He discovers that his T-cell count has dropped significantly. This moment represents an important moment in TV history: a painful aspect of a PWA's quotidian reality is represented as never before. This sequence is followed by one in which Pedro gives a safe-sex and risk-prevention seminar at Stanford University. Puck, always vying for the house's attention, schedules a beachcombing expedition at the same time. Pam and Judd choose to watch and support Pedro while Cory and Rachel join Puck. The show crosscuts both sequences, emphasizing the divisions in the house. Tensions mount during episode nine. Pedro and Sean become engaged and Puck reacts with what is by now predictable homophobia. The house confronts Puck on his behavioral problems in episode eleven. Puck will not listen and Pedro delivers an ultimatum to the house: it is either him or Puck. The members vote, and Puck is unanimously ejected from the house.

In episode eleven, Pedro travels with Rachel to Arizona to meet her Catholic and

Republican family. Pedro is exceedingly diplomatic with the family and connects with them as Latinos. Rachel's parents, both educators at a local school, invite Pedro to talk about AIDS at their workplace. One student asks if he still has sex and whether or not he has a girlfriend. There is a tight shot of Rachel's mother looking worried and seemingly holding her breath. Pedro pauses, then answers that he is in "a relationship" and continues to practice safe sex. There is a cut to a shot of Rachel's mother looking relieved. This maneuver shows what is for many antihomophobic spectators a difficult and problematic moment. Deciding *not* to be out and *not* perform and inhabit his queerness at that moment was a worthwhile compromise in the face of his professional work as an AIDS educator dealing with adolescents in a public school. It can also be understood, at least in part, as a moment of Latino allegiance, where queerness is displaced by the mark of ethnicity. Understanding this disidentification with his queerness as a disservice to queers or his own queer identity would be erroneous in that these shuttlings and displacements are survival strategies that intersectional subjects, subjects who are caught and live between different minoritarian communities, must practice frequently if they are to keep their residences in different subcultural spheres.

Episode thirteen focuses on Pedro's returning home to Miami and his best friend Alex. The homecoming is cut short when Pedro becomes sick. Zamora, in a post–*Real World* interview, explained that he had wanted to show it all, the good days and the bad days.[24] Representing the totality of living with AIDS was very important for his ethics of the self, his performance of being a self *for* others. That episode gives a family history and background. Pedro emigrated to the United States in the Mariel boat lift in 1980. He lost his mother to cancer at the age of fifteen, a tragedy that rocked his family. His family is represented as a very typical blue-collar Cuban-American family. Cuban-Americans, especially Miami Cubans, are associated with right-wing politics and values. It is thus important to see this family embrace their son and brother without hesitation. The image of Cuban-Americans loving, accepting, and being proud of a gay son complicates the map of *latinidad* that is most available within U.S. media. The better-known map that positions Cubans on the far right and Chicanos on the far left, while demographically founded, is nonetheless a reductive depiction of *latinidad.*

Episode sixteen depicts Pedro's bout with pneumonia that eventually leaves him hospitalized. The housemates experience a feeling of helplessness that is common in support communities for people with AIDS. By the next episode, Pedro is out of the hospital and accompanies the rest of the cast on a trip to Hawaii. By the twentieth and final episode, Pedro has become very close to Cory, Pam, and Judd. The cast is shown moving out of the Lombard Street flat.

The second-to-last episode, episode nineteen, points out the restraints that the show's producers put on Zamora's performances and the way in which the young Cuban-American responded to them. Pedro's romance became the major romance of the show; Sean never fell out of the picture the way Norman's and Beth's partners and flirtations did. Sean became part of Pedro's quotidian reality. Both made their presence continuously known in the San Francisco flat. A few weeks into their relationship, Sean proposed marriage to Pedro and Pedro accepted. In response, the show's other "star" presence, Puck, decided to one-up the queer couple by proposing marriage to his new girlfriend Toni. Puck stands as proof that not all counterpublics challenge the way in which the social is organized by the dominant culture. Puck's counterpublic is a juvenile version of rugged individualism; it represents a sort of soft anarchism that relativizes all political struggles as equivalents to his own exhaustive self-absorption. The competing modes of counterpublicity between Pedro and Puck eventually contributed to the breakdown in the domestic space that concluded with Puck's being asked to leave.

Episode nineteen tracks Pedro's and Puck's respective romances. Pedro's queerness is played against Puck's heterosexuality. The episode crosscuts between the two pairings. One questions the producer's rationale for juxtaposing Puck and Toni's romantic relationship with Pedro and Sean's commitment ceremony. Because Puck was ejected from the house, producers continued to film his encounters with his former housemates Cory, Rachel, and Judd. But except for this penultimate episode, there had been no presentation of Puck independent of his housemates.

Early in the episode, Sean and Pedro are shown in bed together as they lie on top of each other and plan their commitment ceremony. To MTV's credit, there has never been any scene of queer sociality like it on television. The scene of two gay men of color, both HIV positive, in bed together as they plan what is the equivalent of a marriage is like none that was then or now imaginable on television. The transmission of this image throughout the nation and the world is a valuable instance of counterpublicity. Edited within this scene are individual video bites by both participants. Sean explains that

> [b]eing with Pedro, someone who is so willing to trust and love and sort of be honest with, is refreshing. I think that knowing that Pedro does have an AIDS diagnosis and has been getting sick makes me recognize the need to be here right now. I know that one of us may get sick at sometime but [it is this] underlying understanding or this underlying feeling that makes it a lot easier.

Sean's statement and his performance in front of the video camera explain their reason for having a formal bonding ceremony as being a response to a radically refigured temporality in the face of AIDS. This, too, is an important instance of nationally broadcast counterpublic theater that provides an important opportunity for the mass public to glimpse different life-worlds than the one endorsed by the dominant ideology.

Yet, the power of this image and Sean's statement is dulled when the program cuts to its next scene. The gay coupling scene is followed by Puck and Toni's coupling ritual. Puck, in a voice-over, announces that he and Toni are made for each other, that they are, in fact, "a matched pair." They go window-shopping for a wedding ring and Toni eyes a ring that she likes; Puck scolds her and tells her that the window item is a cocktail ring, not a traditional wedding ring. He then offers to buy her a tie clip instead. (This footage is of mere window-shopping; later, the other couple is shown actually selecting bands.) Sean's voice-over is narratively matched with the playful Toni who explains that "[w]hen I first met Puck he was stinking and looking for a mate. I think we're in love. I know we're in love." Whereas Sean and Pedro are preparing for an actual ceremony, Toni and Puck are shown hanging out. Toni and Puck are not planning any sort of ceremony. The producers' strategy of matching the story lines and making them seem equivalent is resolved by crosscutting the commitment ceremony with one of Puck's soapbox derby races. Toni is shown cheering Puck on as he races his green boxcar.

Since the inception of *The Real World,* its producers have always hoped for a romance to erupt on the set between cast members. That has yet to happen.[25] In lieu of such a relationship, the producers hope for an interesting relationship between a cast member and outsider. Sean and Pedro's romance emerged early on as the show's most significant relationship. I am arguing that the series producers were unable to let a queer coupling, especially one as radical as Sean and Pedro's, to stand as the show's actual romance. Pedro's and Sean's individual performances and the performance of their relationship were narratively undermined by a strategy of weak multicultural crosscutting that was calibrated to dampen the radical charge that Pedro and Sean gave *The Real World.*

Despite these efforts by the show's producers to diminish the importance of Pedro and Sean's relationship, the ceremony itself stands as an amazingly powerful example of publicly performing an ethics of the self while simultaneously theatricalizing a queer counterpublic sphere.

The ceremony begins with a shot of a densely populated flat. Sean and Pedro are toasted by Eric, a friend of the couple who has not appeared on any previous episodes, and who delivers a touching toast:

> It gives me a lot of pleasure and I see it as a real pleasure to speak on behalf of Sean and Pedro and to them. In your love you remind us that life is about now and love is about being there for one another. It is with real bravery that you open your hearts *to each other* and I think it's with real hope that you promise your lives to each other. *We stand with you* defiantly and bravely and with real hope. To the adorable couple. (My emphasis)

This toast is followed by equally elegant statements by both Pedro and Sean. Eric's statement is significant because it marks the way in which Pedro and Sean's being for themselves ("to each other") is, simultaneously, a being for others ("We stand with you"). This ceremony is like none that has ever been viewed on commercial television. It is a moment of counterpublic theater. The commitment ceremony not only inspires the gathering of spectators at the ceremony to stand together bravely, defiantly, and with hope, but also, beyond the walls of the Lombard Street flat and beyond the relatively progressive parameters of San Francisco, it inspires a world of televisual spectators.

The Real World is overrun by queers. Queer bonds are made manifest in ways that have never been available on cable or broadcast television. Pedro's insistence on mastering the show's format through his monologues, domestic interventions, and continuous pedagogy are relaxed in the sequence just described. Here the public sphere is reimagined by bringing a subaltern counterpublic into representation. The real world is overrun by queers—queers who speak about those things that are terrifying and ennobling about a queer and racialized life-world. The commitment ceremony sequence in many ways sets up the show's closure. Puck's antics, crosscut and stacked next to the commitment ceremony, are narratively positioned to lessen the queer spin put on *The Real World* by Pedro. Such a strategy is concurrent with the show's pluralist ethos. Queer commitments, energies, and politics are never quite left to stand alone.

The way Puck's relationship is used to relativize and diminish the emotional and political impact of Pedro and Sean's relationship is reminiscent of Pedro's selection to be included in the cast *with and in contrast to* Rachel, the young Republican Latina. Again, the ideologically bold move of representing an activist such as Pedro as a representative of *latinidad* is counterbalanced by a reactionary Latina. The fact that Rachel and Pedro later bond as Latinos, despite their ideological differences, is narratively satisfying, producing a sense of hope for the spectator invested in pan-Latino politics.

The performance of a commitment ceremony itself might be read as an aping of heterosexual relationships. Such a reading would miss some important points. In a voice-over before the ceremony, Pedro discusses the need to "risk" being with Sean. He points to the ways in which this relationship, within the confines of his tragically abbreviated temporality, forms a new space of self, identity, and relationality. It is, in Foucault's terms, a new form. The couple form, crystallized as the bourgeois heterosexual dyad, is shattered and reconfigured. Indeed, this is a disidentification with the couple form. When one is queer and knows that his or her loved one is dying, the act of "giving oneself" to another represents an ethics of the self that does not cohere with the prescribed and normative coupling practices that make heterosexuals and some lesbians and gay men want to marry. Pedro and Sean's ceremonial bonding is *not* about aping bourgeois heterosexuality; rather, it is the enacting of a new mode of sociality. Foucault, in an often-cited interview on friendship, suggested that we understand homosexuality not so much as a desire, but rather as something that is *desirable*. He explains that we must "work at becoming homosexual and not be obstinate in recognizing that we are."[26] Homosexuality is desirable because a homosexual way of life allows us to reimagine sociality. The homosexual needs to "invent from A to Z a relationship that is formless" and eventually to arrive at a "multiplicity of relations."[27]

Becoming homosexual, for Foucault, would then be a political project, a social movement of sorts, that would ultimately help us challenge repressive gender hierarchies and the structural underpinnings of institutions. Thus, mark Sean and Pedro's union as something new, a new form that is at the same time formless from the vantage point of established state hierarchies.[28] The new form that Sean and Pedro's performances of self brings into view is one that suggests worlds of possibility for the minoritarian subject who experiences multiple forms of domination within larger systems of governmentality.

When considering Zamora's lifework one is struck by his accomplishments, interventions within the dominant public sphere that had real effects on individuals (such as the woman from South Carolina whose letter was cited at the beginning of this chapter), and other interventions as an activist. Zamora tested positive for HIV while still in high school, a few years after he arrived in the United States with his parents and two siblings in 1980 with some one hundred thousand other Cuban refugees who sailed to Florida in the Mariel boat lift. His activism began not long after he tested positive for the virus. Zamora testified before the Presidential Commission on AIDS and twice before congressional committees, took part in a public service ad campaign for the Centers for Disease Control and Prevention, and was appointed to a Florida government panel on AIDS. He also gave many interviews in the print and electronic media. I first encountered Zamora before his tenure on MTV. I saw him and his father on a local Spanish-language television news program in south Florida while I was visiting my parents during college. As I sat in the living room with my parents, I marveled at the televisual spectacle of this young man and his father, both speaking a distinctly Cuban Spanish, on television, talking openly about AIDS, safe sex, and homosexuality. I was struck because this was something new; it was a new formation, a being for others. I imagined countless other living rooms within the range of this broadcast and I thought about the queer children who might be watching this program at home with their parents. This is the point where I locate something other than the concrete interventions in the public sphere. Here is where I see the televisual spectacle leading to the possibility of new counterpublics, new spheres of possibility, and the potential for the reinvention of the world from A to Z.

Chapter 7

Performing Disidentity: Disidentification as a Practice of Freedom

There are the limits to the strategies, tactics, and performativities that I have been exploring. There is also more to say about disidentification, its nuances, and its intricacies. This chapter will consider questions of publicity and privacy. It will also further elaborate the concept of counterpublicity. Questions that emerge around the public/private thematic will lead me to interrogate "the place" of multiculturalism within the politics of disidentification. I will follow these threads from the preceding chapter on Pedro Zamora's work by considering two other cultural workers (one a conceptual artist, the other a transgender sex worker turned evangelist) who shared similar identity coordinates with Zamora and, more important, employed disidentificatory performances to do their work.

By "limits" I mean something other than failures. Instead, I want to call attention to some of the material and psychic forces that work against the disidentifying subject. I wish to disarm a *pre*critical celebratory aura that might attach itself not only to disidentification but also to some of this book's other key words: *hybridity, queerness, migrancy, autoethnography,* and so forth. Let me be clear about one thing: disidentification is about cultural, material, and psychic survival. It is a response to state and global power apparatuses that employ systems of racial, sexual, and national subjugation. These routinized protocols of subjugation are brutal and painful. Disidentification is about managing and negotiating historical trauma and systemic violence. I have gone to great lengths to explicate, render, and imagine complicated strategies and tactics that enact minoritarian subjectivity. I have wanted to posit that such processes of self-actualization come into discourse as a response to ideologies that discriminate against, demean, and attempt to destroy components of subjectivity that do not conform or respond to narratives of universalization and normalization. The disidentifying subject is not a flier who escapes the atmospheric force field of ideology. Neither is she a trickster figure who can effortlessly come out on top every time. Sometimes disidentification is insufficient.

Failed Transformations

In the Introduction, I wrote that disidentification is not an appropriate strategy for all minoritarian subjects all of the time. *The Transformation* (1996), a follow-up by Susana Aiken and Carlos Aparicio to their powerful 1990 documentary *The Salt Mines* (1990), will serve as an example to help me illustrate the "limits of disidentification."

The Salt Mines worked for me as something of an antidote to Jennie Livingston's famous documentary *Paris Is Burning* (1991). I programmed the film for a queer film collective I worked with in North Carolina in the early 1990s. *Paris Is Burning* presented a highly sensationalized rendering of Latino and black transvestite and transsexual communities. *The Salt Mines* and *The Transformation,* two texts that have received far less critical consideration, have offered a narration of transgender communities of color in New York City that has resisted the impulse to glamorize the experience in the way that *Paris Is Burning* does.[1] Poverty and disease, for instance, have not been sacrificed in these videos for the sake of spectacle and style, as they were in Livingston's film. Thus, I think of the Aiken and Aparicio videotapes as antidotes of sorts to the overexposed *Paris Is Burning.* They offer a much starker and less glamorous rendering of the minoritarian subject: specifically Latino transsexuals. The "salt mines" of the video's title is taken from the name given by its inhabitants to the parking lot of a New York City salt reserve that had been converted into a makeshift transgender village. The video documents the lives of different transvestites and transsexuals who lived in the broken-down garbage trucks at the salt reserve lot. This community of homeless queers of color is not shown voguing in spectacular balls. Instead, the video depicts the queens cooking hamburgers over a campfire, shooting up female hormones, and "reading" each other. Many of the salt mine's population are on crack and a large number are sex workers. Beyond these activities, the queens of the salt mines do quite a bit of talking. One of the best talkers is one of the video's most engaging documentary subjects: Sara. Sara is a transgendered subject who was born male and has been shooting female hormones over the course of many years. Sara and the other queens of *The Salt Mines* are preyed on by missionaries who are interested in winning their souls. The queens are highly skeptical of these mostly white evangelists whose notion of salvation is decidedly antiqueer and homophobic.

The Transformation begins with a letter sent to Aiken and Aparicio by Sara, who now, four years after the events depicted in *The Salt Mines,* has relocated to Texas and is going by the name Ricardo. Ricardo is Sara's male birth name. He has taken on this name in the same fashion that he has taken on a heterosexual identification and a conversion to fundamentalist Christianity. Ricardo has even gone so far as to marry a woman from his church group. Even though Sara had breasts and had undergone years of guerrilla hormone therapy, he is trying to masculinize himself to fit into his new community. This masculinization includes having his implants removed, cutting his hair, and renouncing his homosexual desire.

His job, it would seem, is to be a good husband to his wife and work with the white male evangelical soul hunter who snared him. He works as an assistant and a walking "example." In the course of the documentary, Ricardo and the white man go after two of his former friends from *The Salt Mines* and fail to convert either. One queen, who has just gotten out of jail, rejects the evangelical proposition, explaining that she can never pretend to live as a man. The other queen is no longer living on the street and has returned to her family, who now accept her as a sister, daughter, and aunt. Ricardo strikes out in both his attempts to convert his former friends.

It is not difficult to understand why Ricardo has made this transformation. The chief reason is his health status. Ricardo was living with AIDS. His already tragically shortened life span would have been even more painful if he had continued to live on the street in poverty and malnourished. His choice to leave the street for the relative warmth and comfort of the materially supportive church community is an act of survival that can possibly be understood as a disidentification. Ricardo worked with and on the ideology of born-again Christianity, attempting to benefit from its rewards (material support, supportive communities, companionship) while resisting total cooptation by that discourse. Ricardo's disidentification, like other forms, entailed a series of negotiations. The cost of Ricardo's "transformation" was his breasts, his homosexual desire, and his queerness. He tried his best to perform normative heterosexuality. The interviews with his wife and other members of the Texas community indicated that he had made serious inroads—he was accepted and nurtured. Yet at what cost? It is clear that Ricardo compromised a great deal to reformulate his identity into a form that was legible to and compatible with born-again Christianity.

Yet, Ricardo's attempt at disidentification failed. The video ends with a chilling monologue in which a tired and infirm Ricardo seems especially bitter and sad. His final wish is not to appear ridiculous to others in his illness. He admits that he never successfully negotiated his desire—that he missed the touch of other men tremendously. This last monologue was recorded shortly before his death. The viewer cannot help but feel the stinging sadness of Ricardo's life—compromising his self to the dominant ideology cost too much. The sadness is underscored by a juxtaposition of images of Sara in *The Salt Mines* laughing and indignant in the face of overarching adversity and heartbroken Ricardo's final video monologue.

Sara/Ricardo was not a queer activist like Pedro Zamora, but a traditional documentary subject—which is not to say that he did not, like Zamora, attempt to mess with the protocols of documentary practice. Ricardo's church knew of the previous documentary and Sara's role in it and attempted to use the video artists Aiken and Aparicio to spread "Ricardo's message/example" in a new documentary. Aiken and Aparicio took the church and Ricardo's bait, yet clearly had no intention of being reeled in. Instead of chronicling the triumph and salvation of Ricardo's new life, they recorded the way in which he failed to convert his fellow "salt mines" alumni, the difficulties of his marriage, his persistent yet stifled desire for other men, and the sadness of his death. Ricardo's disidentification was not in the service of a larger practice of freedom like the disidentifications enacted by Zamora. He disidentified with the church that used him, the "salt mines" community, and his own desire as a man who desired other men. He attempted to refashion himself in an attempt to negotiate a homophobic public sphere and a world of poverty that would accelerate his illness.

Any comparison of Sara/Ricardo with Zamora requires a consideration of the class differential between the two. Both emigrated in the Mariel boat lift of 1980. Zamora, a small boy at the time, was raised in the working-class Cuban community of Hialeah. Less is known about Sara/Ricardo. We do know that he came of age in Cuba, and it is likely that he was one of the many homosexuals who were ejected from the island during the boat lift. His immigration eventually led to the life of homelessness depicted in *The Salt Mines.* Although Zamora was essentially working-class, he had access to channels of representation that Sara/Ricardo could never have dreamed of. Zamora's relative class privilege afforded him opportunities and possibilities denied to the older immigrant. It might be hypothesized that strategies and practices that constitute disidentification are, for the most part, more readily available to subjects whose class privilege gives them access to systems of representation.

The story this chapter tells shifts to yet another Cuban-American. Felix Gonzalez-Torres immigrated to the United States in the 1970s via Spain and was able, unlike both Zamora and Sara/Ricardo, to pursue a higher education. He rose to fame in the art world during the late 1980s. He died at the zenith of his fame in January 1996. Gonzalez-Torres rejected the general strictures of identity and what he understood as the constraints of multiculturalism. Sara/Ricardo had no access to the spheres of publicity and culture that Zamora or Gonzalez-Torres operated within. Yet, all three Cuban-Americans, operating in vastly different fields of television, evangelical religion, and the New York City art world, all used disidentificatory performances to remake the self. Whereas Zamora worked to publicize his minoritarian identity within the dominant public sphere while disidentifying with his televisual "Real World" and Sara/Ricardo denied and rejected his minoritarian identification in hopes of crafting a majoritarian self, Gonzalez-Torres rejected the very tenets of identity. Instead, through his disidentificatory performances of self, he achieved what I would provisionally call *disidentity.* I am not positing disidentity as a sort of "anti-identity." Instead, I offer the concept as a heuristic example that aims to help explain a subject such as Gonzalez-Torres, who rejected any route understanding of "identity" but nonetheless called for what I see as a *reconstructed* identity politics. The artist's particular version of identity politics critiqued simplistic pluralism and weak multiculturalism as it called for an engagement with the *question of identity.* Although any of the artist's images might invoke a queer or Latino life-world for minoritarian cognoscenti, such meanings, while central, are not the only available ones. Identity is never pinned downed by representation in Gonzalez-Torres's work; his disidentificatory strategies of cultural production eschew representation for performance, specifically, disidentificatory performance.

Identity against Itself: Felix Gonzalez-Torres and the Limits of Multiculturalism

Like Sara/Ricardo and Pedro Zamora, Gonzalez-Torres was queer, *cubano,* and a person living with AIDS. His work never invoked identity elements in any obvious way. He depended on a minimalist symbolic lexicon that disidentified with minimalism's own self-referentiality. Gonzalez-Torres's minimalism evoked meaning and employed connotation, using the minimalist style to speak to a larger social order and to expanded issues of identity. His refunctioning of minimalism enabled him to rethink identity and instead opt for a disidentity.

I am not the first to mark his nuanced relationship to identity. Robert Storr, for instance, has stated:

> In an art world too often obsessed with simplistic affirmations of origin or essence, Gonzalez-Torres eschews the role of Latin [*sic*] artist or queer artist or even activist artist, while using everything that his experience as a Cuban-born, politically committed gay man has taught him. What he has learned is that in America's presently chauvinist climate, loudly declaiming who you are frequently preempts showing an audience what you see.[2]

Although the artist does not speak from the space of an identity, his work is influenced and shaped by a vision that is always structured through his own multiple horizons of experience. This is true of almost anyone, but in the case of Gonzalez-Torres one needs to consider the ways in which his horizons of experience have been debased and stigmatized within the dominant channels of representation. By refusing to simply invoke identity, and instead to connote it, he is refusing to participate in a particular representational economy. He does not counter negative representations with positive ones, but instead absents himself and his work from this dead-end street. One need not turn to art critics to verify this point; the artist himself spoke eloquently on the subject. Indeed, in all his work, interviews, teaching, and public lectures, he actively rebelled against any reductive understanding of how his identity affects his cultural production. In his response to interviewer and fellow artist Tim Rollins, who asked about the the "content" of his work, Gonzalez-Torres articulated his own understanding of how identity formation is more complicated than most familiar models of multiculturalism:

> TIM [ROLLINS]: I've heard a lot of grumbling, Felix, about the lack of an overt political or Latino content in your work.
>
> FELIX [GONZALEZ-TORRES]: (*laughing*) Well, I just want to start by saying that the "maracas" sculptures are next! I'm not a good token. I don't wear the right colors. I have my own agenda. Some people want to promote multiculturalism as long as they are the promoters, the circus directors. We

> have an assigned role that's very specific, very limited. As in a glass vitrine, "we"—the "other"—have to accomplish ritual, exotic performances to satisfy the needs of the majority. This parody is becoming boring very quickly. Who is going to define my culture? It's not just Borges and García Marquez, but also Gertrude Stein and Freud and Guy Debord—they are all part of my formation.[3]

Gonzalez-Torres foregrounded the complexity of contemporary hybrid identities. Given his Latino ethnicity, a sector of the arts community expected his work to be influenced and shaped by a strong identification with Latin American masters. Identifications with a very queer Anglo-American modernist, the father of psychoanalysis, or a French high theorist of the spectacle are not, according to the critics the interviewer invoked earlier in their dialogue, proper identifications for the artist.

When Gonzalez-Torres, out of frustration, asked, "Who is going to define my culture?" he was expressing a view shared by all the cultural producers considered in this study. The roles that are available within dominant culture for Latino/a and other minority identities are narrow, static, and fixed. These identity constructs are more often than not exotic rituals and performances commissioned by mainstream culture. These accounts of mainstream identity are, in most instances, unable to account for the specificity of black and queer lives or any other collision of two or more minority designations. Gonzalez-Torres's art insisted on speaking queerly and speaking Latino in ways that were oblique. Consequently, his work functioned as a formidable obstacle to facile conceptions of identity. He elaborated forms of representation premised on *invisibility.* Gonzalez-Torres invokes a disidentity that is predicated on transparency and the everyday instead of the more familiar models of minority identity that invoke exotic colors and rituals.

The interviewer's suggestion that Gonzalez-Torres's work is apolitical is a charge leveled at many minority cultural producers who do not critique the dominant culture through predictable routes. Gonzalez-Torres's work enables a discussion of the way in which dominant publicity, especially the interpellating call of multiculturalism—or, as I will specify, reductive multicultural pluralism—is challenged and obstructed by a series of disidentificatory maneuvers that are calibrated to forge an activist anti-identitarian counterpublicity.

Gonzalez-Torres's response to Rollins's question betrays a frustration with the way in which multicultural pluralism disarms the politics of specificity. Multicultural pluralism's rhetoric of inclusion homogenizes difference. Difference becomes part of the race, class, and gender mantra, essentially a form of sloganeering. John Guillory, in his study of the politics of canonization, identifies all the problems of the mantra in relation to the politics of canonization:

> [T]he ubiquitous invocation of these categories of social identity continually defers their theoretical discrimination from each other on the behalf of whatever political work is being done by pronouncing their names in the same breath as

> practice. But what work is that? What political work requires the deferral of theory, despite the fact that one must always gesture to some future, as yet unelaborated, analysis of the *relations* between race, class and gender?[4]

The mantra thus smoothly positions minority identity designations within a syntax of equivocations that defers the work of theorizing relations of power. In this book, I have insisted that critical hermeneutics and political projects that are not sufficiently intersectional are grossly inadequate to the project of mapping and analyzing the social. Optics that are not sufficiently intersectional are thus blinded by severe cultural myopia. Intersectionality should not be confused with multiculturalism. Intersectionality is primarily concerned with the *relations* between different minoritarian coordinates (which include the "mantra" but also allow for nodes of difference that cannot be anticipated). Intersectionality does not, once again, defer analyses, as Guillory suggests multiculturalism does. Instead, it insists on a theoretical apparatus that is located in the "now."

This is not automatically to foreclose the project of multiculturalism. In fact, a crucial distinction needs to be posited between multicultural pluralism (or weak multiculturalism) and what Wahneema Lubiano has referred to as a "radical" multiculturalism. Lubiano admits that multiculturalism can and has often been appropriated by reactionary and liberal ideologies. She nonetheless locates a kernel of transformative political possibility in multiculturalism, leading to a politics that she describes as radical multiculturalism. Lubiano understands the ways in which elites can hijack the form of multiculturalism but maintains:

> If elites manage business as usual and can't call it multiculturalism, they will simply call it something else. We cannot give up the ground because of what they can do in the name of the ground on which we have chosen to fight. The process of normalization or the work of oppositional gestures is an ongoing dynamic of our system and, of course, multiculturalism can be used to continue such management. Radical multiculturalism, however, turns its attention to demystifying just such management and to fighting it. Contestation is the driving force of such a dynamic.[5]

Lubiano's radical multiculturalism is conceived as a counterattack to systems of normalization, as a management of oppositional gestures. For Lubiano, this active, activist, and politicized reconceptualization of multiculturalism is a reaction against corporate multiculturalism. Her writing is designed to be a disidentification with liberalism's outmoded narrative of multiculturalism. Lubiano's narrative of multiculturalism keeps political possibility in motion. Furthermore, unlike the version of multiculturalism that Guillory discusses, radical multiculturalism is focused on the relational or intersectional aspects. Guillory's main reservation about the mantra is that it stands in for politics and disables analysis. Lubiano pushes for a mobilization that synchronizes and choreographs different oppositional gestures, gestures that include different modalities of reading. It also calls attention to the conflicts and strife between identity components, refusing to whitewash such complexities. These writers make the important claim for methodologies that enable critique. Thus, a critical multiculturalism is a far cry from reductive multicultural pluralism. I understand disidentification in a similar fashion and argue that it too offers a system of volitional and semivolitional gestures whose ethos, while always survivalist, is also *critical.* It would be useful to reconsider the term *disidentification* at this juncture.

Disidentification, Social Theory, and the Public/Private Binarism

A question needs to be posed in relation to the theoretical project that this book puts forth: How does one get from discursive analysis to counterpublicity? Disidentificatory performances (here I mean the work of the artists I read *and* my own readings) resist the social matrix of dominant publicity by exposing the rhetorical/ideological context of state power. To elucidate this point, it is useful to return to the work of Michel Pêcheux, one of the conceptual and philosophical linchpins of this book's theoretical apparatus. Slavoj Žižek, one of Pêcheux's most interesting commentators, elaborates the relation between discourse analysis and state power:

> Michel Pêcheux . . . gave a strict linguistic turn to Althusser's theory of interpellation. His work is centered on the discursive mechanisms that generate the "evidence" of Sense. That is to say, one of the fundamental stratagems of ideology is the reference to some self-evidence—"Look, you can see for yourself how things are!" "Let the facts speak for themselves" is perhaps the arch-statement of ideology—the point being, precisely, the facts *never* "speak for themselves" but are always *made to speak* to a network of discursive devices. Suffice to recall the notorious anti-abortion film *The Silent Scream*—we "see" a foetus which "defends" itself, which "cries," and so on, yet what we "don't see" in this very act of seeing is that we "see" all this against the background of a discursively pre-constituted space. Discourse analysis is perhaps at its strongest in answering this precise question: when a racist Englishman says "There are too many Pakistanis on our streets!", *how—from what place—does he "see" this*—that is, how is his symbolic space structured so that he can perceive the fact of a Pakistani strolling along a London street as a disturbing surplus? That is to say, here one must bear in mind Lacan's motto that *nothing is lacking in the real*: every perception of a lack or a surplus ("not enough of this," "too much of that") always involves a symbolic universe.[6]

Žižek's gloss on Pêcheux assists in the visualization of the "work" that disidentification does within the social. Disidentification permits the subject of ideology to contest the interpellations of the dominant ideology. Thus, a subject who is hailed by the ideology cops' cry of "hey, you" may respond with a *tactical misrecognition* like the one that Molina offers Valentín in Manuel Puig's *Kiss of the Spider Woman.* Valentín commands his gay cell mate to "Be a man!" Molina, a seasoned *loca,* responds to his command by exclaiming: "A man! Where do you see a man!" Such a tactical misrecognition permits a subject to demystify the dominant publicity, exposing it as a "discursively pre-constituted" space that often maintains strict and oppressive hierarchies within the social. Counterpublicity is thus born from a modality of disidentification that is essentially an act of *tactical misrecognition* that serves as a bulwark against the effects of dominant publicity.

The performances and installations of Gonzalez-Torres achieve a tactical misrecognition of dominant publicity's public/private binary. Gonzalez-Torres was a shrewd tactician and an excellent philosopher of publicity. Nancy Fraser, a leading U.S. philosopher of the public sphere, succinctly explicates the ways in which the public/private binary bolsters the dominant public. She explains that the public/private split "enclave[s] certain matters in specialized discursive arenas so as to shield them from general debate." She concludes: "This usually works to the advantage of dominant groups and individuals and to the disadvantage of their subordinates."[7] Fraser's proposition is tailored to speak to the ways in which the public/private binarism has been used to historically "enclave" women's experience and perpetuate their subordination. Gonzalez-Torres shared these feminist concerns, but his own horizon of experience was that of a gay man—a gay man whose identity was, from the vantage point of the dominant culture, a "don't ask, don't tell" issue. He was also a person living with AIDS who had lost his adored lover, Ross, in the pandemic. Gonzalez-Torres refused to limit his grief to a privatized self.

The artist's interrogation of a public/private binary also served as a critique of the universalized individual subject. Mónica Amor has read the artist's work, especially his word sculptures that represent public and personal dates and words in seemingly random order, as providing an "indiscriminate intersection of both public and private" that "subverts the Western myth of a self-sufficient subjectivity," which allows her to conclude that the artist suggests that we are "historical and cultural products as well as individuals."[8] The artist often worked with oblique images that were strategically invisible to the hostile public but visible to those inside different counterpublics.[9] These oblique images share similar aesthetic philosophies with the art of ACT-UP and other queer/ HIV/AIDS-activist groups. Douglas Crimp's reading of the famous Silence = Death logo outlines some of the strategies of that movement:

> Our emblem's significance depends on foreknowledge of the use of the pink triangle as the marker of gay men in concentration camps, its appropriation by the gay movement to remember a suppressed history of our oppression, and, now, an inversion of its positioning (men in the death camps wore a pink triangle that pointed down; SILENCE = DEATH's points up). SILENCE = DEATH declares that silence about the oppression and annihilation of gay people, *then and now*, must be broken as a matter of our survival. As historically problematic as an analogy of AIDS and the death camps is, it is also deeply resonant for gay men and lesbians, especially insofar as the analogy is already mediated by the gay movement's adoption of the pink triangle. But it is not merely what SILENCE = DEATH says, but also how it looks, that gives it its particular force. The power of this equation under a triangle is the compression of its connotation into a logo, a logo so striking that you ultimately *have* to ask, if you don't already know,

> "What does that mean?" And it is the answers we are constantly called upon to give to others—small, everyday direct actions—that make SILENCE = DEATH signify beyond a community of lesbian and gay cognoscenti.[10]

The work of Gonzalez-Torres was in sync with many of these AIDS activist postmodern strategies. Consider the billboards that Gonzalez-Torres installed throughout New York City depicting an empty and unmade bed, two pillows marked with the indention of two absent heads. This vague, roundabout image, when considered from a Latino or queer perspective (to name only two communities under siege, composed of people who Crimp described as cognoscenti), is a comment on the current crisis that shapes such identities. For some spectators, what is suggested is nothing but a mundane image from everyday life. Yet, there is something about the image, blown up and relocated in the public sphere, that casts a shadow of enigma over the picture. Spectators out of the "know" are put in the position where they "*have* to ask, if [they] don't already know, 'What does that mean?'" For others, those touched by the catastrophe of HIV and other genocidal epidemics, the image is an allusion to the loss, absence, and negation that blankets queer lives, Latino/a lives, and many other communities at risk or people who share this structure of feeling. The billboards powerfully challenge notions of publicity and privacy. The image, repeated throughout the city, is one that represents not a presence, an identity, but instead an absence, a lacuna, a void gesturing to something valuable, loved, and missing. *Private loss is restructured and becomes public art.*

The "cognoscenti" who might "get" the way in which the image speaks to the AIDS epidemic are not subjects who simply "identify" with the image. There is in fact nothing to identify with—no figure, no text, no gesture, barely an object, only an absence. What is evoked is a "structure of feeling" that cuts through certain Latino and queer communities but is in no way exclusive to *any* identitarian group. I am suggesting that the image connotes a *disidentity,* a version of self that is crafted through something other than rote representational practices, produced through an actual disidentification with such practices and the public/private binary.

Other arts, especially painting and photography, are, as Peggy Phelan has noted, "increasingly drawn to performance."[11] Gonzalez-Torres's project utilized performance as a central element. Actual live performances were sometimes included in his work. Yet, even when these performances were not at the center of his installations, the work called on the spectator to become an active participant in his project. The interaction of the spectator to the art object is, as Phelan put it, "essentially performative." This point is uniquely illustrated by Gonzalez-Torres's thematization of "the interactive exchange between the art object and viewer."[12] The artist's stacks of paper and his giant spills of candy, pieces of art that invite the spectators literally to take a piece of the work with them, call on the spectators to move and physically engage the art object. This is equally true on a more symbolic level as the artist's work takes the space of the gallery or museum, remakes it into a performance space, and asks the visitor to become an active interlocutor with the work.

Felix Gonzalez-Torres, *Untitled*, 1991. View of billboard. Photo by Peter Muscato. Dimensions variable. Gallery credit: As installed for the Museum of Modern Art, New York. "Projects 34: Felix Gonzalez-Torres," May 16–June 30, 1992, in twenty-four locations throughout New York City. Courtesy of the Andrea Rosen Gallery, New York. Collector credit: The Werner and Elaine Dannheisser Collection, on long-term loan to the Museum of Modern Art, New York.

An untitled installation by Gonzalez-Torres from 1991 serves as a glaring example of this movement toward performance and the restructuring of gallery space into performance space. The installation positions a dark young man, who is probably Latino, go-go dancing on a platform surrounded with lights.[13] He wears jockey shorts and a red T-shirt that he strips off during his routine. This Latino body, recontextualized within the space of the art gallery, disrupts its space. The dancer's performance is not the type of activity that usually would be glimpsed in a downtown New York gallery. This image would usually be available to the consumer of such spectacles in the Times Square area of New York, at clubs such as the Eros or the Gaiety Burlesque.[14] Gonzalez-Torres's installation is reminiscent of some of the queer pop art practices that Andy Warhol pioneered in the 1960s. Warhol's films brought Times Square hustlers to the realm of gallery art and art house cinema, and former hustlers such as Joe Dallesandro starred in many of his films from that period.[15] This recontextualization challenges the integrity of distinctions between lowbrow erotic entertainment and high culture. The queer life-worlds of the go-go palace and the Soho gallery are occluded. In this instance, through this sexy performance, queer identity is dis-organized and dis-placed.

The installation also provided a commentary on the location of *latinidad* in gay male culture. In commercialized gay male culture, bodies like those of the go-go boy on the platform are consumed in the privacy of home video screenings and in the semiprivacy of dark clubs such as the Eros.[16] Gonzalez-Torres's installation dislocates the Latino body from its standard location in gay male culture, at once revealing and deconstructing a fixed notion of the role of *latinidad* in queerness. It makes the privatized and compartmentalized desire for Latino/a bodies a public issue. It also functions as public sex act that publicizes queer sexual performance, elevating it from the position of private vice.

Gonzalez-Torres's work did not identify in clear or pronounced ways with the politics of AIDS and illness management *or* with the hyperstratification of art and the eroticized body of color. Yet, as the readings I have offered suggest, *he did exactly that,* which is to say that through his nimble practice of disidentifying with the public/private binary, he was able to perform activist politics. The negotiation between identification and counteridentification in the artist's work is, primarily, a mode of critical performativity, one that I am identifying as tactical misrecognition of the public/private grids that structure the social.

We can further track the disidentificatory impulse in his work if we consider the ways in which he deals with issues of exile and ethnos. His *Untitled (Madrid 1971)* is composed of two jigsaw puzzles in cellophane bags, stacked next to each other. The first jigsaw is the picture of the artist as a boy; next to him is a photo of a statue, what appears to be a monument, shot from the perspective of someone looking up, perhaps a child. Matched, these two images represent aspects of the artist's biography—in this instance, when he was separated from his parents at age nine so he could leave

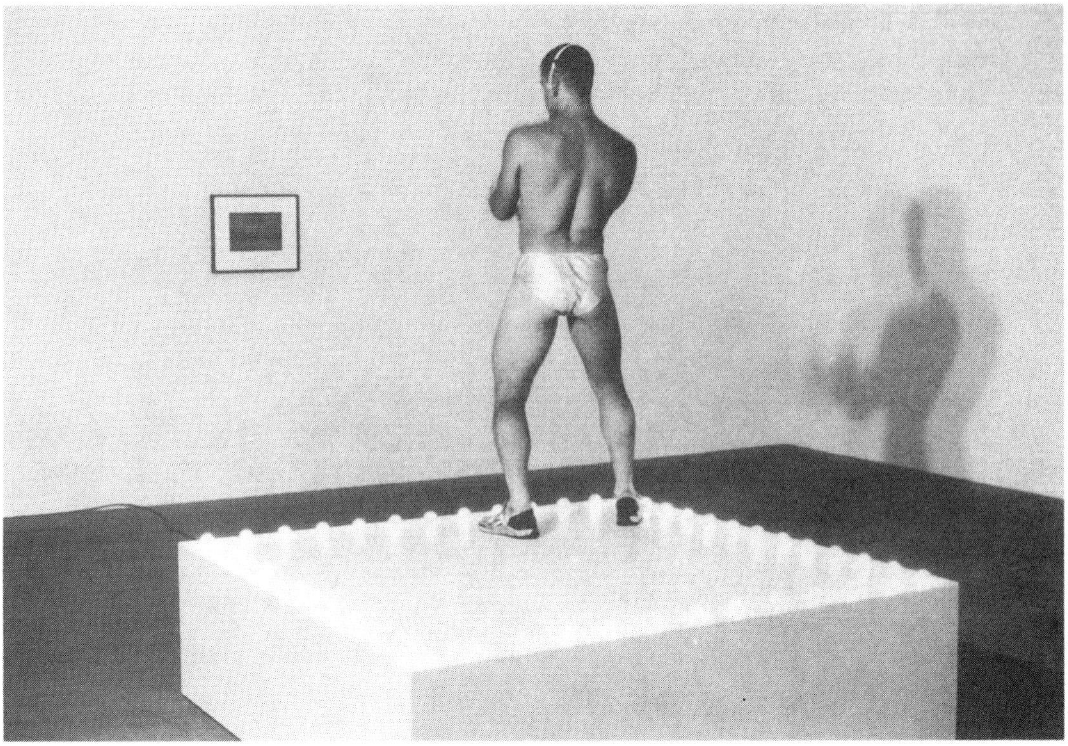

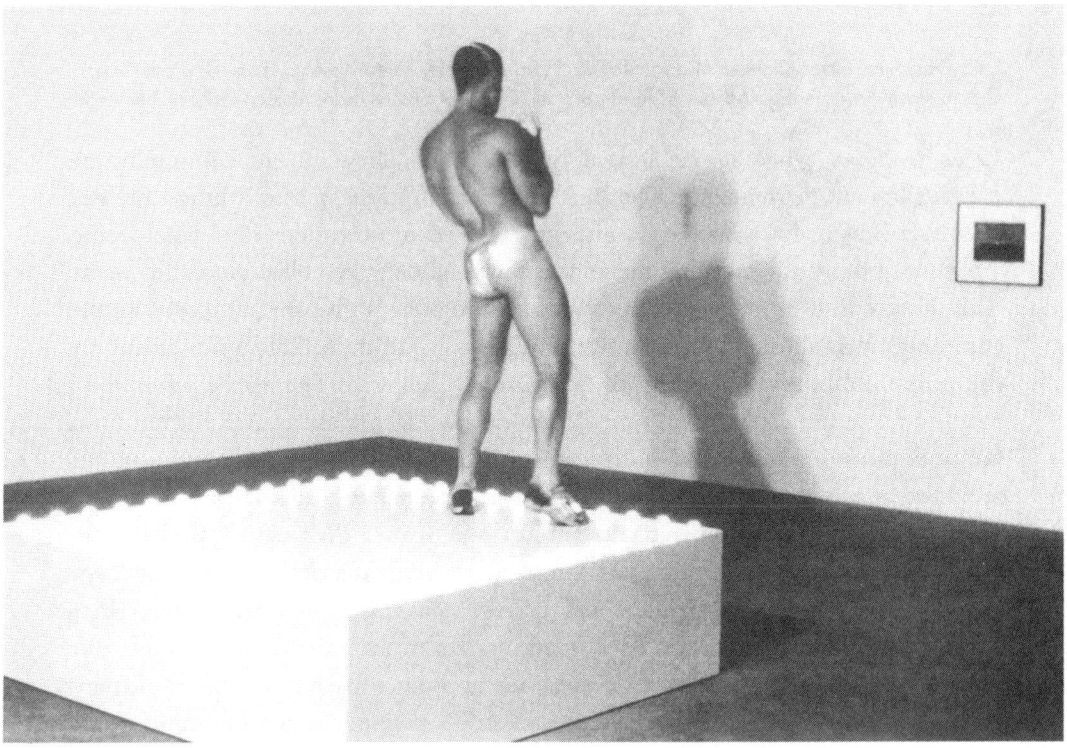

Felix Gonzalez-Torres, *Untitled (Go-Go Dancing Platform)*, 1991. Photo by Peter Muscato. 21½ x 72 x 72 inches. Courtesy of the Andrea Rosen Gallery. Installation view: Felix Gonzalez-Torres, "Every Week There Is Something Different," May 2–June 1, 1991. Week Two.

Felix Gonzalez-Torres, *Untitled (Madrid 1971)*, 1988. Photo by Peter Muscato. 15 x 18 inches. Two C-print jigsaw puzzles in plastic bags, and Letra set. Courtesy of the Andrea Rosen Gallery, New York.

Cuba for Spain, where he was housed by the church. These images connote memory's fragility and permanence. The small puzzles remind us of a few things: the ways in which images form memories and, in turn, memories themselves fall together. They foreground the fact that memory is always about the collection of fragments. The constellation of memory is also made through an active spectator who pushed pieces together, like a child with a puzzle. The image of the self alongside the imposing statue connotes the feeling of being small, helpless. The statue looks like a memorial to another place and time. Memorials work to make cogent the fictions of nationalism and individual national culture. The pairing of a photo of the artist as an innocent and sweet-looking boy next to a cold metal sculpture performs, through a calculus of contradiction, the vulnerability of a dismantling of the public/private binary. The piece gestures to the fashion in which one's identity is eclipsed by a system of national signs that do not constitute one's citizenship but instead one's alienation, displacement, and exile. This image speaks to exile and ethnicity in a voice that is evocative and suggestive. It does not announce itself as a cultural artifact. Instead, it renders queerness, ethnicity, and AIDS through a circuitous and roundabout fashion. These connotations are powerful ones that engage the spectators in a way that makes them into interactive interlocutors, half of a performance that is

Felix Gonzalez-Torres, *Untitled (Me and My Sister)*, 1988. Photo by Peter Muscato. 7½ x 9½ inches. C-print jigsaw puzzle in plastic bag. Courtesy of the Andrea Rosen Gallery, New York.

completed with the art object. Yet, I am not *implying* that these are the only available meanings. Amor has contended that "[t]he majority of his works are untitled, while a word in parenthesis suggests a meaning related to experiences of the artist's life, *but* always open and multivalent."[17]

Another piece, *Untitled (Me and My Sister),* is another small snapshot converted into a jigsaw puzzle. The image's black-and-white tones of gray mark it as being from the fifties or early sixties. The visual effect transports the spectator to another temporality and a different spatiality. Without announcing itself, this image becomes emblematic of exile, the lost home and territory, the lost childhood, and a gilded and fragile recollection of it. Private and individual ephemera are loaded with publicness, once again offsetting the public/private binarism. Identity, ethnic or exilic, is not rendered in these two pieces through representation. The images are obscure in their meaning, mediated through the jigsaw-puzzle effect and the plastic bag.

Storr and other critics have gestured to the many ways in which the artist rejected minoritized identity labels. This is certainly true, but it is not the end of the story. More than simply counteridentify/reject identity, Gonzalez-Torres's cultural production disidentified with the representational protocols of identity. Pieces like the one

Felix Gonzalez-Torres, *Untitled (Ross and Harry)*, 1991. Photo by Peter Muscato. 7½ x 9½ inches. C-print jigsaw puzzle in plastic bag. Courtesy of the Andrea Rosen Gallery, New York.

I have just described hail from the locus of an ethnic and exilic past but do not simply reproduce identity. Performance avoids reproductive economies, and the disidentificatory performances of Gonzalez-Torres are no different.[18] Artful mediation, evidenced by the jigsaw strategy or the plastic bags I have described, points to the ways in which reproduction, representation, and any rote understanding of identity they engender are insufficient. Instead, the mediation of puzzle pieces and plastic bags offers a view of a *disidentity* that potentially informs an *anti-identitarian identity politics* in which commonality is not forged through shared images and fixed identifications but fashioned instead from connotative images that invoke communal structures of feelings. The structures of feeling that are invoked point to a world in which exile and ethnicity are not stigmatized aberrations, but instead everyday aspects of national culture.

The jigsaw-puzzle strategy is also employed to connote a queer life-world. For instance, *Untitled (Ross and Harry)* and *Untitled (Loverboy)* are monuments to Gonzalez-Torres's lover Ross, who died before him in 1991. These too are pictures from a private life, in this instance a specifically queer life, made public. This work, then, challenges dominant protocols that relegate queerness, and other minoritarian histories and philosophies of the self, to a forced exile in the private sphere. Once

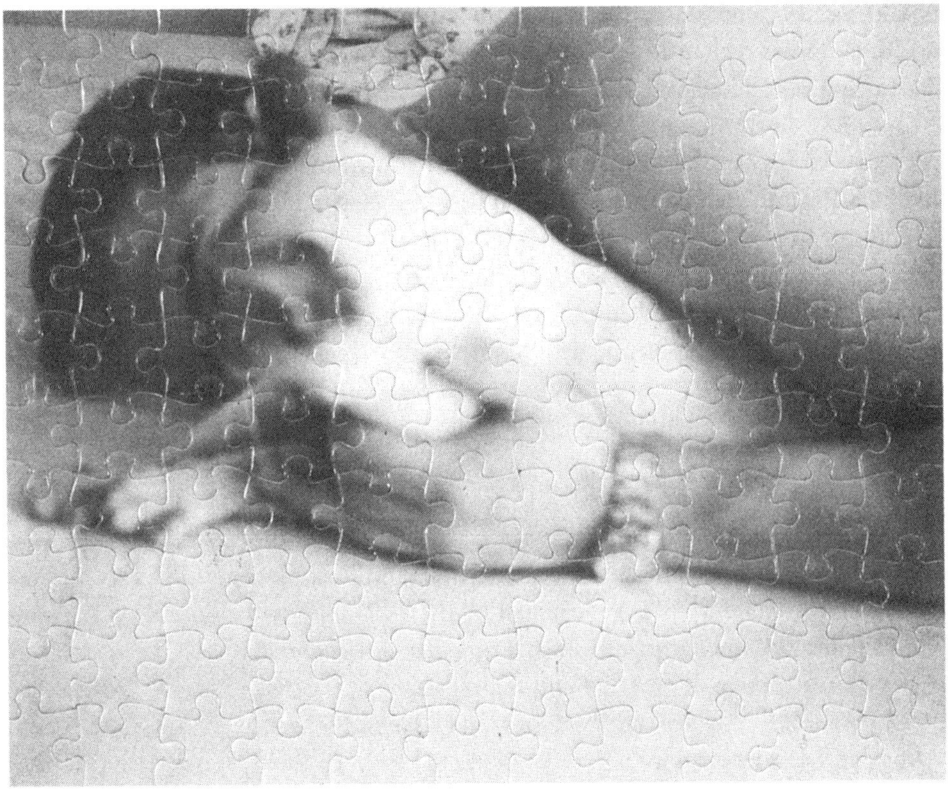

Felix Gonzalez-Torres, *Untitled (Loverboy)*, 1988. Photo by Peter Muscato. 7½ x 9½ inches. C-print jigsaw puzzle in plastic bag. Courtesy of the Andrea Rosen Gallery, New York.

again, the jigsaw images achieve a disidentificatory status through the determined negation of direct representational routes, a turn toward a strategic obliquity that is anti-identitarian in the service of a reconstructed identity politics.

Puzzle images of Ross resonate alongside a puzzle photo of Oscar Wilde's tomb, *Untitled (Oscar Wilde's Tomb)*, as a disidentificatory performance that imagines, renders, and signals a queer life-world into visibility by rendering a queer icon, a romantic image from the history of queer politics and culture in the mass public space. This mode of visualizing and portraying private loves and public heroes is a style of disidentificatory portraiture that trades in connotations, connotations that can be described as "almost articulate."

The same disidentificatory and anti-identitarian impulse toward portraiture is located in the artist's spill sculptures, in which spills of candy are weighed to the exact weight of an individual, of whose "portrait" this spill is a rendering. Those candies are then offered to spectators as souvenirs and treats. Through the course of an exhibition, the spills are literally consumed by spectators. The spills are then replenished, symbolically restoring the subject of the piece, who, further along in this symbolic circuit, stands for a sick loved one brought back from a nightmare of wasting illness.

Bodies are also represented through chains of lightbulbs that burn out one by one. Again, bulbs are replenished, rendering a dream in which the dying "lights" of one's life are fantastically reignited.

Whereas Zamora used identity as a stage to perform media-savvy counterpublicity and Sara/Ricardo seemed utterly trapped within the restraints of identity, attempting to perform heterosexuality and failing, Gonzalez-Torres seemingly rejected the politics of identity altogether. Yet, as my readings have indicated, *disidentity* is held in his project through deep disidentification with identity's very tenets. Gonzalez-Torres presents images of the epidemic by offering its cognoscenti a portrait of loss and sadness through mass-produced public art: he "reveals" his own loved object (Ross) and snapshots of his exilic childhood through the heavy mediation of the jigsaw puzzle; he approaches the identity-centric genre of portraiture through the abstraction of his spills and his light strings. Gonzalez-Torres was, as the interview cited earlier indicated, deeply weary of identity. He was especially critical of multiculturalism's narrative of identity. Nonetheless, his work ultimately held on to some aspect of identity. That remaining component of "self" is mined by the artist and used to narrate a transformative politics of the self that enabled a "practice of freedom."

Within the context of AIDS cultural criticism and activism, Simon Watney has called for an "ethically grounded politics of gender and sexuality" in the service of enabling "practices of freedom": "'For what,' he asked 'is morality, if not the practice of liberty, the deliberate practice of Liberty?' Rather than assuming a natural, inevitable unity among gay men, or between gay men and lesbians, such an approach grounds our experience, in all its diversity and complexity, within a wider ethical context."[19] Watney extracts this notion of a practice of freedom from Foucault's late interviews.[20] Ethics for Foucault (a concept that is vastly different than notions of morality floated in contemporary U.S. culture by the religious right) is achieved through the care of the self. I am suggesting that Gonzalez-Torres's distanced and nuanced rendering of the self, what I have been calling *disidentity,* functions as counterpublicity that provides pictures of possible future relations of power. The self of disidentity is ultimately an *impersonal self.* Following the lead of Paul Veyne, who discussed the self in Foucault's final writings as "a strategic possibility," David Halperin suggests that "To practice a stylistics of the self ultimately means to cultivate that part of oneself that leads beyond oneself, that transcends oneself: it is to elaborate the strategic possibilities of what is the most *impersonal* dimension of personal life—namely, the capacity to 'realize oneself' by becoming other than what one is."[21] Self cultivated in the work of Gonzalez-Torres visualizes "the strategic possibilities of what is the most *impersonal* dimension of personal life." Furthermore, the impersonal self that is produced in his oeuvre challenges the always already reductive self that is mass-produced in the discourse of multiculturalism. Finally, this self, fashioned through strategic disidentifications with dominant discourses on "selfness," presents the potential to ultimately "cultivate that part of oneself that leads beyond oneself, that transcends oneself." This moment of transcendence is the moment in which counterpublics become imaginable; it is a moment brimming with the possibility of transformative politics.

Disidentification's use-value is only accessible through the transformative politics that it enables subjects and groups to imagine. Counterpublics are not magically and automatically realized through disidentifications, but they are suggested, rehearsed, and articulated. Disidentifications are strategies that are called on by minoritarian subjects throughout their everyday life. The cultural productions and performances I have considered in this book amplify and often explicate these everyday practices. They offer a metanarrative on disidentification that at once further atomizes and further transmits these practices. This book is thus meant to complement this cultural work and further push the envelope. My desire is to perpetuate disidentification and offer it as not only a hermeneutic but also as a possibility for freedom.

Chapter 8

Latina Performance and Queer Worldmaking; or, *Chusmería* at the End of the Twentieth Century

for Tony

Our *Chusmas*, Our Selves

Readers outside the realm of the Caribbean Latina/o experience might require an introduction to *chusmería* if they are to follow this book's final chapter. Those who grew up in and around Spanish-speaking Caribbean communities probably have encountered the term as an admonishment: "¡No sea tan chusma!" (Don't be such a *chusma*!). This reprimand plays into a stigmatized understanding of Latina identity held both inside and outside those communities. By turning to the theatrical text under consideration, Carmelita Tropicana's play *Chicas 2000,* one can locate an efficient explication of the term.[1]

Chicas 2000 features four actors playing various roles. The play narrates the future adventures of Carmelita Tropicana, the performance artist persona of Alina Troyana, whose solo performance work was discussed in chapter 5.[2] The play's two opening scenes are fictive TV programs: *Opinions of the Hoi Polloi* and *Homo Decorum.* Both are deliberately tacky and ribald. Both are interrupted when they are abruptly pulled off the air in mid-"broadcast." An offstage voice indicates that "due to the offensive nature" of both shows they have been "taken off the air." The play's next scene features another televisual voice-over monologue that this time explains the state's decision to clamp down on *chusmería.* Two *chusma* fashion police perform a *chusma*-esque pantomine during this scene.

The next few scenes tell the tale of the *chusma* protagonist's abduction by a mad scientist, his cloning of two mini-Carmelitas, and Carmelita's ray gun-wielding retaliation against the demented geneticist. Our heroine is then arrested by the *chusma*-detaining arm of the state power apparatus. She serves time in the big house with her televisual sidekick from *Homo Decorum,* the lovely Desiree. Carmelita keeps herself busy behind bars by engaging in a jailhouse romance with the mysterious and feral

Rodesia. The play then shifts from the star's plight to the now-adult clones' flight from captivity. The sisters are accidentally reunited and, after identifying each other as two of a matched pair, decide to go on a quest for their their *chusma* parent/source, the performance artist Carmelita Tropicana. The girls eventually run into their "source" through a series of mishaps, but they do not recognize her until the play's conclusion when the mad doctor, their evil "father," pits the younger woman against Carmelita in a field of combat. The play ends with a comedic family reunion. The entire drama is a tacky affair, a spectacle of Latina excess and gaudiness.

From this thumbnail sketch of the play's action, the codes of conduct that make up *chusmería* come squarely into view: *chusmería* is a form of behavior that refuses standards of bourgeois comportment. Chusmería is, to a large degree, linked to stigmatized class identity. Within Cuban culture, for instance, being called *chusma* might be a technique for the middle class to distance itself from the working class; it may be a barely veiled racial slur suggesting that one is too black; it sometimes connotes gender nonconformity. In the United States, the epithet *chusma* also connotes recent immigration and a general lack of "Americanness," as well as an excessive nationalism—that one is somewhat over the top about her Cubanness. The sexuality of individuals described as *chusmas* is also implicated. The prototypical *chusma*'s sexuality is deemed excessive and flagrant—again, subverting conventions. There is something monstrous about the *chusma*. In this chapter, I will read Tropicana's play and its thick description of the *chusma* and her "ways" to further outline my theory of disidentification. This case study will allow me to pay special attention to the unique features of disidentificatory live performance. I will also mark the way in which subaltern subjects negotiate what I call the "burden of liveness," which I describe as a particular hegemonic mandate that calls the minoritarian subject to "be live" for the purpose of entertaining elites. This "burden of liveness" is a cultural imperative within the majoritarian public sphere that denies subalterns access to larger channels of representation, while calling the minoritarian subject to the stage, performing her or his alterity as a consumable local spectacle. Thus, the story this chapter tells is the tale of *chusma*'s disidentifications with the "burden of liveness."

A consideration of the play's logic of censorship allows us to understand the threat that *chusmería* presents to the dominant public sphere. The censorship mechanism is seen in the play's third scene, which features three of the play's four cast members: Carmelita Tropicana plays a newscaster, while Ana Margaret Sanchez and Rebecca Sumner-Burgos begin the scene as stiff FBI agents who flank the equally uptight-looking newscaster. (Although the latter two performers' outfits, snug-fitting silk miniskirts and tops, do not connote their positions as FBI agents, the costumes do signal a fantastic transformation that both characters will soon experience.) The newscaster's monologue introduces the play's setting and the general style of the play:

> On December 31, 1999, TV shows like these were taken off the air. They were symbolic of the social ills gripping the nation. It was in response to these shows

DIXON PLACE PRESENTS
CHICAS 2000
"This comic spitfire cheerfully sticks her spiked heels into both Cuban and American eyeballs." -The New York Post
"A Carmen Miranda cloaked in dangerous fruits." -Mas Magazine
WRITTEN BY CARMELITA TROPICANA
DIRECTED BY UZI PARNES
STARRING CARMELITA TROPICANA, REBECCA SUMNER BURGOS, ANA MARGARET SANCHEZ & UZI PARNES
JUNE 6–21, 1997
THU, FRI & SAT AT 8:00PM
RESERVATIONS: 219-3088

Poster for *Chicas 2000*, written by Carmelita Tropicana, directed by Uzi Parnes. (left to right) Rebecca Sumner-Burgos, Carmelita Tropicana as Pingalito, and Ana Margaret Sanchez. Photo by Paula Court. Courtesy of Carmelita Tropicana.

> that the FBI DNA RA BMU was created, the DNA Remodeling Agency and Behavior Modification Unit. Its mission: better the human race through designer genes. Genes responsible for antisocial behavior were coded and classified. Among the deviant genes heading the list: the *chusma* gene, that which gives rise to a disease known as *chusmería*—shameless, loud, gross, tacky behavior, in short, tasteless attitude.

At this point in the performance, the two agents' body movements and general countenance abruptly change. The two are no longer rigid with their hands crossed behind their lower backs; instead, their arms swing loosely at their sides and their erect posture fades as they rest one hand on a hip. While the announcer explains that "Individuals with the *chusma* gene are known to favor Egyptian head movement from side to side," Sanchez illustrates this characteristic as her own head swivels back and forth in a symmetrical fashion. The announcer then makes a fashion commentary: "They wear clothes that are too tight for their weight category, with emphasis on the chest and posterior." Sumner-Burgos walks to center stage and lasciviously clutches her breasts; she then turns her back to the audience and pats her buttocks. The announcer concludes this definition of the corporeality of the *chusma* by explaining that "when excited [*chusmas* are] known for wild gesticulations of their extremities." At this point the two performers cut loose. They mutter in Spanish as they swing their hips and pick their teeth. The announcer drones the final lines of her monologue in an arid make-believe "white woman" voice as the newly born *chusmas* carry on:

> The *chusma* gene is found in Latin America with high concentration in the Caribbean, although the gene has crossed over to North America. U.S. citizens classified with the gene are: Shelly Winters, Dennis Rodman, Roseanne, Tonya Harding, and Martha Stewart. The latter is a perfect example of the gene in remission. Although the *chusma* gene cannot be eradicated or its disease cured, it can be controlled. The government has stepped up its efforts to combat the *chusma* gene and a disease called *chusmería.*

As the newscaster mouths the last word of the monologue, *chusmería,* the *chusmas* yell it out in unison. The word sounds like a battle cry and the women fly toward the audience. Their body movements are bawdy as they tour the assembled spectators. They pick out an audience member (during one of the performances I attended, I was one of the unfortunate targets) and harass her or him, commenting on his or her fashions, claiming to be the "*chusma* fashion police," and threatening to arrest the perpetrator as they shake their fingers, sashay their hips, and practice their "Egyptian" head movements.

The examples of *chusma* cultural crossovers are interesting as they target queerly valenced icons in the popular culture. The non-Latina/o pantheon of *chusmas* includes figures of exaggeration who practice "inappropriate" and antinormative behavior. Although some of these figures embody a corporate ethos that is camouflaged as subversive (Rodman, Stewart, Roseanne), their reception through *chusma* eyes enables models of identity that contest hegemonic models of citizenship.

The *chusma*'s identity is thus a Goffmanian spoiled identity.[3] The work that Carmelita Tropicana's play carries out, then, follows a disidentificatory path that I have traced in the work of other cultural workers in this book. Disidentification is a mode of performance whereby a toxic identity is remade and infiltrated by subjects who have been hailed by such identity categories but have not been able to own such a label. Disidentification is therefore about the management of an identity that has been "spoiled" in the majoritarian public sphere. This management is a critical negotiation in which a subject who has been hailed by injurious speech, a name, or a label, reterritorializes that speech act and the marking that such speech produces to a self. Judith Butler has argued that although injurious speech "may appear to fix or paralyze the one it hails," it often, paradoxically, inaugurates in speech a subject who comes to use language to counter an offensive call.[4] Indeed, this story is at least as old as one of English literature's most enduring fables of disidentification, William Shakespeare's *The Tempest.* In that play, Caliban, who learned how to fully inhabit his monstrousness, used that stigmatized designation—"monster"—as a site from which to curse Prospero, the oppressive force who brought him into language in the first place. Rather than counteridentify with Prospero (refusing to speak his language) or identify with his master (to speak like Prospero), he chooses to disidentify by recomposing Prospero's idiom and making it his own.

There is in fact something quite Calibanistic and, as I have suggested, monstrous, about the *chusma. Chicas 2000* offers several representations of monstrous women, starting with the diva herself. In this play, Carmelita is a blue-haired freak who has been detained for a number of years at the FBI DNA RA BMU—the DNA Remodeling Agency and Behavior Modification Unit. While in that facility, a love affair ignites between Rodesia (also played by Sumner-Burgos), another monstrous creature, and the captive *chusma.* Rodesia, a butch woman whose behavior is greatly influenced by the fact that her heart is the transplanted heart of a brown bear. Rodesia's condition is a comical send-up of the postcolonial hybrid. Her position in the play is a commentary on the general condition of "exilic hybridity" that characterizes the majority of Latina/o America.[5] Rodesia is a monstrous creation whose heart does not correspond to her exterior self. We are reminded of a tradition of exile sentimentality where crooners and poets wax on about having left their hearts in their native land. Her queerness can be located not only in her butch demeanor, but also in the very fact that her heart and body do not line up.

The play's engagement with monstrousness also signifies upon recent updates in reproductive technologies that are deemed "evil" by proponents of heteronormative reproduction. Hysteria about the monstrous practice of cloning, a potential mode of queer reproduction, is manifest in the characters of Clana and Cluna. Clana and Cluna (played by Sanchez and Sumner-Burgos) are the blue-haired *chusma* clones of

Carmelita. Carmelita was captured and detained in the FBI DNA RA BMU after an altercation with the play's sinister villain. In the fourth scene, Carmelita is kidnapped by the evil Dr. Igor (performed by the play's director, Uzi Parnes), a mad *chusma* wannabe who wished to possess the play's heroine. Tropicana refused to submit to the deranged scientist, who retaliates with the nonconsensual cloning of cells forcefully extracted from her buttocks. (The buttock, as the earlier monologue indicates, is a privileged site on the *chusma*'s body.) Carmelita's monstrous progeny grow up separately in BMUs located in two hubs of *chusma* culture: Miami and the Bronx. They do not meet each other until they simultaneously escape from their prisons and become illegal immigrants on the run.

The plight and flight of Clana and Cluna, while hilariously funny, manage to articulate a poignant social critique. The two clones literally bump into each other as they flee the law. They almost instantly recognize each other as twin sisters. (Much of the humor in this scene is derived from a sight gag: the two women who play Clana and Cluna, Sanchez and Sumner-Burgos, are dressed in almost identical outfits, wear similar wigs, but physically look completely different.) Once the cloned sisters meet, they begin to contemplate their "bio-original." Clana asks Cluna if she ever wonders about their bio-original, to which Cluna responds: "Every day. I think, why did she make us knowing we would always be illegal? Once illegal, always illegal." In this speech, a pivotal fact about the status of U.S. Latina/o existence becomes painstakingly apparent: "once illegal, always illegal." The U.S. Latina/o holds the place of the perpetually "illegal" immigrant in the national imagination. This fact is apparent both in the channels of majoritarian representation and in federal legislation as the civil rights of U.S. Latina/os, both "illegal" and "legal," continually erode. In post–Proposition 187 North America, the U.S. Latina/o is constantly scapegoated as the invader and outsider who is ruining the prosperity of "real" citizens. Legislation has reached the floor of the U.S. House of Representatives that calls for a curtailing of benefits and social services to immigrants who are deemed "illegal" by the state apparatus. Hence, one of the *Chicas 2000*'s most salient points: *Once illegal, always illegal.*

Similar social commentary undergirds the entire play. The postmillennial setting of the play speaks of the massive (and continually accelerating) class stratification of New York City. The play's science-fiction chronology is set in a not-too-distant future in which most of the island of Manhattan has become a posh elite residential district. The only exception to this ultragentrification is a small section of the Lower East Side, an area that has come to be known as "*Chusma*town." Chusmatown is an apartheid-like settlement inhabited exclusively by *chusmas.* Clana and Cluna's quest for their bio-original takes them to the fabled Chusmatown. The ghetto-like neighborhood is a site of government relocation, and in this way the play calls attention to the U.S. government's history of internal colonization—specifically, the forced "removals" of indigenous peoples to reservations and the practice of detaining Japanese-Americans in internment camps during World War II.

"The Burden of Liveness": Toward a Minoritarian Performance Theory

This future Chusmatown is besieged by massive inflation. The clone "sisters" and the bio-orginal both opt to work in a Chusmatic Casino, a coliseum/entertainment complex where *chusma* gladiators fight as entertainment for the non-*chusma* elite. Fighting in the Chusmatic Casino is an *illegal* profession. By performing in this space, the *chicas* participate in an alternative "outlaw economy." Again, the far-flung future scenario remarks upon the contemporary social plight of Latinas and other disenfranchised people of color. Late capitalism represents the dwindling of possibilities for the racialized working class. Under such hegemony, women of color compete over low-wage positions within the shrinking service economy. Individuals who reject this constrained field of possibility often choose to survive by entering alternative economies involving sex work or the drug trade. The *chusmas*' move into the illicit coliseum represents a dystopic vision of what the continuation of late capitalism will mean for Latinas and other people of color. The illegality of the space also represents the overdetermination of such positions for the always "illegal" subject. Clana is taken aback by Cluna's suggestion that they work in the Chusmatic Casino. She protests by pointing out that the casinos are illegal. Within Cluna's justification of working in the "illegal" performance space one can trace the same social forces that lock "immigrants" into criminal or exploitative labor situations today:

> So are we [illegal]. They have *chusma* wrestling. It's packed on Fridays with *chusmas* and well-dressed respectable non-*chusmas*. Their lives are so dull they gotta come for cheap *chusma* thrills. I read about it in the *Daily Chusma* while you were doing number 3. Clana, with your physical ability and my mental strategy, we could do it. Without money we can't live and finish our mission. What do you say?

An illegal establishment such as the Chusmatic Casino is the space allotted for the *chusma* (non)citizen within the national economy. The only activity that the *chusmas* are permitted to perform is that of "live performance" for the *chusma* and non-*chusma* elite. Once again the dystopic picture rendered by the play has direct parallels that bear considering.

Live performance for an audience of elites is the only imaginable mode of survival for minoritarian subjects within the hegemonic order that the *chusmas* live within *and* in opposition to. This fact correlates with what I call the "burden of liveness" that inflects the experience of postcolonial, queer, and other minoritarian subjects.[6] The story of "otherness" is one tainted by a mandate to "perform" for the amusement of a dominant power bloc. If there is any acceptable place for "queers" in the homophobic national imaginary, it certainly is onstage—being "funny" for a straight audience. The minoritarian subject is always encouraged to perform, *especially* when human and civil rights disintegrate. This point is evidenced in chapter 4 of this study, which surveys the paradox of contemporary drag and queer performance's current boom in an age of escalating state-sponsored homophobia. The same is true in the United States for people of color who are lauded as performers and entertainers but are still met with recalcitrant racism in everyday life. If we consider the colonial condition, we might again turn to *The Tempest* and recall that, upon meeting Caliban, a drunken Stephano immediately thinks of bringing the indigenous monster home to Naples as a prize and amusement for his emperor.

The female subject who is both racialized and queer is triply susceptible to the "burden of liveness." Elin Diamond has suggested that "women, especially lesbians and women of color, have struggled to appear, to speak, be heard, be seen. In the history of Western metaphysics the female body is represented as both crude materiality and irreparable lack."[7] Although the minoritarian subject experiences pressures to perform a live and "crude materiality," this fact nonetheless does not register within the larger context of the dominant culture. Diamond points to a fact that is important to index here: "Socially and culturally, however, all performances are not equal."[8] Some performances are structured through historically embedded cultural mandates that the body of color, the queer body, the poor body, the woman's body perform his or her existence for elite eyes. This performance is positioned within the dominant culture as a substitute for historical and political representation. Thus, performing beyond the channels of liveness and entering larger historical narratives seems especially important.

Perhaps the best way to understand the "burden of liveness" that shadows the minoritarian subject is to consider the far-reaching implications of what Coco Fusco has called "the other history of intercultural performance."[9] Fusco discloses that Dadaist events were not the first instances of performance art in the West. Fusco has suggested instead that the history of performance art is as old as the European "conquest" when indigenous people were transported to the metropole as scientific curiosities and popular amusements. She and Guillermo Gómez-Peña offered a metacommentary on this history with their controversial 1992 "Couple in a Cage" performance. The artists toured museums around the world posing as Amerindians from the fictitious land of "Guatinau," an island in the Gulf of Mexico that had miraculously escaped the notice of imperial eyes for five centuries. While audiences looked on, the "Guatinauis" ate, slept, and marveled at the wonders of modern technology. They also danced, told stories, or exposed their genitals for nominal fees. The performance served as a "reverse ethnography" that made the audience the object of critical scrutiny. Fusco's essay and the performance both debunk any notions of the history of intercultural performance as one of fair and mutually beneficial exchange. Furthermore, they also expose the ways in which the other is constructed as a live performing other whose place is that of entertaining the dominant order. The Chusmatic Casino is a fictional performance space that, like the couple's golden cage, comments on the burden of live performance that is sutured to minoritarian subjects. Both cage and casino call attention to the audience, interrogating the spectator's racial, class, and gender privilege. The casino mirrors the actual reception of the play. The audience at Dixon Place is implicated by this scenario and implicitly asked to question how it might be or not be one of those *chusmas* or non-*chusma* elites who consume *chusmería* as spectacle or amusement.

My interest in schematizing a trope like the "burden of liveness" is nothing short of the disarming of a celebratory precritical aura that shrouds some performative research. It is important to keep in mind that not all performances are liberatory or transformative. Performance, from the positionality of the minoritarian subject, is sometimes nothing short of forced labor. The most obvious and relevant example of performance as forced labor from a U.S. perspective is certainly chattel slave performance. But this history does not stop there. It in fact reaches into our present context. Minoritarian subjects do not always dance because they are happy; sometimes they dance because their feet are being shot at.

It is equally important to understand the ways in which the "burden of liveness" structures temporality. The "burden of liveness" affords the minoritarian subject an extremely circumscribed temporality. To be only in "the live" means that one is denied history and futurity. If the minoritarian subject can only exist in *the moment,* she or he does not have the privilege or the pleasure of being a historical subject. If that subject needs to focus solely on the present, it can never afford the luxury of thinking about the future.

It is important to offset the "burden of liveness" by employing a performance theory that disentangles a reified linkage between performance and liveness. In this book, I have attempted to assemble a performance-studies lens that reads the performance of minoritarian subjectivity in live manifestations and in other aspects of visual culture such as film, photography, video, and painting. I have thus mapped disidentificatory performances across fields of cultural production. I have chosen to interrogate disidentification's always already performative properties in both live and mediated manifestations because it is not the liveness of disidentificatory performance in and of itself that bestows it with its worldmaking properties. I am interested in disidentificatory performance's power of critique and its vision of transformative politics. This is what constitutes the power and relevance of disidentification. Furthermore, we run the risk of making liveness something of an obstructive fetish when we position it as the central trope of performance or performance studies. The burden of liveness makes us cognizant of the burden to always already be live that the minoritarian subject must continually negotiate.

Philip Auslander has worried about the binary between "liveness" and media culture. He warns against discourses that privilege a "liveness" that is imagined as a "pristine state uncontaminated by mediatization." Instead, Auslander points to the unavoidable and often *productive* imbrication between technological media and performance:

> I would argue that the live and the mediatized exist in a relation of mutual dependence and imbrication, not one of opposition. The live is, in a sense, only a secondary effect of mediating technologies. Prior to the advent of those technologies

> (e.g., photography, telegraphy, phonography) there was no such thing as the "live," for the category has meaning only in relation to an opposing possibility.[10]

I share with Auslander this belief that technological mediation is not performance's end. Furthermore, the insistence on a binarized opposition between live performance and mediatized performance can lead not only to a dangerous reification of performance, which would contribute to the "burden of liveness" that haunts minoritarian subjects in the dominant public sphere, but also to an ossification of performance's potential to enact social critique. Although "liveness" and "performance" are rich theoretical and political concepts, both are lessened by any *intractable* and *essentialized* linkage to each other.

The culture of mass media has made significant inroads into performance and vice versa. This is true of the feminist video surveillance work of Julia Scher and the incorporation of video images in the solo performance work of Idris Mignot, to name just two examples from a wide field of technologically imbricated performances. Television, or, more nearly, the phenomenon of television, plays a role in *Chicas 2000.* By indexing the televisual, the play gestures to the importance of media culture for the performed enactment of minoritarian counterpublics. The play opens with this premise: Pingalito Betancourt, a seventy-year-old Cuban man with a cigar who identifies himself as a "retired transportation official," has been given a cable access show.[11] His show is titled *Opinions of the Hoi Polloi.* Pingalito's career in public transportation encompassed his tenure as a bus driver in Havana, where he was affectionately known as the Socrates of the M15. This experience as bus driver/philosopher has prepared Pingalito for his current role as televisual public intellectual. Pingalito's topic for the day is "Puritanism." The play uses this opportunity to launch a social critique of the United States' foundational mythology. Pingalito misreads and misrecognizes the attributes "Self-reliance," "Industry," and "Frugality." He understands his own self-reliance, for instance, as his ability to repair his eyeglasses with the skillful application of duct tape and a safety pin. These "attributes," which have been invoked by the nation as justifications for the gutting of public assistance, are mocked and satirized, revealed as ridiculous concepts that justify greed and foreclose the possibility of an ethical and just state system.

Pingalito eventually parts company with Puritanism—even his misrecognized Puritanism—when the topic of sex is broached. The elder Cuban statesman recommends the example of the Bonobo monkey as a positive rewriting of Puritanical sexuality. The Bonobos, he explains, utilize sex for various purposes: "They have sex for procreation, recreation, to relieve stress, anxiety, boredom." Pingalito then challenges the audience to imagine a human culture that was patterned after Bonobo society:

> Can you imagine, ladies and gentlemen, what kind of world this would be if you got up in the morning and your doorbell rang. It's the UPS girl with a package. You are tired and sleepy and to wake you up she starts to rub against

you; and at the bank you find yourself overdrawn and the bank teller starts to fondle your privates to make you feel better. Eh. What a world this could be!

Lolita, a female Bonobo, joins Pingalito on stage for a duet of "To All the Girls I've Loved Before." A woman in an ape suit jumps on stage. She is exceedingly frisky with the senior citizen, and before things become too risqué the stage blacks out. The announcer's voice explains that because of the show's tastelessness, it has been taken off the air. Televisual censorship is thus positioned as the first explicit maneuver in a war against *chusmas. Chusmas* are denied access to televisual performance and any media stage and are, instead, rerouted to the Chusmatic Casino, where their performances of self are staged exclusively for elites who can afford to consume spectacles and resist the political pedagogy of *chusma* performance. This opening skit locates the time and place of the production, of the *live* play, as that of media culture. The lesson to be extracted is this: performance exists within media culture and the media culture has a life inside of performance. Behind the absurd humor of this opening scene, we begin to glimpse an important truism: a critical optic that does not calculate the imbrication of both modes of expression will fail to see the future of performance *and* media.

*Chusma*esque politics informs my decision to look far and wide for disidentificatory performances. I have paid great attention to performances of disidentification that have been strategically embedded in other media and mediums. The methodology I am performing can be understood as a critical *chusmería*—a tactical refusal to keep things "pristine" and binarized, a willful mismatching of striped and floral print genres, and a loud defiance of a rather fixed order. In this sense, I am following Pingalito's lead by rejecting a live performance puritanism. This critical *chusmería* allows me to resist subscribing to a stabilized notion of performance that can be primarily defined by its relationship to presence. My *chusma*like disruption of performance as unsullied by alternative representational media is meant to counteract the burden of liveness that haunts intercultural and minoritarian performance. The "burden of liveness" informs this maneuver insofar as it understands the need to dislodge the minoritarian subject from a theoretical apparatus that positions her as only legible as a live and immediate presence and not as a historicized and representable entity.

Disidentificatory Iconicity: Loving La Lupe

Although I am arguing against a performance puritanism, I am nonetheless invested in what I call a notion of "pure performance." A *chusma*'s life is one in which drama and performance reign supreme. This is certainly true of the *chicas* and their *chusma* foremothers. A climatic scene in the Chusmatic Casino helps us understand a *chusma*esque understanding of pure performance. The Chusmatic Casino is run by the twisted Dr. Igor, who, realizing the relation of Clana and Cluna to Carmelita, pits the masked clones against their also masked bio-original in the arena. The play's resolution occurs when the match's participants realize each other's identities and subsequently turn on Dr. Igor. It is thus the moment when the Other looks beyond the audience and sees the "otherness" of those who have been cast as one's enemy within a majoritarian script that liberation is achieved. *Chicas 2000* concludes with a musical number—a stirring lip-synching of Cuban diva La Lupe's rendition of "My Life." The song choice brings a crucial point to light: it is only when a subject is brought to light that the constitution of a self ("a life") is possible.

The closing song pays homage to the troubled iconicity of La Lupe, a figure who reigns supreme in the history of *chusmería.* La Lupe's live performances in prerevolutionary Cuba and in *el exilio* were legendary for their excess. The singer was known to shudder and convulse as she sang. Her stage movements often included writhing on the floor. A few witnesses have reported that she concluded her performances by banging her head against the wall. If one considers the history of strategic shock effects and theatricalized violence that characterize performance art, La Lupe emerges as an important precursor of that artistic movement. Thus, the play offers an alternative genealogy of performance art, one in which a Caribbean queen reigns supreme.

Carmelita herself names La Lupe "Latin America's first performance artist." She further expounds on La Lupe's critical importance when she declares that she was:

> A woman whose singing was a censored sensation;
> A woman who gave us not Dada art but mama art;
> A woman who showed the way for many a little boy
> letting them find meaning in life through eyelashes,
> sequins and mascara. The one and only: La Lupe!

This ode to the Cuban songstress identifies her not only as an outlaw artist and an unappreciated avant-gardist, but also as a disidentificatory icon for queer little boys who had little hope of achieving the linear gender identifications that heteronormative culture decrees. La Lupe was a *chusma* diva and the monstrous excess of her femininity proved to be an accommodating and rich site for many a queer boy's psychic attachments and investments.

Citing La Lupe and giving her the position of the play's patron saint or chief divinity establishes a productive link between theater and everyday life. La Lupe's live performance and songs thematized performance in everyday life. One of her most famous songs, "Puro teatro," presents a scorned lover who turns to her partner and shrieks, "Teatro, lo tuyo es puro teatro" (Theater, your life is pure theater). Her accusations continue to fly and she indicates that her loved one's behavior is "estudiado simulacra" (studied simulacra). Of course, it takes one to know one, and La Lupe's deep read of her lover sounds as though she is talking about herself. More broadly, it sounds as though she is describing the *chusma* condition, an aspect of the Cuban condition not covered in Gustavo Pérez Firmat's study by that name.[12] The *chusma*'s life is *pure performance*; it is about studied excess and overblown self-fashioning. It rejects constraints on the self that are mandated for the "good immigrant" by Anglo culture. *Chusmería* also responds to reactionary aspects of Latino culture that suggest that a Latino should not be too black, too poor, too sexual, too loud, too emotional, or too theatrical.

Carmelita turns to La Lupe for the purposes of establishing a Latina self who is not lessened by restrictive codes of conduct. Santa La Lupe serves as a beacon; through her model and her shining example, an identity that has been spoiled is newly reinhabited and recomposed as a site of possibility and transformation. *Chusmería* is "puro teatro" or pure performance. This pure performance salvages something that has been disparaged and rendered abject. This pure performance, this divine *chusmería,* as realized in *Chicas 2000,* helps build a queer world.

Picuo: A Queer Thing about *Chusmería*

This idea of pure performance is familiar to many a queer subject who understands her or his existence, with campy composure, as an ongoing drama. *Chusmas* and queers are not one and the same, but they do share a drama queen's identifications. Yet, *chusmería*'s relation to the discourse of queerness is not that of "stand-in." *Chusmería*'s discourse of loudness and deliberate tackiness does not necessarily connote practices of same-sex desire or queer self-actualization. Conversely, queerness, while sometimes a very camp enterprise, does not usually pride itself on its regard for (mis)matching stripes and floral patterns. I have already pointed to the excess of *chusmería,* and certainly similar discourses of excess saturate queerness. A gay man's nonmonogamy and willful promiscuity and a butch dyke's masculine style both register, under a heteronormative criterion, as excessive. Yet, excess is not the only entrance into a consideration of links between queerness and *chusmería;* the key word *shame* might also be considered.

Chusmas who fail to be properly reconditioned with the FBI DNA RA BMU are treated to all manner of torture and punishment. Take, for instance, the fate that befell Desiree (played by Sanchez), Carmelita's sensuous assistant on her censored *Homo Decorum.* Carmelita instantly understands what Desiree has gone through when she encounters the trembling young *chusma* in the FBI DNA RA BMU's common space during scene 8. The play's protagonist describes the "tank" and Desiree's three-hour stay in the torture chamber:

> The tank is where they stick you when you break the dress code and then they flash slides of *chusmas* in *chusma* outfits. Every time a slide comes on they whisper "Shame," and the voices keep getting louder and the slides go faster and faster. There are slides of *chusma* men with bellies in tank tops with big gold medallions drinking beer from cans, and *chusma* men and women smiling with their gold teeth; and *chusmas* that don't know how to match outfits—floral prints with stripes; and even ancestral *chusma* women in housedresses with big fat foamy curlers going to the corner bodega for a pack of Marlboros and pork *chuletas* [chops] in *chancletas* [flip-flop-like sandals].

Desiree falls apart after the senior *chusma*'s description of the "tank." As she drops to the floor, Desiree yells "Shame, Shame, Shame" in a thick accent. Her crime: the wearing of *chancletas.* In this scene, one discerns that *chusmería* is, in part, stigmatized by its refusal to be shamed and, furthermore, its shamelessness. Shame, on the other hand, is an effect that shares a particularly dense history with "queerness." *Queer* itself is a taking back of the shaming epithet that does not participate in what Eve Kosofsky Sedgwick has called "deontological closure" or cleansing, but, instead, recomposes shame as an inhabitable and potentially enabling identity site.[13] The mind programmers who torture the *chusmas* in the tank strive to reestablish a damaging and inhibiting shame. *Chusmas,* like queers, have managed a spoiled identity by disidentifying with shame, making it a source of energy as opposed to an occasion for devaluation. Thus, both *chusmas* and queers make a world through performances that disidentify with shame.

Chicas 2000 is a theatrical text that includes many shame-laden *chusma* performances. *Chusmería* also permeates the production on the level of costumes and acting. The costumes are loud, bright, and revealing. These semiobscene outfits complement the simple yet gaudy set design and go with the inexpensive Fourteenth Street wigs that the actors also wear.[14] The acting is deliberately overindulgent; all four actors turn in performances reminiscent of the over-the-top antics of Charles Ludlam's legendary Ridiculous Theatrical Company.

The entire production is deeply *picuo. Picuo* is a word that sends me on a more personal journey between queerness and *chusmería.* I remember walking into my father's house one Saturday afternoon. He had just come home from work. This incident occurred during my late teens, at about the time I manifested my "difference" from my family by beginning to dress "punk." This particular afternoon I had donned a pair of bright red sunglasses that I had shoplifted from the drugstore where I worked after school. As I entered the house, my father took one look at me and asked why I was wearing such glasses. At this stage of my adolescence, my father's displeasure in me often progressed to anger. What I wanted to say was that I had enlisted these red sunglasses in an attempt to see the world differently, to look beyond the universe of my family and ethnicity, perhaps to see things they never wanted me to see. Of course, I said no such thing. Instead, I offered some lame defense—claiming that my ruby lenses were some new style or fashion. My father, with equal measures of disgust and exhaustion in his voice, said that the sunglasses were simply *picuo.* I instantly knew that this was one of those old-fashioned Cuban words that had not completely traveled to Miami. I was not sure what it meant, but I feared the worst. By now it was clear to all parties concerned that I would *not* be following the path of Cuban-American heterosexuality that had been so neatly laid out for me. I would instead be traveling my own route, with my own friends, and, most probably, with these scarlet sunglasses. My father's temper storms and the increasingly frequent tone of disgust in his voice indicated that he suspected what my general destination was.

He was none too happy about this. I instantly felt the shaming properties of *picuo* and imagined that I was being called the faggot I was about to become. Weeks later I summoned the courage to ask my mother what *picuo* meant. She explained that the word meant tacky. The clothing *chusmas* wore was, for example, *picuo. Chusmas* I knew from. I remembered stories of our loud and quarrelsome neighbor Hilda La Flaca (skinny Hilda), who lived next door to us in Havana. According to my parents, her *chusmería,* which was most often evidenced by tales of her street brawls with her husband, was legendary. (It certainly was to me.) So *picuo* did not mean what I thought (and secretly hoped) it would mean. But I was nonetheless still stung by my father's shaming. Although he could not call me the *maricón* (faggot) I was, he found another way of inducing the same shame in me without having to own his son's queerness by performing so direct a speech act. His lips were spared the indignity of speaking my name and performatively confirming what for him was the worst. I was left shamefaced and *picuo.*

The fact that *picuo* meant tacky, yet I feared that it might mean queer, reveals what is for me a point of convergence between these two different forms of alterity. Both the queer and the "tacky" poor have failed to properly be hailed by heterosexuality and capitalism. Both share this sense of "failure" when hailed by the call of normativity.

This recollection also concretizes what for me are the powerful and inescapable links between *chusmería* and queerness. The play's politics and performances are located at these links. All the performers and most of the characters are queer; Carmelita and Rodesia, for instance, have a star-crossed bear-girl hybrid/*chusma* affair. Alterity is not performed via the route of queerness but is instead articulated through *chusmería.* The discourse of queerness has mostly been employed by white performers. Performers of color who work through this concept often feel the need to define themselves against the overarching whiteness of "queer." *Chusmería* becomes a mode of articulating a *queer world* (for the world of Chusmatown is most certainly that) through the auspices of Latina performance. *Chusmería* provides Carmelita and her collaborators an occasion to speak queer *and* beyond.

Performance, Politics, and the Making of Queer Worlds

A central contention of this study is that minoritarian performance labors to make worlds—worlds of transformative politics and possibilities. Such performance engenders worlds of ideological potentiality that alter the present and map out a future. Performance is thus imbued with a great deal of power in my study. But what is meant precisely by "worldmaking"? The concept of worldmaking delineates the ways in which performances—both theatrical and everyday rituals—have the ability to establish alternate views of the world. These alternative vistas are more than simply views or perspectives; they are oppositional ideologies that function as critiques of oppressive regimes of "truth" that subjugate minoritarian people. Oppositional counterpublics are enabled by visions, "worldviews," that reshape as they deconstruct reality. Such counterpublics are the aftermath of minoritarian performance. Such performances *transport* the performer *and* the spectator to a vantage point where transformation and politics are imaginable. Worldmaking performances produce these vantage points by slicing into the facade of the real that is the majoritarian public sphere. Disidentificatory performances opt to do more than simply tear down the majoritarian public sphere. They disassemble that sphere of publicity and use its parts to build an alternative reality. Disidentification uses the majoritarian culture as raw material to make a new world.

Nelson Goodman, among the first writers to employ the term *worldmaking,* has remarked that "composition and decomposition" are central to that process. Other aspects of worldmaking that he lists include revisionary "weighing" and "ordering" of reality as well as practices of "deletion and supplementation," and, finally, "deformation."[15] In this book, I have outlined the ways in which minoritarian performances have done all of this work. *Chicas 2000* has offered an oppositional public where a stigmatized identity is simultaneously decomposed and recomposed; where values and tastes are reordered and reweighed utilizing alternate criteria; where a degree of editing, deletion, and supplementation is applied to an oppressive social script; and where a fundamental deformation of the dominant public sphere is achieved. All of this is the work of disidentification.

Performance is capable of providing a ground-level assault on a hegemonic world vision that substantiates the dominant public sphere. Disidentificatory performance willfully disavows that which majoritarian culture has decreed as the "real." The force of performances that I collect in this book is performative as opposed to epistemological energy. Disidentificatory performance's performativity is manifest through strategies of iteration and *re*iteration. Disidentificatory performances are performative acts of conjuring that deform and re-form the world. *This reiteration builds worlds.* It proliferates "reals," or what I call worlds, and establishes the groundwork for *potential* oppositional counterpublics.

Such performances transport both audience and performer, equally integral components of any performance, to another *space.* In his classic treatise on the liminal space of convergence between theater and anthropology, Richard Schechner has pointed out two modalities of performance: performances of transportation and performances of transformation.[16] Transportation is more typically associated with theater, whereas transformation is linked to the realm of ritual. Performances of transportation move the spectator from the space of the ordinary world to a performative realm. After the performance has expired, the spectator is returned to the realm of the ordinary at about the same place he or she entered. Individuals who have experienced transport performance have encountered some minimal change in their lives. Performances of transformation include bar mitzvahs and other initiations into adulthood. Transformation performances do not merely "mark" a change, they effect a change through the performative act. Schechner is quick to point out that these two modalities of performance are not always discrete categories and the same performance will often include components of both. *Chicas 2000,* a performance that I have been describing as a queer worldmaking performance, initiates both spectator and performer into *chusma*hood—a very queer and racialized ontology. It transports the spectator to Chusmatown, a performative world where *chusmería* is not a toxic identity characteristic, but instead an emergent American identity. This transformation makes inroads on the "real world."

Schechner's project maps out a "point of contact" between performances of transformation and performances of transportation. In his paradigm, the transported (the actor, performer, cultural worker) imprints change onto the transformed (who might be a spectator or a performer in a ritual). I am suggesting that the imprint left on both performer and audience is laden with queer worldmaking potentialities. These imprints or marks are "loaded with power" and potentially "bind a person to his community; anchor him to an identity"; and "are at once intimate and public."[17]

Disidentificatory performance's ability to move a subject through political and symbolic space is only one of its particularities worth noting. The performances I collect in this text also possess extremely special temporalities in that they exist in both *the future and the present.* This phrase, "the future and the present," echoes the work of the great Marxist theoretician C. L. R. James, whose first volume of collected writing was titled *The Future in the Present.*[18] This title riffs on an aspect of Hegelian dialectics that suggests that the affirmation known as the future is contained within its negation, the present. In another text, his coauthored *Facing Reality,* James argues that a socialist future could be glimpsed by observing worker interaction and sociality within the space of the industrialized factory. Furthermore, he explains, the shop floor was *an actually existing socialist reality in the present.* His most striking proof for this thesis considers the case of an anonymous worker at an unnamed factory:

> In one department of a certain plant in the U.S. there is a worker who is physically incapable of carrying out his duties. But he is a man with wife and children and his condition is due to the strain of previous work in the plant. The workers have organized their work so that for ten years he has had practically nothing to do.[19]

James looks to this situation and others like it throughout the world as examples of an already existing socialist present outside of the bureaucracy that characterized the Eastern bloc. James argues that "the fundamental task" is "to recognize the socialist society and record the facts of its existence"; thus, the scenes he describes are to be read as "outposts of a new society." This notion of the future in the present is manifest in James's post-Trotskyist workerism, which has been critiqued widely. Two of James's most famous collaborators denounced this notion as delusional and naive.

Cornelius Castoriadis (who contributed to the book under his pen name Pierre Chaulieu) countered James's claims by explaining, "It is not difficult to understand that if socialist society already existed people would have noticed it"; and Raya Dunayevskaya, who, with James, founded the Johnson-Forest Tendency in American Marxism, stated that "the man who can write 'It is agreed that the socialist society exists' need never face reality."[20] These are harsh words from allies and friends; yet, despite these damning critiques, I am still drawn to this idea in James and its emphasis on the factory worker, particularly its framing of the social performer as something more than a cog. I contend that James's dialectical utopianism can tell us something about the temporality of disidentificatory performance, which I have described as worldmaking performance. I have suggested that *Chicas 2000* maps a future in which the *chusma* citizen subject (who represents the minoritarian citizen subject) resists escalating state repression by performing the very shame-laden excessive affect that the state indexes as justification for discrimination. But such a future-oriented claim fails to properly consider the time and place of the present in the performance, that actual sensuality of the present moment witnessed during the actual moment of performance.[21] If disidentificatory performance transports us across symbolic space, it also inserts us in a coterminous time where we witness a new formation within the present and the future. In this fashion, the temporality of disidentificatory performance disrupts the mandates of the "burden of liveness" that shadows the minoritarian subject in that the "burden of liveness" labors to relegate this minoritarian citizen subject to the live and the present and thus evacuates such personages from history. The coterminous temporality of disidentificatory performance exists within the future and the present, surpassing relegation to one temporality (the present) and insisting on the minoritarian subject's status as world-historical entity. *Chicas 2000* is more than a vision of a future moment; it is also about something new emerging in the actuality of the present, during the scene of performance. The stage, like the shop floor, is a venue for performances that allow the spectator access to queer life-worlds that exist, importantly and dialectically, within the future and the present.

James's workerist theory allows me to think of the minoritarian performer as a worker and the performance of queer worldmaking as labor. This notion of performer as avant-garde worker is calibrated to derail limited essentialist *or* constructionist understandings of the worker. Queer and gender theories that employ performance and performativity are, according to Cindy Patton, primarily responses to critiques of essentialized identity and debates about the end of identity politics. The problem that Patton detects with this direction in those larger bodies of theory is what she perceives as an "overemphasis on the actant-subject and a relative lack of consideration of the stage or content or field of the performance or performative act."[22] For Patton, performativity and performance are important critical terms for social theory. Performativity, for instance, can also discern the role of institutions and the state as players in a performative scene; for it is not only counterpublic cultural workers who utilize different modes of performance, but also the ideological state apparatus and other aspects of the hegemonic order that perform. Disidentificatory performances sometimes mimic and remake those performances with a critical worldmaking difference, but such performances are some among many. The social is both a stage and a battlefield. Different performances attempt to order reality and prescribe "truth" and organize hierarchies. Opposing players also use competing discourses that need to be understood (and countered) as performative. Whiteness, heteronormativity, and misogyny are performative projects and disidentification is a counterperformativity.

Ngugi wa Thiong'o has also stressed the state's status as a performing entity within the context of colonial and postcolonial regimes. He has argued that "The struggle between the arts and the state can be seen in performance in general and in the battle over the performance space in particular."[23] In that essay-opening sentence, Ngugi describes, with different terminology, the manner in which disidentificatory performances (by postcolonial artists) serve as counterpublicity that contests the performances of majoritarian regimes (by empire or the neocolonial state).

The stakes in the conflict between performing forces is the world, or, better put, the world to be made. Ngugi further specifies the performance of the state: "The state has its areas of performance; so has the artist. While the state performs power, the power of the artist is solely in the performance. Both the state and the artist have a different conception of time, place, content, goals, either of their own performance or of the other, but they have the audience as their common target."[24]

The performances and performative energies located in Marga Gomez's imaginary talk show, Jean-Michel Basquiat's pop art paintings, Isaac Julien's revisionary history of the Harlem Renaissance, Richard Fung's reconstructed porn and ethnography, Vaginal Davis's white masculinity stage show, Ela Troyano's Latina camp, Pedro Zamora's version of *The Real World,* Felix Gonzalez-Torres's "disidentity politics," all share a common goal with the repressive regimes of truth they counter: they all aim to make worlds. Ngugi's distinction is key: the state performs power but the artist's power comes through performance. Thus, all the disidentificatory performances I have chronicled have been enactments of power in the face of repressive truth regimes and the state power apparatus.

Chicas 2000 enacts power and attempts to make a world by imagining a dystopic scenario that critiques the present by imaging its teleological future. The play visualizes a "worst-case scenario" that is well within the limits of our contemporary imaginations and then locates a kernel of counterpublic resistance within that nightmare future. The production builds a present in the future and, dialectically, a future in the present. This temporality helps counter the "burden of liveness" mandate that stalks the minoritarian subject insofar as time and space transport is made available and the disidentifying player and spectator are freed from the holding cell that is the strictly live, local, and present world. Politics is enabled and propelled by humor and extravagance. *Chicas 2000* makes visible the performative ideology of the state by exaggerating it, causing it to balloon to ridiculous proportions. Through its enactment of comedy, Ludlamesque ridiculousness, and satire, Carmelita Tropicana's play extrapolates a queer world within a very antiqueer future.

This book has insisted on the need to read disidentificatory performances in manifestations both live and not so live. The priority has been to describe the performative politics of disidentificatory performances, which is to say that I have opted against an epistemological approach to disidentification and have instead attempted to offer descriptions of what disidentification *does within the social.* Rather than pit performativity against performance or stack them next to each other in a less than interactive fashion, I have chosen to employ a methodology that stresses the performativity of *or* in performance. It is my contention that *the doing* that matters most and the performance that seems most crucial are nothing short of the actual making of worlds.

Disidentification is a point of departure, a process, a building. Although it is a mode of reading and performing, it is ultimately a form of building. This building takes place *in the future and in the present,* which is to say that disidentificatory performance offers a utopian blueprint for a possible future while, at the same time, staging a new political formation in the present. Stakes are high. People of color and queers are scapegoated, targeted, and assaulted in all manner of ways. Through the "burden of liveness," we are called to perform our liveness for elites who would keep us from realizing our place in a larger historical narrative. Queers of color and other minoritarians have been denied a world. Yet, these citizen subjects are not without resources—they never have been. This study has tracked utopian impulses made manifest by the performers, cultural workers, and activists who are *not* content merely to survive, but instead use the stuff of the "real world" to remake collective sense of "worldness" through spectacles, performances, and willful enactments of the self for others. The minoritarian subject employs disidentification as a crucial practice of contesting social subordination through the project of worldmaking. The promises made by disidentification's performance are deep. Our charge as spectators and actors is to continue disidentifying with this world until we achieve new ones.

Notes

Preface: Jack's Plunger

1. *Normal Love* was never finished—Smith explained that his films took decades to complete. The "restored" version of the film I screened was a reconstruction of Smith's text, not a finished film that he completed.

2. See J. Hoberman, "Jack Smith: Bagdada and Lobsterrealism," introduction to *Wait for Me at the Bottom of the Pool: The Writings of Jack Smith* (New York and London: Serpent's Tail, 1997), p. 20.

3. Inderpal Grewal discusses the binary of home and harem that structured colonial rhetoric. The fantasy of the exotic and decadent harem helped the colonialist imaginary secure the symbolic pace of "home" (*Home and Harem: Imperialism, Nationalism and the Culture of Travel* [Durham, N.C.: Duke University Press, 1996]). Smith wanted nothing to do with home, home being the universe of his despised "pasty normals," and instead worked with fantasies of the stigmatized and "excessive." Smith did not simply remake racist fantasies of the other, but instead his performances recycled these tropes and made them lush opportunities for queer worldmaking.

4. Stefan Brecht, *Queer Theatre* (New York: Methuen, 1978), p. 9.

5. Jack Smith, "Capitalism of Lotusland," in *Wait for Me at the Bottom of the Pool,* p. 11. The monologue is taken from "Irrational Landlordism of Bagdad," presented at the Cologne Art Fair 1977.

6. Ibid.

7. Hoberman, "Jack Smith," p. 18.

8. Michael Warner, "Introduction," *Fear of a Queer Planet: Queer Politics and Social Theory* (Minneapolis: University of Minnesota Press, 1993).

9. Lisa Duggan develops this idea in her tentatively titled monograph *The Incredible Shrinking Public Sphere.*

Introduction: Performing Disidentifications

1. Néstor García Canclini, "Cultural Reconversion," in *On Edge: The Crisis of Contemporary Latin American Culture,* ed. George Yúdice, Jean Franco, and Juan Flores (Minneapolis: University of Minnesota Press, 1992), p. 32.

2. William E. Connolly, *Identity\Difference: Democratic Negotiations of Political Paradox* (Ithaca, N.Y.: Cornell University Press, 1991), p. 163.

3. These debates are meticulously outlined in Diana Fuss, *Essentially Speaking: Feminism, Nature and Difference* (New York and London: Routledge, 1989).

4. For an important intervention on this front, see Essex Hemphill, "If Freud Had Been a Neurotic Colored Woman: Reading Dr. Frances Cress Welsing," in *Ceremonies* (New York: Penguin, 1992), pp. 52–61.

5. Norma Alarcón, "Conjugating Subjects in the Age of Multiculturalism," in *Mapping Multiculturalism*, ed. Avery F. Gordon and Christopher Newfield (Minneapolis: University of Minnesota Press, 1996), p. 129.

6. Jean Laplanche and Jean-Bertrand Pontalis, *The Language of Psychoanalysis*, trans. Donald Nicholson-Smith (New York: W. W. Norton, 1973), p. 206.

7. Eve Kosofsky Sedgwick, *The Epistemology of the Closet* (Berkeley and Los Angeles: University of California Press, 1990), p. 61.

8. Kimberle William Crenshaw, "Beyond Racism and Misogyny: Black Feminism and 2 Live Crew," in *Words That Wound: Critical Race Theory, Assaultive Speech, and the First Amendment*, ed. Mari J. Matsuda et al. (Boulder, Colo.: Westview Press, 1993), pp. 111–32.

9. Frantz Fanon, *Black Skins, White Masks* (New York: Grove Press, 1967), p. 180.

10. John Champagne, "'Anthropology—Unending Search for What Is Utterly Precious': Race, Class, and *Tongues Untied*," in *The Ethics of Marginality: A New Approach to Gay Studies* (Minneapolis: University of Minnesota Press, 1995). Champagne's text, in its frantic mission to attack important black queer culture makers such as the late Marlon Riggs and Essex Hemphill, attempts to link Riggs's critique of the Castro's white normativity as a critique of S/M and, furthermore, as being closely aligned with antiporn movements. Champagne accuses Hemphill of having cried during a reading of his on the exploitative dimensions of the late Robert Mapplethorpe's work's mythification of black men as exotic kink. Champagne's reductive critical lens equates a critique of a major artist with the antiporn censorship of Andrea Dworkin and John Stoltenberg. In doing this, Champagne seems to betray his ignorance of the body of Hemphill's cultural production, which includes poetry and prose that the likes of Dworkin and Stoltenberg would immediately denounce as porn. Champagne declines to engage actual antiporn movements and instead makes weak accusations that gay African-American cultural workers who engage white racism and the exclusion of bodies of color from many aspects of white gay culture are actually antiporn activists. Hemphill's tears during his presentation are interpreted as a manipulative act of bad faith. This accusation indicates the ways in which the critic is dulled to the history of subjugation that black bodies have experienced under the influence of whites.

11. Yvonne Yarbro-Bejarano, "Expanding the Categories of Race and Sexuality in Lesbian and Gay Studies," in *Professions of Desire: Lesbian and Gay Studies in Literature*, ed. George E. Haggerty and Bonnie Zimmerman (New York: MLA, 1995), pp. 128–29.

12. Louis Althusser, *Lenin and Marxism and Other Essays*, trans. Ben Brewster (New York: Monthly Review Press, 1971), pp. 127–87.

13. Michel Pêcheux, *Language, Semantics and Ideology* (New York: St. Martin's Press, 1982).

14. Judith Butler, *Bodies That Matter: On the Discursive Limits of "Sex"* (Routledge: New York, 1993), p. 219. Žižek's discussion of disidentification can be found in Slavoj Žižek, *The Sublime Object of Ideology* (New York: Verso, 1991).

15. Butler, *Bodies That Matter*, p. 219.

16. One of Freud's accounts of identification can be found in *Group Psychology and the Analysis of the Ego*, trans. James Strachey (New York: W. W. Norton, 1959). In this book Freud schematizes three types of identification: the first type is the original emotional tie with an object that is central to the the-

ory of the Oedipus complex; the second variant is identification with a substitute for a libidinal object; and the third mode is a nonerotic identification with a subject who shares common characteristics and investments. The first route is clearly the road to normative heterosexual identity formation. The second notion of identification is the pathologized and regressive possibility that can account for the taking on of various queer object choices. In this mode of identification, the object is not sucessfully transferred as it is in the Oedipal identificatory circuit, but instead what I understand as a *queer* introjection occurs and circumvents such identifications. The final mode allows for identifications that are same-sex and decidedly nonerotic, thus permitting same-sex group identifications that are not "regressive" or pathological. Throughout Freud's writing, there is a curious interlacing of desire and identification. Identification with a same-sex model is necessary for the process of desiring an opposite-sex object choice. Desire, for Freud, is, then, a term that is reserved for normative heterosexuality, and homosexual emotional and erotic connections are talked about in terms of identification. The theory of disidentification proposed here is offered, in part, as a substitute to this Freudian model, even though its workings also depend on certain forms of introjection, as described in Freud's second modality of identification. In what follows, I make links between my understanding of disidentification and the Freudian and post-Freudian understanding of melancholia. Melancholia is a process that also depends on introjection. In my analysis, this introjection is described as the "holding on to" or incorporation of or by a lost object.

17. Eve Kosofsky Sedgwick, "Queer Performativity: Henry James's *The Art of the Novel*," *GLQ* 1:1 (fall 1993): 13.

18. Diana Fuss, "Fashion and the Homospectatorial Look," *Critical Inquiry* 18:4 (summer 1992): 713–32.

19. Ibid., p. 730.

20. Teresa de Lauretis, *The Practices of Love: Lesbian Sexuality and Perverse Desire* (Bloomington and Indianapolis: Indiana University Press, 1994), p. 190.

21. Diana Fuss, *Identification Papers* (New York: Routledge, 1995), p. 11.

22. James Baldwin, *The Devil Finds Work* (New York: Dial Press, 1976), p. 7. For an intriguing discussion of Baldwin's complicated and queenly identification with Davis, see Jane Gaines, "On Being Green" (unpublished manuscript presented at the MLA, December 1992).

23. For an important critique of Rodriguez's work and assimilationist politics, see Ramón Saldívar's *Chicano Narratives: The Dialectics of Difference* (Madison: University of Wisconsin Press, 1990). See Richard Rodriguez, *Hunger of Memory: The Education of Richard Rodriguez* (New York: Bantam Books, 1983).

24. Michel Foucault, *The History of Sexuality*, vol. 1, *An Introduction*, trans. Robert Hurley (New York: Random House, 1980), pp. 100–101.

25. David Leeming, *James Baldwin: A Biography* (New York: Alfred A. Knopf, 1994), pp. 333–34.

26. James Baldwin, *Just Above My Head* (New York: Dial Press, 1979), p. 550.

27. Ibid., p. 552.

28. Leeming, *James Baldwin*, p. 332.

29. An especially troubling genealogy of queer theory is Annamarie Jagose's *Queer Theory* (New York: New York University Press, 1996), a book that attempts to historicize queer discourse by narrating its debt to the homophile movement and lesbian feminism, and yet almost completely ignores queer theory's debt to radical women and men of color.

30. Norma Alarcón, "The Theoretical Subject(s) of *This Bridge Called My Back* and Anglo-American Feminism," in Gloria Anzaldúa, *Making Face, Making Soul/Haciendo Caras: Creative and Critical Perspectives by Feminists of Color* (San Francisco: Aunt Lute Books, 1990), pp. 356–69.

31. Ibid., p. 360.

32. Ernst Bloch and Theodor W. Adorno, "Something's Missing: A Discussion between Ernst and

Theodor W. Adorno on the Contradictions of Utopian Longing," in Ernst Bloch, *The Utopian Function of Art: Selected Essays,* trans. Jack Zipes and Frank Mecklenburg (Cambridge: MIT Press, 1988), pp. 1–17. For more on the idea of queer utopianism, see my essay "Ghosts of Public Sex: Utopian Longings, Queer Memories," in *Policing Public Sex: Queer Politics and the Future of AIDS Activism,* ed. Dangerous Bedfellows (Boston: South End Press, 1996), pp. 355–72.

33. Stuart Hall, "Encoding/Decoding," in *Culture, Media, Language,* ed. Stuart Hall, Dorothy Hobson, Andrew Lowe, and Paul Willis (London: Unwin Hyman, 1980), p. 136.

34. Ibid., p. 137.

35. Christian Metz, "The Imaginary Signifier," trans. Ben Brewster, *Screen* (summer 1975): 14–76.

36. Laura Mulvey, "Visual Pleasure and Narrative Cinema," *Screen* 16:1 (winter 1975): 6–18.

37. For a critique of the Metzian/Mulveyan paradigm, see Gaylyn Studlar, "Masochism and the Perverse Pleasures of the Cinema," in *Movies and Methods: An Anthology,* ed. Bill Nichols (Berkeley: University of California Press, 1985), pp. 602–21.

38. Laura Mulvey, "Afterthoughts on 'Visual Pleasure and Narrative Cinema,' Inspired by *Duel in the Sun,*" *Framework* 15:17 (1981): 29–38.

39. *Degaying* is a term I borrow from Cindy Patton, who uses it in her *The Invention of AIDS* (New York: Routledge, 1990) to discuss the ways in which government health-care agencies and some HIV/AIDS service groups have worked to disassociate the AIDS epidemic from its connection to gay culture.

40. Miriam Hansen, *From Babel to Babylon: Spectatorship in American Silent Film* (Cambridge: Harvard University Press, 1991).

41. Ibid., p. 281.

42. For an excellent survey of these developments, see Judith Mayne, *Cinema and Spectatorship* (New York: Routledge, 1993).

43. Manthia Diawara, "Black Spectatorship," in *Black American Cinema,* ed. Manthia Diawara (New York: Routledge, 1993), p. 215. Bell hooks, in her essay "The Oppositional Gaze: Black Female Spectatorship" in the same volume, challenges Mulvey's formulations from an uncompromising and powerful black feminist position.

44. This is not to say that other variables such as age or ability do not register. They do not take their place in the familiar litany I rehearse here because they do not significantly figure in the history of critical writing on filmic identification that I am narrating.

45. Chris Straayer, "The Hypothetical Lesbian Heroine," in *Deviant Eyes, Deviant Bodies: Sexual Re-orientations in Film and Video* (New York: Columbia University Press, 1996), p. 10.

46. Michele Wallace, "Race, Gender, and Psychoanalysis in Forties Film: *Lost Boundaries, Home of the Brave* and *The Quiet One,*" in Diawara, *Black American Cinema,* p. 257.

47. Ibid., p. 264; my emphasis.

48. Toni Morrison, "Unspeakable Things Unspoken: The Afro-American Presence in American Literature," *Michigan Quarterly Review* 28:1 (winter 1989): 14. Morrison further delineates these ideas in her study *Playing in the Dark: Whites and the Literary Imagination* (Cambridge: Harvard University Press, 1992).

49. Eve Kosofsky Sedgwick, "Across Gender, Across Sexuality: Willa Cather and Others," in *Displacing Homophobia: Gay Male Perspectives in Literature and Culture,* ed. Ronald R. Butters, John M. Clum, and Michael Moon (Durham, N.C.: Duke University Press, 1989), p. 65.

50. Butler, *Bodies That Matter,* pp. 143–66.

51. Wayne Koestenbaum, *The Queen's Throat: Opera, Homosexuality, and the Mystery of Desire* (New York: Vintage Books, 1993), pp. 84–85.

52. Craig Owens, one of postmodernism's most astute theorists, summarizes postmodernism's

identity crisis in his important essay on postmodernism and otherness as follows: "Decentered, allegorical, schizophrenic . . . however we choose to diagnose the symptoms, postmodernism is usually treated, by its protagonists and antagonists alike, as a crisis of cultural authority, specifically the authority vested in Western Culture and its institutions" ("The Discourse of Others: Feminism and Postmodernism," in *Beyond Recognition: Representation, Power and Culture* [Berkeley and Los Angeles: University of California Press, 1992], p. 166).

53. Gayatri Chakravorty Spivak, *Outside in the Teaching Machine* (New York and London: Routledge, 1993), p. 252.

54. Rodriguez comes out in a somewhat oblique fashion in his second book, *Days of Obligation: An Argument with My Mexican Father* (New York: Viking Press, 1992).

55. Arturo Islas, *Migrant Souls* (New York: Avon, 1990), p. 41.

1. Famous and Dandy like B. 'n' Andy

1. Although the racism that Basquiat encountered in the 1980s art world (or even now in his work's critical reception) is not this study's primary concern, it is important to mention the adverse climate that he was, in part, responding to. This case has been documented in many of the essays published in the catalog of the Whitney Museum of American Art's retrospective of Basquiat's work. See *Jean-Michel Basquiat,* ed. Richard Marshall (New York: Whitney Museum of American Art, 1992). Bell hooks discusses the racist slant in art journalism concerning Basquiat in her essay "Altar of Sacrifice: Re-membering Basquiat," *Art in America* (June 1993): 68–117. Greg Tate eloquently defended Basquiat in his important essay "Flyboy in the Buttermilk: Jean-Michel Basquiat, Nobody Loves a Genius Child," *Village Voice,* November 14, 1989; reprinted in *Flyboy in the Buttermilk: Essays on Contemporary America* (New York: Simon and Schuster, 1992). In that essay, Tate produces a damning indictment of the New York art world: "No area of modern intellectual life has been more resistant to recognizing and authorizing people of color than the world of the 'serious' visual arts. To this day it remains a bastion of white supremacy, a sconce of the wealthy whose high-walled barricades are matched only by Wall Street and the White House and whose exclusionary practices are inforced *24-7-365.* It is easier for a rich white man to enter the kingdom of heaven than for a Black abstract and/or conceptual artist to get a one-woman show in lower Manhattan, or a feature in the pages of *Artforum, Art in America* or *The Village Voice*" (234).

2. Fred Brathwaite, "Jean-Michel Basquiat," *Interview* (October 1992): 112.

3. Conference presentations at "Re-reading Warhol: The Politics of Pop," Duke University, January 1993.

4. Greg S. McCue and Clive Bloom, *Dark Knights: The New Comics in Context* (Boulder, Colo.: Pluto Press, 1993), p. 20.

5. Ibid.

6. Sander Gilman, *The Jew's Body* (New York: Routledge, 1991), p. 53.

7. A disidentification with the superhero form, operating on an entirely different cultural register, can be seen in the emergence of *Milestone Comics.* Milestone has rewritten Superman, for instance, in the form of Icon, an alien child who was not found by white mid-westerners but instead by slaves on a nineteenth-century plantation in the United States. The shapeless alien took on the racial characteristics of the earth people who discovered him and "passes" as an African-American human. It is also interesting to note that the Milestone comic book universe is also populated with more gay, lesbian, Asian, and Latino characters than any other major U.S. comic company. For an informative journalistic account of the Milestone revolution in comics and a survey of the African American superhero, see Gary Dauphin, "To Be Young, Superpowered and Black, Interdimensional Identity Politics and Market Share: The Crisis of the Negro Superhero," *Village Voice,* May 17, 1994, pp. 31–38.

8. Warhol himself, as Moon has shown us, was also not content to just "reproduce" Superman's image. He also let the paint splashes rupture the illusion of comic book perfection. Basquiat, in my estimation, follows this lead in his "homages" to childhood heroes.

9. Lucy Lippard, *Pop Art* (New York: Praeger, 1966).

10. Susan Stewart, *Crimes of Writing: Problems in the Containment of Representation* (New York: Oxford University Press, 1991), p. 207.

11. Paul Gilroy, "Whose Millennium Is This? Blackness: Pre-Modern, Post-Modern, Anti-Modern," in *Small Acts: Thoughts on the Politics of Black Cultures* (New York: Serpent's Tail, 1993), p. 164.

12. Ibid.

13. Lauren Berlant, "National Brands/National Bodies: *Imitation of Life*," in *Comparative American Identities: Race, Sex, and Nationality in the Modern Text*, ed. Hortense Spillers (New York: Routledge, 1991), p. 121.

14. Tate, *Flyboy in the Buttermilk*, p. 231.

15. Stewart, *Crimes of Writing*, p. 227.

16. Andy Warhol, *The Andy Warhol Diaries*, ed. Pat Hackett (New York: Warner Books, 1989), p. 572.

17. Ibid.

18. Quoted by Brathwaite, "Jean-Michel Basquiat," p. iii.

19. See Philip Brian Harper, "Eloquence and Epitaph: Black Nationalism and the Homophobic Impulse in Response to the Death of Max Robinson," *Social Text* 28, no. 9.3 (1991): 68–86, for an excellent discussion of the African-American reception of Robinson's life and death.

20. Jean Laplance and Jean-Bertrand Pontalis, *The Language of Psychoanalysis*, trans. Donald Nicholson-Smith (New York: W. W. Norton, 1973).

21. Hooks, "Altar of Sacrifice," p. 71.

22. Hooks rightfully explains that "In Basquiat's work, flesh on the black body is almost always falling away" (ibid.).

23. Ibid., p. 74.

24. For an interesting discussion of the "black life-world," see Manthia Diawara, "*Noir* by *Noirs*: Towards a New Realism in Black Cinema," in *Shades of Noir*, ed. Joan Copjec (New York: Verso, 1993), pp. 261–79.

25. Hooks, "Altar of Sacrifice," p. 74.

26. Tate also points out the occlusion of black women in Basquiat's art, but he arrives at a very different understanding of this trend in the painter's work: "If you're black and historically informed there is no way you can look at Basquiat's work and not get beat up by the black male's history as property, pulverized meat, and popular entertainment. No way not to be reminded that lynchings and minstrelsy still vie in the white supremacist's imagination for the black male body's proper place" (*Flyboy in the Buttermilk*, p. 238). Tate's statement should not be seen as an attempt to deny the history of the black female body's exploitation under white supremacy. Rather, I see his statement, like Basquiat's paintings, as an explication of the specific position of black men in the dominant culture's imagination.

27. Hortense Spillers, "Mama's Baby, Papa's Maybe: An American Grammar Book," *Diacritics* 2 (summer 1987): 65–81.

28. Daniel P. Moynihan, *The Negro Family: The Case for National Action* ("The Moynihan Report") (Washington D.C.: U.S. Department of Labor, 1965), in *The Moynihan Report and the Politics of Controversy: A Transaction Social Science and Public Policy Report*, ed. Lee Rainwater and William L. Yancey (Cambridge: MIT Press, 1967), pp. 47–94.

29. Spillers, "Mama's Baby, Papa's Maybe," p. 80.

30. Toni Morrison's novel *Jazz* (New York: Alfred A. Knopf, 1992) is a cultural text that examines

the workings of mourning and melancholia from a female perspective. Like this chapter's final section, her novel is inspired by a James Van DerZee photograph. It is set in 1927, seven years after armistice. Its location is Harlem. A door-to-door salesman who is married and fifty meets and falls in love with an eighteen-year-old woman. The affair ends with the older man, Joe Trace, sick and mad with love, shooting the young woman Dorcas in a fit of passion. The tragedy becomes even more profound when Joe's wife, Violet, in a fit of blinding madness, lashes out with a knife during the funeral and mutilates the beautiful light-skinned young woman's face as mourners look on horrified. This is where the book begins. It goes on to tell the story of the way in which Dorcas's face, captured in a photograph on the mantelpiece, haunts Joe and Violet. The character of Violet embodies an aspect of African-American female mourning. Like the Basquiat paintings discussed in this section, her story is a meditation on the workings of mourning in African-American culture.

31. The next chapter, "Photographies of Mourning: Melancholia and Ambivalence in Van DerZee, Mapplethorpe, and *Looking for Langston,*" reproduces an account of the specificities of black male mourning in twentieth-century U.S. cultural production.

2. Photographies of Mourning

1. Judith Halberstam, *Female Masculinity* (Durham, N.C.: Duke University Press, 1998).

2. Sylvia Wynter, "Rethinking 'Aesthetics': Notes Towards a Deciphering Practice," in *Ex-Iles: Essays on Caribbean Cinema,* ed. Mbye Cham (Trenton, N.J.: African World Press, 1992), pp. 266–67.

3. Raymond Williams first used the phrase "structure of feeling" in his study *Marxism and Literature* (New York: Oxford University Press, 1978). For Williams, a structure of feeling was a *process* of relating the continuity of social formations within a work of art. Williams explains: "The hypothesis has a special relevance to art and literature, where true social content is in a significant number of cases of this present and affective kind, which cannot be reduced to belief systems, institutions, or explicit general relationships, though it may include all these as lived and experienced, with or without tension, as it also evidently includes elements of social and material (physical or natural) experience which may lie beyond or be uncovered or imperfectly covered by, the elsewhere recognizable systematic elements. The unmistakable presence of certain elements in art which are not covered by (though in one mode, might be reduced to) other formal systems is the true source of the specializing category of 'the aesthetic', 'the arts', and 'imaginative literature'. We need, on the one hand, to acknowledge (and welcome) the specificity of these elements—specific dealings, specific rhythms—and yet to find their specific kinds of sociality, thus preventing the extraction from social experience which is conceivable only when social experience itself has been categorically (and at root historically) reduced" (p. 133).

4. Arnold Rampersad, *The Life of Langston Hughes,* vols. 1 and 2 (New York: Oxford University Press, 1986, 1988).

5. Rampersad also fails to explore the paths of an orientation that might be primarily autoerotic or in some way "bisexual" or perhaps even a non-"traditional" gender identification. In an interview, gay Harlem Renaissance figure Bruce Nugent himself refers to Hughes as "asexual." I do not wish to rule out the "asexual" possibility in the same way that Rampersad refuses to seriously consider any sexual option but compulsory heterosexuality. If one were to envision asexuality as more of a practice than a primary orientation, I do not see a necessary contradiction in being both queer and asexual. My intention is not to rule out the asexual as a species, but instead to decipher the ways in which asexuality is deployed from a normative heterosexual register as a mechanism to cancel queer possibility. For an excellent example of African-American biography writing that engages the queerness of its subject and the Harlem Renaissance, see Wayne F. Cooper, *Claude McKay: Rebel Sojourner in the Harlem Renaissance* (Baton Rouge: Louisiana State University Press, 1987).

6. Joan W. Scott, "The Evidence of Experience," *Critical Inquiry* 17 (summer 1991): pp. 773–97.

7. Sergei Eisenstein, *Film Form: Essays in Film Theory* (New York: Meridian Books, 1957), p. 58.

8. Fredric Jameson, *Signatures of the Visible* (New York: Routledge, 1991), p. 78.

9. Gayl Jones, *Liberating Voices: Oral Tradition in African American Literature* (Cambridge: Harvard University Press, 1991), p. 197. For another useful account of call-and-response in twentieth-century African-American cultural production, see John F. Callahan, *In the African American Grain: Call-and-Response in Twentieth-Century Black Fiction* (Middletown, Conn.: Wesleyan University Press, 1988).

10. Langston Hughes, "Poem," in *Black Men/White Men: A Gay Anthology*, ed. Michael J. Smith (San Francisco: Gay Sunshine Press, 1983).

11. Houston Baker Jr., *Blues, Ideology, and Afro-American Literature: A Vernacular Theory* (Chicago: University of Chicago Press, 1984), pp. 3–4.

12. Paul Gilroy, "Nothing but Sweat inside My Hand: Diaspora Aesthetics and Black Arts in Britain," in *ICA Documents 7: Black Film, British Cinema*, ed. Kobena Mercer (London: ICA, 1988), p. 46.

13. Roland Barthes, *Camera Lucida*, trans. Richard Howard (New York: Hill and Wang, 1974), p. 93.

14. Sigmund Freud, "Mourning and Melancholia," in *General Psychological Theory*, trans. James Strachey (New York: Collier Books, 1963), p. 243.

15. My thinking about melancholia is enabled by the work of Judith Butler, who, in *Gender Trouble: Feminism and the Subversion of Identity* (New York: Routledge, 1990), describes the melancholic as a subject who "refuses the loss of the object, and internalization becomes a strategy of magically resuscitating the lost object, not only because the loss is painful, but because the ambivalence felt toward the object requires that the object be retained until differences are settled" (p. 58).

16. Paul de Man, "Autobiography as De-facement," in *Rhetoric of Romanticism* (New York: Columbia University Press, 1984), pp. 75–76.

17. Peggy Phelan has written about this particular ontology of performance in *Unmarked: The Politics of Performance* (New York: Routledge, 1993), pp. 33–70.

18. James Van DerZee, *The Harlem Book of the Dead* (New York: Dutton, 1974), p. 83.

19. Barthes, *Camera Lucida*, p. 112.

20. Michael Moon, "Memorial Rags, Memorial Rages," unpublished manuscript.

21. Tony Fischer, "Isaac Julien: Looking for Langston," *Third Text* 12 (1990): 59–70.

22. Stuart Hall, "Cultural Identities and Cinematic Representations," in *Ex-Iles*, p. 133.

23. Fischer, "Isaac Julien," p. 67.

24. Dominick Dunne, "Robert Mapplethorpe's Proud Finale," *Vanity Fair* (February 1989). See Robert Mapplethorpe, *Black Book*, Foreword by Ntozake Shange (New York: St. Martin's Press, 1986).

25. Isaac Julien and Kobena Mercer, "True Confessions: A Discourse on Images of Black Male Sexuality," in *Male Order: Unwrapping Masculinity*, ed. Rowena Chapman and Jonathan Rutherford (London: Lawrence and Wishart, 1988); reprinted in *Brother to Brother: New Writings by Black Gay Men*, ed. Essex Hemphill and Joseph Beam (Boston: Alyson Publications, 1991), p. 170.

26. The "black male porn" I am referring to is nothing like lesbian erotica, porn produced for lesbians by lesbians. It is, in fact, just the opposite: porn made by white men for a primarily white audience. One could tentatively imagine that the pro-gay, pro-black, pro-sex charge that a black male porn produced by black men might create would indeed be powerful.

27. Kobena Mercer, "Looking for Trouble," *Transition* 51 (1991): 189.

28. This is not to imply that only gay men of color can disidentify with Mapplethorpe's images. Jane Gaines has written about the pleasure that straight white women can extract from Mapplethorpe. Gaines narrates her suspicion that "there may be fantasies of defiance as well as fantasies of discovery

worked out over these 'borrowed' and shared love objects" ("Competing Glances: Who Is Reading Robert Mapplethorpe's *Black Book*," in *New Formations* 16 [spring 1992], p. 39). The working out that transpires in Gaines's account is, then, an ambivalent working through, what in the terms of this study would be understood as a disidentification with a complex object.

29. Phelan, *Unmarked*, p. 51.

30. Judith Butler, "The Force of Fantasy: Feminism, Mapplethorpe, and Discursive Excess," *Differences* 2:2 (1990): 105–25. Butler's formulations in this instance are informed by the work of Jean Laplanche and Jean-Bertrand Pontalis, *The Formation of Phantasy*, ed. Victor Burgin, James Donald, and Cora Kaplan (London: Methuen, 1986).

31. Jeff Nunokawa, "'All the Sad Young Men': AIDS and the Work of Mourning," *Yale Journal of Criticism* 4:2 (1991): 2.

32. Kobena Mercer, "Dark and Lovely Too: Black Gay Men in Independent Film," in *Queer Looks: Perspectives on Lesbian and Gay Male Film and Video*, ed. Martha Gever, John Greyson, and Prathiba Parmar (New York: Routledge, 1993), pp. 253–54.

33. Douglas Crimp, "Mourning and Militancy," *October* 51 (1989): 18.

3. The Autoethnographic Performance

1. Homi K. Bhabha, *The Location of Culture* (New York and London: Routledge, 1994), p. 86.

2. Eve Kosofsky Sedgwick, *Tendencies* (Durham, N.C.: Duke University Press, 1993), p. 3.

3. Ella Shohat, "Notes on the Post-Colonial," *Social Text* 31–32 (1992): 110.

4. Bruno Latour, *We Have Never Been Modern*, trans. Catherine Porter (Cambridge: Harvard University Press, 1993), p. 34; emphasis added.

5. Fredric Jameson, *Signatures of the Visible* (New York and London: Routledge, 1992), p. 1.

6. This coauthored essay appears in Bill Nichols's collection *Representing Reality: Issues and Concepts in Documentary* (Bloomington and Indianapolis: Indiana University Press, 1991), pp. 201–28.

7. For further discussion of "pornotopia," see Linda Williams, *Hardcore: Power, Pleasure, and the "Frenzy of the Visible"* (Berkeley and Los Angeles: University of California Press, 1989).

8. The idea of the "native informant" has been discredited in contemporary anthropology and is now only written within scare quotes. The idea of indigenous people serving as informants to First World ethnographers has been critiqued throughout anthropology, critical theory, and postcolonial studies.

9. In contemporary gay culture, *top* and *bottom* are words used to describe people's sexual proclivities. Women or men who prefer to be penetrated in sexual acts are bottoms; those whose identification is connected with acts of penetration are usually referred to as tops. The words *top* and *bottom* do not capture the totality of one's sexual disposition, but instead work as a sort of cultural shorthand. Asian gay men, as will be explained later in this chapter, are stereotypically labeled as strictly bottoms in the erotic image hierarchy of North American gay porn.

10. Judith Butler, *Bodies That Matter: On the Discursive Limits of "Sex"* (New York: Routledge, 1993), pp. 226–27.

11. Jacques Derrida, *Limited Inc.*, trans. Samual Weber and Jeffery Mehiman (Evanston, Ill.: Northwestern University Press, 1988), p. 18.

12. Bhabha, *The Location of Culture*, p. 245.

13. Françoise Lionnet, *Autobiographical Voices: Race, Gender, and Self-Portraiture* (Ithaca, N.Y., and London: Cornell University Press, 1989), pp. 99–100.

14. Ibid., p. 102.

15. The phrase "figural anthropology" is developed in the work of Michel Serres, *The Parasite*, trans. Lawrence R. Schehr (Baltimore: Johns Hopkins University Press, 1982), p. 6.

16. Mary Louise Pratt, *Under Imperial Eyes: Travel Writing and Transculturation* (New York and London: Routledge, 1992), pp. 6–7.

17. Jim Lane has argued for the utility of literary theories of autobiography when considering the historical and theoretical underpinnings of autobiographical film. Lane's article also provides a good gloss of the autobiographical film after 1968. See "Notes on Theory and the Autobiographical Documentary Film in America," *Wide Angle* 15:3 (1993): 21–36.

18. For a historical overview of documentary video, see Deirdre Boyle, "A Brief History of American Documentary Video," in *Illuminating Video: An Essential Guide to Video Art,* ed. Doug Hall and Sally Jo Fifer (New York: Aperture Bay Area Video Coalition, 1990), pp. 51–70. Boyle's most significant elision in the summary is the omission of gay, lesbian, queer, and HIV/AIDS activist video documentary.

19. Lane, "Notes on Theory."

20. See Marcos Becquer, "Snapthology and Other Discursive Practices in *Tongues Untied,*" *Wide Angle* 13:2 (1991), for a fine reading of Riggs's black and queer performance and production.

21. Chris Holmlund has discussed Benning's videos as autoethnographies in "When Autobiography Meets Ethnography and Girl Meets Girl: The 'Dyke Docs' of Sadie Benning and Su Friedrich," unpublished manuscript, presented at Visible Evidence, Duke University, September 1993.

22. Stuart Hall, "Cultural Identity and Cinematic Representations," in *Ex-Iles: Essays on Caribbean Cinema,* ed. Mbye Cham (Trenton, N.J.: African World Press, 1992), p. 133.

23. Michelle Wallace has argued forcefully against the trend to produce negative/positive critiques in critical race theory in her book *Invisibility Blues: From Pop to Theory* (New York and London: Verso, 1990), pp. 1–13.

24. Richard Dyer, "Male Gay Porn: Coming to Terms," *Jump Cut* 30 (1985): 27–29.

25. Chris Straayer, "The She-Man: Postmodern Bi-Sexed Performance in Film and Video," *Screen* 31:3 (1990): 272.

26. The term *contact zone* is borrowed from Pratt, *Under Imperial Eyes,* pp. 6–7.

27. The tradition of white male spectators, firmly positioned in a superior hierarchical position, dates back to the very first photographic male pornography. An article on six gay male pornographic photographs, retrieved from the Kinsey Institute for Research in Sex, Gender, and Reproduction, identifies an orientalist motif in the images of two men with turbans and "oriental" robes having oral and anal sex in front of the artificial backdrop of exoticized palm trees. The article's author argues that orientalism has long occupied an important position in gay male pornography (Todd D. Smith, "Gay Male Pornography and the East: Re-orienting the Orient," *History of Photography* 18:1 [1994]).

28. See Richard Fung, "Looking for My Penis: The Eroticized Asian in Gay Video Porn," in *How Do I Look?: Queer Film and Video* (Seattle: Bay Press, 1991), pp. 145–60. In this essay, Fung explains an orientalism that Edward Said's seminal study could not imagine. Fung surveys the different racist constructions of Asian men that dominate gay male pornography, and tentatively imagines a pornography that affirms rather than appropriates Asian male sexuality.

29. Edward Said, *Orientalism* (New York: Random House, 1979), pp. 2–3.

30. Homi K. Bhabha, "The Other Question: The Stereotype of Colonial Discourse," *Screen* 24:6 (1983); reprinted in Bhabha, *The Location of Culture.* Tom Hastings offers the most interesting and sustained critique of the heterosexist blind spots in Said's study in his "Said's Orientalism and the Discourse of (Hetero)Sexuality," *Canadian Review of American Studies* 23:1 (1992): 130.

31. Lisa Lowe, *Critical Terrains: French and British Orientalism* (Ithaca, N.Y., and London: Cornell University Press, 1991), p. 5.

32. Pratt, *Under Imperial Eyes,* p. 7.

33. See, for example, C. L. R. James, *Beyond a Boundary* (London: Stanley Paul, 1963).

34. Vijay Mishra and Bob Hodge touch on Canada's ambiguous postcolonial status in their essay "What Is Post-Colonialism?" *Textual Practices* 15:3 (1991): 339–414. Canada is also covered in the important primer by Bill Ashcroft, Gareth Griffiths, and Helen Tiffin, *The Empire Writes Back: Theory and Practice in Post-Colonial Literatures* (London and New York: Routledge, 1989).

35. The colonization of Canada's "French-Other," Quebec, by a decidedly North American (here meant to include Anglo-Canadian and mainstream U.S.) culture has been touched on by Robert Schwartzwald in his essay "Fear of Federasty: Quebec's Invented Fictions," in *Comparative American Identities: Race, Sex, and Nationality in the Modern Text,* ed. Hortense Spillers (New York: Routledge, 1991), p. 181. Fung's Asian queer community can be understood as another "Other-Canada" that experiences a cultural colonization under the sign of North America.

36. Antonio Benítez-Rojo, *The Repeating Island: The Caribbean and the Postmodern Perspective,* trans. James E. Maranisis (Durham, N.C.: Duke University Press, 1992), p. 11.

37. Fung's videos are available through Video Data Bank, School of the Art Institute of Chicago, 112 South Michigan Avenue, Suite 312, Chicago, IL 60603 (Telephone: 312-345-3550).

4. "The White to Be Angry"

1. Barney Hoskyns, *Waiting for the Sun: Strange Days, Weird Scenes and the Sound of Los Angeles* (New York: St. Martin's Press, 1996), p. 307.

2. George Lipsitz, *Dangerous Crossings: Popular Music, Postmodernism and the Poetics of Space* (New York and London: Verso, 1994), p. 17.

3. Tommy Gear and Mike Glass, "Supremely Vaginal," *aRude* 1:2 (fall 1995): 42.

4. Ibid.

5. Kimberle William Crenshaw, "Beyond Racism and Misogyny: Black Feminism and 2 Live Crew," in *Words That Wound: Critical Race Theory, Assaultive Speech, and the First Amendment,* ed. Mari J. Matsuda et al. (Boulder, Colo.: Westview Press, 1993), pp. 111–32.

6. Félix Guattari, *Soft Subversions,* ed. Sylvère Lotringer, trans. David L. Sweet and Chet Wiener (New York: Semiotext[e], 1996), p. 37.

7. Julian Fleisher, *The Drag Queens of New York: An Illustrated Field Guide to Drag* (New York: Riverhead Books, 1996).

8. "Realness" is mimetic of a certain high-feminine style in standard realist terms.

9. Many of the performers I have just mentioned appear in the film documentation of New York's annual drag festival, *Wigstock: The Movie.*

10. Gear and Glass, "Supremely Vaginal," p. 77.

11. Antonio Gramsci, "The Formation of Intellectuals," in *The Modern Prince and Other Writings,* trans. Louis Marks (New York: International Publishers, 1959), p. 181.

12. Here I do not mean homogeneity in its more quotidian usage, the opposite of heterogeneous, but instead in a Gramscian sense that is meant to connote social cohesion.

13. John Fiske, "Opening the Hallway: Some Remarks on the Fertility of Stuart Hall's Contribution to Critical Theory," in *Stuart Hall: Critical Dialogues in Cultural Studies,* ed. David Morley and Kuan-Hsing Chen (New York: Routledge, 1996), pp. 213–14. Also, for an analysis that uses what is in part a Gramscian lens to consider group formations, see Dick Hebdige's classic analysis of subcultures, *Subculture: The Meaning of Style* (London: Routledge, 1979).

14. Miss Guy's image was featured in designer Calvin Klein's CK One ad campaign. Her androgynous, nontraditional drag was seen all over the nation in print and television advertisements. This ad campaign represented a version of gender diversity that was not previously available in print advertising. Yet, this diversity only, once again, led to a voyeuristic absorption with gender diversity and no real engagement with this node of difference.

15. Queercore writer Dennis Cooper, in an attempt to out the "real" Davis in *Spin* magazine, implied that Hilliard was the artist's true identity. The joke was on Cooper because her professional identity as Hilliard was another "imagined identity." Davis has explained to me that her actual birth name is Clarence, which will be an important fact as my reading unfolds.

16. An alternate, yet complementary, reading of the name Clarence would link this white militiaman and the act of cross-race minstrelsy to the George Bush-appointed Supreme Court justice Clarence Thomas, an African-American who has contributed to the erosion of civil rights within the nation.

17. Here I risk collapsing all antigovernment militias with more traditional domestic terrorists such as the Klu Klux Klan or neo-Nazis. Not all militiamen are white supremacists and the vast majority of white supremacists are not in a militia. But Davis's Clarence is definitely concerned with racist militias whose antigovernment philosophies are also overtly xenophobic and white supremacist.

18. Eric Lott, *Love and Theft: Blackface Minstrelsy and the American Working Class* (New York: Oxford University Press, 1993), p. 25.

19. Antonio Gramsci, *Selections from the Prison Notebooks* (New York: International Publishers, 1971), p. 14.

20. Ibid., p. 348.

21. For an example of this divide in classical Marxism, see Karl Marx, "Theses on Feuerbach," in *The Marx-Engels Reader,* ed. Robert Tucker (New York: W. W. Norton, 1972), p. 145.

22. Mark Simpson, ed., *Anti-Gay* (London: Freedom Editions, 1996).

23. Ibid., p. xix.

24. Ibid.

25. Stuart Hall, "Gramsci's Relevance for the Study of Race and Ethnicity," in Fiske, *Stuart Hall,* p. 433.

26. Michael Omi and Howard Winant, *Racial Formation in the United States: From the 1960s to the 1990s* (New York: Routledge, 1994), p. 81.

27. Hall, "Gramsci's Relevance," p. 439.

28. Cornel West, "Afro-American Oppression and Marxism," in *Marxism and Interpretation,* ed. Cary Nelson and Lawrence Grossberg (Urbana: University of Illinois Press, 1988).

29. Ibid., p. 440.

5. Sister Acts

1. See Jill Dolan's review of Carmelita Tropicana's work at the Chandelier Club, "Carmelita Tropicana Chats at the Club Chandelier," *TDR: The Drama Review* 29:1 (1985): 26–32; and C. Carr, *On Edge: Performance at the End of the Twentieth Century* (Hanover, N.H.: Wesleyan University Press, 1993), pp. 78–84.

2. Camp is most often discussed as a mode of reception. I do not want to deny that camp is often a powerful subcultural lens for viewing the dominant culture, but I suggest that camp is also a style, even a means toward the enactment of self in an adverse cultural climate.

3. This is not to suggest that Sontag theorized a specifically gay male sensitivity; she was, in fact, interested in explaining how camp was, or at least could be, more than just a homosexual phenomenon. This universalizing gesture elided the issue of how other minority communities might enact a camp discourse in favor of how (white) heterosexuals could develop a camp sensibility. See Susan Sontag, "Notes on Camp," in *Against Interpretation* (New York: Delta, 1979). For a critique of Sontag's urbane homophobia, see D. A. Miller, "Sontag's Urbanity," *October* 49 (1989): 21–101.

4. The term *Loisaida* has been used to describe a neighborhood in the Lower East Side of New York City where *el barrio* meets bohemia.

5. Celeste Olalquiaga, *Megalopolis: Contemporary Cultural Sensibilities* (Minneapolis: University of Minnesota Press, 1992).

6. The store's name, not insignificantly, signifies upon one of the first Latino characters that made it into the popular American imagination. The hybrid child of Ricky Ricardo (Desi Arnaz) and Lucy (McGillicuddy) Ricardo (Lucille Ball) embodied the mixing and literal miscegenation that occurs when cultures collide or otherwise meet. Interestingly, the birth of Little Ricky on *I Love Lucy* became a national event in which fiction and real life coincided.

7. Andrew Ross, *No Respect: Intellectuals and Popular Culture* (New York: Routledge, 1989), p. 145. Ross explains that "kitsch, has serious pretensions to artistic taste, and, in fact, contains a range of references to high or legitimate culture which it apes in order to flatter the consumer. Kitsch's seriousness about art, and its aesthetic chutzpah, is usually associated with the class aspirations of and upper mobility of a middlebrow audience, insufficient in cultural capital to guarantee access to legitimate culture" (ibid.).

8. Eve Kosofsky Sedgwick, *The Epistemology of the Closet* (Berkeley and Los Angeles: University of California Press, 1990), p. 156. For a keen gloss on Sedgwick's reading of kitsch and camp as a binarism, see James Creech, *Closet Writing/Gay Reading: The Case of Melville's* Pierre (Chicago: University of Chicago Press, 1993), pp. 45–51.

9. Esther Newton, *Mother Camp: Female Impersonators in America* (Chicago: University of Chicago Press, 1972), p. 105.

10. Pamela Robertson, "'The Kinda Comedy That Imitates Me': Mae West's Identification with Feminist Camp," *Cinema Journal* 32:2 (winter 1993): 57.

11. Ibid.

12. Carr, *On Edge*, p. 79.

13. Ibid., p. 83.

14. Michael Moon, "Flaming Creatures," *October* 51 (winter 1989): 37. Moon's essay is the best account of the politics of Smith's queer performance and filmic production. Other useful accounts include Richard Dyer, *Now You See It: Studies on Lesbian and Gay Film* (New York: Routledge, 1990), pp. 145–49; Carel Rowe, *The Baudelairean Cinema: A Tend within the American Avant-Garde* (Ann Arbor: UMI Press, 1982), pp. 39–40; and David James, *Allegories of Cinema: American Film in the Sixties* (Princeton, N.J.: Princeton University Press, 1989), pp. 119–27.

15. Carr, *On Edge*, p. 83.

16. Pepito, when he is shown at the film's end, is revealed to be Asian. This is significant insofar as the three siblings are all of different races, yet all Cuban and Latina/o. This fact confounds U.S. popular understandings of just what a Latino might look like. It also depicts the three largest racial groups on the island of Cuba.

17. Eve Kosofsky Sedgwick, *Tendencies* (Durham, N.C.: Duke University Press, 1993), pp. 5–9.

18. Interestingly, Ela Troyano portrays the object of a nun's desire in Su Friedrich's video *Damned if You Don't*.

19. Judith Butler, *Bodies That Matter: On the Discursive Limits of "Sex"* (New York: Routledge, 1993), p. 226.

20. Sue-Ellen Case, "Towards a Butch-Femme Aesthetic," in *Making a Spectacle: Feminist Essays on Contemporary Women's Theater*, ed. Lynda Hart (Ann Arbor: University of Michigan Press), pp. 282–99.

21. Kate Davy, "Fe/Male Impersonation: The Discourse of Camp," in *The Politics and Poetics of Camp*, ed. Moe Meyer (New York: Routledge, 1993), p. 142.

22. Wayne Dynes, *Encyclopedia of Homosexuality* (New York: Garland Publishing, 1990).

23. Davy, "Fe/Male Impersonation," p. 145.

24. Cathy Griggers, "Lesbian Bodies in the Age of (Post)Mechanical Reproduction," in *The Lesbian Postmodern*, ed. Laura Dolan (New York: Columbia University Press, 1993), p. 128; my emphasis.

25. Homi K. Bhabha, "Of Mimicry and Man: The Ambivalence of Colonial Discourse," in *The*

Location of Culture (New York and London: Routledge, 1993), pp. 85–92; originally published in *October* 28 (1984): 125–33.

26. Fernando Ortiz, *Glosario de Afronegrismo* (Havana: Imprenta "El Siglo XX," 1924), p. 185. The translation I use is taken from Gustavo Pérez Firmat, used in his study *Literature and Liminality: Festive Readings in the Hispanic Tradition* (Durham, N.C.: Duke University Press, 1986), p. 99.

27. Pérez Firmat, *Literature and Liminality*, p. 108.

28. Jorge Mañach, *Indignación del Choteo* (Miami: Mnemosyne Publishing, 1969), p. 18.

29. For a masterful reading of Mañach and other manifestations of *choteo*, see Pérez Firmat, *Literature and Liminality*, pp. 53–108.

30. Gloria Anzaldúa, *Borderlands: La Frontera* (San Francisco: Aunt Lute Books, 1987), pp. 84–85.

31. Ella Shohat and Robert Stam, *Unthinking Eurocentrism: Multiculturalism and the Media* (New York: Routledge, 1994), p. 42.

32. Griggers, "Lesbian Bodies," p. 126.

33. There is a wealth of valuable interventions by lesbians of color that have challenged the ingrained white normativity of lesbian and gay identities. The work of Gloria Anzaldúa, Audre Lorde, Cherríe Moraga, and Barbara Smith come to mind as thinkers who radicalized notions of gay and lesbian identity in an antiracist fashion.

6. Pedro Zamora's *Real World* of Counterpublicity

1. Michel Foucault, *The History of Sexuality*, vol. 3, *The Care of the Self*, trans. Robert Hurley (New York: Vintage Books, 1986). Also see Michel Foucault, "The Ethic of the Care of the Self as a Practice of Freedom," in *The Final Foucault*, ed. James Bernauer and David Rasmussen, trans. J. D. Gauthier (Cambridge: MIT Press, 1987).

2. Michel Foucault, "On the Genealogy of Ethics: An Overview of Work in Progress," in *Ethics: Subjectivity and Truth*, ed. Paul Rabinow, trans. Robert Hurley (New York: New Press, 1997), p. 269.

3. George Yúdice, "Marginality and the Ethics of Survival," in Andrew Ross, ed., *Universal Abandon? The Politics of Postmodernism* (Minneapolis: University of Minnesota Press, 1988), p. 220.

4. Ibid., p. 229.

5. It is important to clarify that my use of public-sphere theory and the notion of a counterpublic sphere is indebted to Oskar Negt and Alexander Kluge and Anglo-American commentators on Jürgen Habermas. One can thus characterize my deployment of this critical vernacular as being post-Habermasian.

6. Nancy Fraser, "Rethinking the Public Sphere," in *The Phantom Public Sphere*, ed. Bruce Robbins (Minneapolis: University of Minnesota Press, 1993), p. 4.

7. Oskar Negt and Alexander Kluge, *Public Sphere and Experience: Toward an Analysis of the Bourgeois and Proletarian Public Sphere* (Minneapolis: University of Minnesota Press, 1993).

8. Miriam Hansen, "Foreword," in ibid., p. xxxvii.

9. For an excellent reading of the political and philosophical disjunctures between Foucault and Habermas, see Jon Simmons, *Foucault and the Political* (New York: Routledge, 1995).

10. Ibid., p. 103.

11. Fredric Jameson, "On Negt and Kluge," in *The Phantom Public Sphere*, p. 49.

12. Hillary Johnson and Nancy Rommelmann, *The Real* Real World (New York: MTV Books/Pocket Books/Melcher Media, 1995), p. 158.

13. Ibid.

14. Hansen, "Foreword," pp. xxxviii–xxxix.

15. Zamora has continued to be, even after his death, a beacon of queer possibility thanks to MTV's policy of continuously airing *The Real World* reruns, from all five seasons.

16. Both Ricardo and Zamora are figures of ambivalence in that although they both held pioneering roles in the history of Latino representation in the media, they also seemed to have no qualms about performing for white people. Of course, this comparison falls apart when one considers the motivations that organized these performances for whites. Zamora's motivations were not about promoting an individual career, but instead about being an activist and a pedagogue in a larger health emergency. But both men are icons, and their iconicity is a troubling thing; one might wish that they had been less willing to assimilate, but one cannot discount the influence of their work on a larger cultural imaginary. This note is a response to a conversation with Jorge Ignacio Cortiñas, a Cuban-American activist and cultural worker whose astute skepticism and critical ambivalence have helped me nuance this discussion of Zamora's work. Cortiñas also urged me to consider a comparison between Ricardo and Zamora.

17. Johnson and Rommelmann, *The Real* Real World, p. 90.

18. Joseph Hanania, "Resurgence of Gay Roles on Television," *Los Angeles Times,* November 3, 1994, p. 12.

19. Ibid.

20. Ibid.

21. The show used only first names. Thus, when I discuss the narratives of actual episodes, I will employ "Pedro," and when I refer mostly to the man and cultural worker outside of the show's narrative, I will use "Zamora."

22. I use the term *Mexican-American* to describe Rachel because I imagine that her political ideology would not be aligned with the politics of the Chicana/o movement.

23. The confessional is a room where house occupants perform a personal monologue for a stationary camera. The confessional footage is later intercut with the show's narrative.

24. Hal Rubenstein, "Pedro Leaves Us Breathless," *POZ* 1:3 (August–September 1994): 38–41, 79–81.

25. Judd and Pam did eventually begin dating, but only after the show stopped filming. Failed on-the-set couplings include Eric and Julie during the first season, Puck and Rachel in the third, and Kat and Neil in the fourth.

26. Michel Foucault, *Foucault Live,* ed. Sylvère Lotringer, trans. John Johnston (New York: Semiotext[e], 1989), p. 204.

27. Ibid.

28. The Pedro Zamora Memorial Fund was established after his death. The fund was set up to educate women, young people, minorities, and the poor about HIV/AIDS, and to fund AIDS service organizations. The fund, part of AIDS Action, can be reached at 202-986-1300 ext. 3013.

7. Performing Disidentity

1. For more on these films, see Chris Straayer, *Deviant Eyes, Deviant Bodies: Sexual Re-orientations in Film and Video* (New York: Columbia University Press, 1996).

2. Robert Storr, "Setting Traps for the Mind and Heart," *Art in America* 84:1 (January 1996): 73.

3. Tim Rollins, "Interview with Felix Gonzalez-Torres," in *Felix Gonzalez-Torres,* ed. William S. Bartman (New York: A.R.T. Press, 1993), p. 19.

4. John Guillory, *Cultural Capital: The Problems of Literary Canon Formation* (Chicago: University of Chicago Press, 1994), p. 11.

5. Wahneema Lubiano, "Like Being Mugged by a Metaphor: Multiculturalism and State Narratives," in *Mapping Multiculturalism,* ed. Avery Gordon and Christopher Newfield (Minneapolis: University of Minnesota Press, 1996), p. 69.

6. Slavoj Žižek, "The Specter of Ideology," in *Mapping Ideology* (London: Verso, 1994), p. 11.

7. Nancy Fraser, "Rethinking the Public Sphere," in *The Phantom Public Sphere,* ed. Bruce Robbins (Minneapolis: University of Minnesota Press, 1993), p. 22.

8. Mónica Amor, "Felix Gonzalez-Torres: Towards a Postmodern Sublimity," *Third Text,* no. 30 (1995): 73.

9. See Lauren Berlant, "National Brands/National Body: *Imitation of Life,*" in *The Phantom Public Sphere,* ed. Bruce Robbins (Minneapolis: University of Minnesota Press, 1993), pp. 173–208, for a compelling reading of public invisibility and private visibility in the public sphere.

10. Douglas Crimp, *AIDSDEMOGRAPHICS* (Seattle: Bay Press, 1990), p. 14.

11. Peggy Phelan, *Unmarked: The Politics of Performance* (New York and London: Routledge, 1993), p. 146.

12. Ibid.

13. I do not know for certain that the dark-haired olive-skinned man I am discussing is Latino. Because Latinos can be of any racial group, a dark-skinned black man, an Asian man, or a blond Anglo could also be Latino. But I read this particular installation as calling on the iconography of the Latino go-go boy. This iconography is familiar to those acquainted with gay New York's bar and club culture; the latino go-go boy is a coveted and fetishized "type" within these circles. Gonzalez-Torres also used female go-go dancers but, from what I can discern, did so less frequently. Most of the documentations of these performances represent male dancers (young men with dark hair and gym-built bodies) that correspond to this "Latino go-go boy" iconography.

14. The Eros was shut down by Mayor Rudolph Giuliani in 1997 as part of his "quality of life campaign" that has targeted the sex industry and queer public sex culture as well as the homeless and families living on public assistance.

15. Michael Moon has discussed some of Warhol's filmic engagements with the 1960s hustler culture in his rich essay "Outlaw Sex and the 'Search for America': Representing Male Prostitution and Perverse Desire in Sixties Film (*My Hustler* and *Midnight Cowboy*)," *Quarterly Review of Film and Video* 15:1 (1993): 27–40.

16. An article in the *Village Voice* focuses on the Latino Fan Club porn company that specializes in homeboy Latinos having sex with each other and the occasional desiring white man in fantasy scenarios such as prisons and drug rehab centers. The author makes a more general point about the relationship between Latino men and white men in gay male consumer culture: "The relationship of gay white men and Latinos, whether mutual attraction or mutual exploitation, has its lore, its literature, and plenty of anecdotal evidence" (Vince Aletti, *Village Voice,* June 28, 1994, pp. 30–31).

17. Amor, "Felix Gonzalez-Torres," p. 73; my emphasis.

18. See the last chapter of Phelan's *Unmarked,* "The Ontology of Performance: Representation without Reproduction" (pp. 146–66), for a persuasive argument for performance's ability to offer representation without reproduction.

19. Simon Watney, *Practices of Freedom: Selected Writings on HIV/AIDS* (Durham, N.C.: Duke University Press, 1994), p. 156.

20. See, for example, Michel Foucault, "The Ethic of Care of the Self as a Practice of Freedom: An Interview," trans. J. D. Gauthier, in *The Final Foucault,* ed. James Bernauer and David Rasmussen (Cambridge: MIT Press, 1994).

21. Paul Veyne, "The Final Foucault and His Ethics," trans. Catherine Porter and Arnold I. Davidson, *Critical Inquiry* 20 (autumn 1993): 1–9; David Halperin, *Saint Foucault: Towards a Gay Hagiography* (New York: Oxford University Press, 1995), p. 75; emphasis in original.

8. Latina Performance and Queer Worldmaking

1. The play was first performed at Dixon Place in New York City in June 1997. Dixon is a small performance space located on Manhattan's Bowery. The space is also Dixon Place director Ellie Covan's living room. Much of the performance that goes on at Dixon Place represents minoritarian communi-

ties. I have seen a lot of theater and performance at Dixon Place. The space has enabled the work of emergent artists such as Idris Mignot and Dan Bacalzo and has continued to promote the work of established performers such as Holly Hughes and Carmelita Tropicana.

2. For an elucidating take on Carmelita's relationship with Alina, see David Román's excellent interview with the artist, "Carmelita Tropicana Unplugged," *Drama Review* 39:3 (fall 1995): 83–93.

3. Irving Goffman, *Stigma: Notes on the Management of Spoiled Identity* (Englewood Cliffs, N.J.: Prentice Hall, 1963).

4. Judith Butler, *Excitable Speech: A Politics of the Performative* (New York and London: Routledge, 1997), p. 2.

5. Within the context of Latin American exile, it is significant that her heart is not her own. Rodesia's condition reminds us of the exilic subject who has left her heart in Cuba or Chile or Mexico or some other romanticized homeland.

6. Conversations with May Joseph about the challenge that post-colonial studies presents to the performance-studies paradigm have helped me to develop this concept.

7. Elin Diamond, *Unmaking Mimesis* (New York and London: Routledge), p. 152.

8. Ibid.

9. Coco Fusco, "The Other History of Intercultural Performance," *Drama Review* 38:1 (spring 1994): 143–67.

10. Philip Auslander, "Liveness: Performance and the Anxiety of Simulation," in *Performance and Cultural Politics,* ed. Elin Diamond (New York and London: Routledge, 1996), p. 198.

11. See chapter 5 for more on the indefatigable Pingalito.

12. Gustavo Pérez Firmat, *The Cuban Condition: Translation and Identity in Modern Cuban Literature* (Cambridge: Cambridge University Press, 1989).

13. Eve Kosofsky Sedgwick, "Queer Performativity: Henry James's *The Art of the Novel*," *GLQ* 1:1 (summer 1993): 13.

14. Fourteenth Street is a famous discount *chusma* shopping strip in lower Manhattan. It is also the place the low-budget drag queens go searching for a wig.

15. Nelson Goodman, *Ways of Worldmaking* (Indianapolis: Hackett, 1978), pp.1–23.

16. Richard Schechner, *Between Theatre and Anthropology* (Philadelphia: University of Pennsylvania Press, 1985), especially pp. 117–50.

17. Ibid., p. 131. Peggy Phelan has gestured to the difference between her own methodology and Schechner's in this respect: "Schechner refers positively to the power of performance to 'invent' the real. I am arguing that actually performance admits and tries to face the impossibility of seizing/seeing the real anywhere anytime" (Peggy Phelan, *Unmarked: The Politics of Performance* [New York and London: Routledge, 1993], p. 192 n. 2). The performance theory that I am employing shares similarities with both scholars' approaches. The methodology that I have been elaborating in *Disidentifications* suggests that disidentificatory performances do in fact *critique* the real, or at least what passes for the real within majoritarian culture's hegemonic order, and, furthermore, go on to "invent" alternate realities or worlds that further this critique and make worlds of political possibility.

My usage of the word *real,* with a lowercase "r," needs to be distinguished from Peggy Phelan's "Real," which is a psychoanalytic understanding of "the Real" extrapolated from her reading of Jacques Lacan. Her project stresses that representation and the image itself are limited by their partial and phantasmic engagement with what Lacanian psychoanalysis posits as the Real, as full Being itself. Part of *Unmarked*'s contribution is its analysis of the ways in which competing discourses within representation characterize themselves as the "Real-real." I would venture to say that Phelan's project and my own converge in our understanding of performance's ability to disrupt hegemonic notions of the Real-real or the true-Real. Although I agree with Phelan's thesis that performance faces up to the "impossibility of seizing/seeing the real anywhere anytime" (ibid.), the power of performance for me exists not only in this epistemological revelation, but also within what I understand to be *disidentificatory performance's performativity*, which is to say the performative (as opposed to epistemological) force of performance within the social.

18. C. L. R. James, *The Future in the Present: Selected Writings* (Westport, Conn.: Lawrence Hill, 1977).

19. C. L. R. James, Grace Lee, and Pierre Chaulieu, *Facing Reality* (Detroit: Bewick Editions, 1974), p. 137.

20. Both cited in Kent Worcester, *C. L. R. James: A Political Biography* (Albany: State University of New York Press, 1996), p. 141. These critiques of James and his coauthors represent the manifesto's negative reception. *Facing Reality* is also regarded as a classic document of the American left. Paul Buhle has claimed that "James and his collaborators may very well have predicted Polish Solidarity a quarter century before its arrival; certainly, the mass-mobilization origins and the form that the action took more nearly resembled the projects of *Facing Reality* than any traditional left perspective" (Paul Buhle, *C. L. R. James: The Artist as Revolutionary* [London: Verso, 1988], p. 122).

21. The "sensuality of performance" is a phrase I borrow from a conversation with Fred Moten about this chapter. I am grateful to him for the suggestion of turning to James and his amazing intellectual camaraderie.

22. Cindy Patton, "Performativity and Spatial Distinction: The End of AIDS Epidemiology," in *Performativity and Performance,* ed. Andrew Parker and Eve Kosofsky Sedgwick (New York: Routledge, 1995), p. 181.

23. Ngugi wa Thiong'o, "Enactment of Power: The Politics of the Performance Space," *Drama Review* 41:3 (fall 1997): 11.

24. Ibid., p. 12.

Index

José Esteban Muñoz is assistant professor of performance studies, Tisch School of the Arts, New York University. He serves on the board of directors for the Center for Lesbian and Gay Studies, City University of New York, and the New Festival, the New York Gay and Lesbian Festival. He is a member of the editorial collective for *Social Text* and series editor of *Sexual Cultures: New Directions in Gay and Lesbian Studies from CLAGS.* He coedited *Pop Out: Queer Warhol* and *Everynight Life: Culture and Music in Latina/o America,* as well as special issues of the journals *Social Text* and *Women and Performance.*